RAIDERS

Also By Ross Kemp

Moving Target
Devil to Pay
Warriors: British Fighting Heroes
Gangs
Gangs II
Ross Kemp on Afghanistan
Ganglands: Brazil
Pirates
Ganglands: Russia

ROSS
KEMP

RAIDERS

CENTURY

Published by Century 2012

2 4 6 8 10 9 7 5 3 1

First published in Great Britain in 2012 by
Century
Random House, 20 Vauxhall Bridge Road,
London SW1V 2SA

www.randomhouse.co.uk

Addresses for companies within The Random House Group Limited can be found at:
www.randomhouse.co.uk

The Random House Group Limited Reg. No. 954009

A CIP catalogue record for this book
is available from the British Library

ISBN: 9781780890555

The Random House Group Limited supports The Forest Stewardship Council (FSC®), the
leading international forest certification organisation. Our books carrying the FSC label are
printed on FSC® certified paper. FSC is the only forest certification scheme endorsed by
the leading environmental organisations, including Greenpeace. Our paper procurement
policy can be found at www.randomhouse.co.uk/environment

Typeset by Palimpsest Book Production Limited, Falkirk, Stirlingshire

Printed and bound in Great Britain by CPI Group (UK) Ltd, Croydon CR0 4YY

Contents

Foreword

For the first four years of the Second World War, Britain was in no position to be able to launch a significant offensive against the Axis forces. Fighting over so many fronts, from the North Atlantic to the Far East, her resources and manpower were stretched to the limit. The country's factories and dockyards were manufacturing warships, tanks, aircraft, weapons and equipment as fast as they could, but it was going to take time to build up, train and re-equip the Allied forces to be strong enough to carry the fight to Germany in a long, concerted campaign. Within days of the Dunkirk evacuation, Prime Minister Churchill, unhappy at the thought of sitting back in a defensive posture for so long, ordered his Chiefs of Staff to come up with ideas for some form of offensive operations against the enemy. It was not in the British Prime Minister's nature to pursue a policy of passive defiance. He wanted to harass Hitler's hordes relentlessly, never letting them settle in the new homes they had acquired for themselves in Western Europe through the Blitzkriegs of 1939 and 1940.

Churchill called for the British to launch a 'reign of terror' against Germany, and he envisaged it being executed in two ways: through a pan-European campaign of sabotage by irregular, covert operatives, and through a series of raids carried out by elite regular troops along the Atlantic Wall. The practical aim of the latter was to force Hitler to strengthen his defences along the western coast of Europe by diverting men and materials urgently required elsewhere. But there was a wider, less tangible purpose, whose dividends could not be calculated in an accounts ledger or a casualty list – and Churchill understood it better than anyone: morale. Britain's newspapers offered little cheer over the breakfast table at this time. The nation's cities were being battered by the Luftwaffe and every day seemed to bring news of a fresh setback from one corner or another of the globe. The sinking mood could only be lifted by the knowledge that there was still some fight left in the country. Even the smallest hit-and-run raid, no more than an irritating distraction to the Nazi war machine, would at least show the British people – and the Germans – that the war in Europe was not quite decided yet.

'How wonderful it would be if the Germans could be made

to wonder where they were going to be struck next instead of forcing us to try to wall in the Island and roof it over!' Churchill wrote. As a result, the Commandos and airborne troops were brought into existence and the tri-service Combined Operations was established. Thousands of the country's best fighting men were soon taking part in intensive training courses; specialist weaponry and equipment was rolling out of the factory gates, and audacious plans for hit-and-run assaults were being sketched out in the planning rooms. The British might have been hopelessly ill-prepared for the Second World War, but they certainly made up for their dithering with a colossal national effort. The raiding forces that were launched against the Nazis were the sharp end of that effort and, as the war ground on, the toll they took on the enemy mounted significantly. The British quickly proved themselves to be masters of the 'raid' as well as irregular warfare. The Commandos caused so much trouble that Hitler issued his famous order: if captured, Britain's elite troops were to be summarily executed, even if they were wearing uniform and had tried to surrender.

Four of the six chapters in *Raiders* tell stories of daring amphibious or airborne operations against targets along the western frontier of Nazi-occupied Europe. Operation ARCHERY was a Combined Operation assault on a Norwegian coastal town that had consequences far beyond the expectations of those who had planned it. Operation BITING, a cross-Channel raid into France, was the first major attack by the British Airborne Division and its first battle honour. Operation GUNNERSIDE was a dramatic demolition assault on Hitler's atomic bomb plant in Norway, carried out by a Norwegian unit of British Commandos. Operation CHARIOT, an amphibious assault on the heavily defended French port of St Nazaire, has been known ever since as 'the greatest raid of all'.

The other two raids described here are of a slightly different nature, but are no less compelling and extraordinary. Operation JUDGEMENT, in which obsolete British biplanes attacked the Italian Fleet at anchor in Taranto, was one of the most spectacular efforts of the entire conflict and altered the balance of the war in the Mediterranean and North Africa. Operation DEADSTICK is the story of a small party of British airborne troops, the first Allies into the fray on D-Day, tasked with seizing and holding two bridges to prevent an armoured German counterattack against the beach landings.

The six stories, each with their own distinctive character, are not just dry, step-by-step accounts of events that will be of interest only to students of military history. As in *Warriors*, my book about individual British war heroes of the two world wars, in *Raiders* I have tried to draw out the human element of these spectacular, dramatic operations, carried out by small groups of fervently patriotic, tough young men, who expected to die for the country they loved and for the freedom of their friends.

Operation Judgement

'It was a beautiful, picture-postcard evening; there were only a few wisps of cloud below us, otherwise the sky was clear, and littered with a blaze of stars; to the south a three-quarter moon was throwing a golden pathway across the calm sea; the air was smooth giving hardly a judder. It would have been the most perfect evening to enjoy flying, had it not been for the reason for our flight.'

Lt John Wellham

When Mussolini declared war on Britain on 10 June 1940, the Royal Navy's Mediterranean Fleet found itself in an extremely vulnerable position. At a stroke, Britain's ability to maintain control over a region vital to its survival was plunged into serious jeopardy. Outnumbered and outgunned, many of Admiral Sir Andrew Cunningham's antiquated ships, impressive though they looked, were clapped out and close to the end of their operational usefulness. The Italians, by contrast, boasted dozens of new and impeccably renovated ships and submarines in a huge fleet, backed up by a large air force with hundreds of very good-quality aircraft. Mussolini liked to refer to the Med as 'Mare Nostrum' (Our Sea) and, on paper at least, it was his Royal Navy, not Britain's, that ruled its waves.

Since Nelson's time, the Mediterranean Fleet had been regarded by British admirals as the finest command of them all, but nine months into Hitler's War, it had become something of a Cinderella service. Most of its best ships had been rushed back to defend home waters: the Dunkirk evacuation had begun at the end of May, the Battle of Britain raged overhead, the Atlantic convoys were being sunk in great numbers by German U-boats, and Norway needed help too. What ships could be spared for the Med were past or fast approaching their scrapping date.

This might not have mattered had the Mediterranean been a backwater command irrelevant to Britain's war effort. But that was far from the case. Control of the 2,400-mile-long sea was vital to British interests and it had to be held at all costs. The Mediterranean was the main corridor for all British imperial assets and territories in North Africa, the Middle East, the Far East and Australasia. The alternative passage from the UK to India, around the Cape of Good Hope, was 4,000 miles longer, which added several more weeks to the journey time.

Gibraltar had no airfield at the time and Malta, the Royal Navy's other major base in the region, lay a short flight from a string of Italian air bases. Over a two-year period, the tiny island and its British naval base was to be subjected to more than 3,000 bombing raids. There was no other good-quality naval base or anchorage in the 6,000 or so miles between Malta and Singapore. The Navy had adopted Alexandria out of necessity rather than choice: the Egyptian port's defences and facilities were poor and the fleet was vulnerable there.

With all her capital ships drawn off for more pressing engagements, by the end of 1939 the once formidable Mediterranean Fleet consisted of three small cruisers and a few destroyers of World War One vintage. The reinforcements that arrived by the time Mussolini decided that Britain was a spent force, ripe for picking off, were welcomed, but they brought little more than the appearance of strength. A fleet is only as powerful as its biggest guns – that is, its battleships – and against Italy's six modern battleships, only HMS *Warspite* could hope to hold her own in an old-fashioned slugging match. Possession of just two of her modern battleships, supported by its cruiser and destroyer squadrons, would have been sufficient to give the Italians the upper hand in the Mediterranean. Half a dozen of them was a luxury that Britain could only envy – and fear. The Royal Navy was also very short of ammunition and, if major repairs were needed to a ship, she would have to return to the UK or make the long, dangerous passage to the United States or Canada.

In short, Britain's days in the Med were numbered. Not for two centuries had one of Britain's enemies had a better opportunity to defeat a fleet of the fabled Royal Navy in open battle. And yet the Italians never tried. There were two reasons for this. Firstly and frankly, they simply didn't fancy it. The reputation alone of the Royal Navy was formidable enough to keep the Italian Fleet in the safety of its heavily defended bases. Secondly, even with the odds stacked in their favour, they didn't need to risk a confrontation. In spite of his ageing fleet's technical inferiority, Admiral Cunningham, a fighting man to the tips of his well-polished shoes, never stopped trying to invite the Italians out into the open. But they never came. When, once, the two forces ran into each other, after a brief engagement the Italians quickly ran for the sanctuary of their harbours.

It wasn't so much cowardice as common sense that persuaded Admiral Riccardi, Chief of the Italian Naval Staff, to keep his big ships out of harm's way. Italian submarines and aircraft of the Regia Aeronautica were causing quite enough damage to British interests as it was. Malta was hanging on by a thread; British submarines were being sent to the bottom faster than they could be replaced; Allied supply convoys to North Africa were being harassed to distraction, and Italian seaplanes, with virtually no opposition in the air, were providing information about every British move in the Med. Riccardi simply had to wait for the overstretched, obsolete Royal Navy fleet to burn itself out before sailing forth to administer the knockout blow.

Admiral Cunningham and his senior commanders understood

the danger. They knew they had to act before it was too late. With the RAF tied up defending Britain from a German invasion, Britain's air assets in the Med were pathetically inadequate for the job of defending the fleet and her bases. There was barely a dozen aircraft available to patrol almost one million square miles of air space, an area the size of the UK, France, Spain, Portugal, Germany, Italy, the Lowlands, Poland and Greece combined.

Old-school Navy characters – and there were a great many of them – were yet to fully grasp the strategic importance of 'air' to navies in modern warfare. Some even thought it was unchivalrous for one Navy to attack another with anything but the guns on her ships. But, whether they knew it or not, the days when two fleets took up position and knocked lumps out of each other from a distance were over. To devastatingly destructive effect, the Luftwaffe divebombers had recently shown in their attacks against the Royal Navy in Norway that a few dozen small aircraft, produced at a fraction of the cost of a warship, were able to locate enemy ships at sea with ease and then set about them with powerful, precisely delivered bombs. The Royal Navy, with its outdated, inaccurate AA guns, never stood a chance in the doomed Norwegian campaign (by coincidence, the campaign came to an end the day Italy declared war on Britain).

A letter in May 1940 from Sir Dudley Pound, the First Sea Lord, Cunningham's predecessor in the Med, confirmed what the new Commander-in-Chief already knew. It read: 'I am afraid you are terribly short of "air", but there again I do not see what can be done because . . . every available aircraft is wanted in home waters. The one lesson we have learnt here is that it is essential to have fighter protection over the fleet whenever they are within the range of enemy bombers. You will be without such protection, which is a very serious matter, but I do not see any way of rectifying it.' At the time of his writing, the ancient aircraft carrier HMS *Eagle* was on its way from the Far East with a small squadron of biplanes in its hangar, but that was next to no comfort to the naval chiefs. Carriers, warships and aircraft were being built at a frenetic rate back in Britain's shipyards and factories, but whether there would still be a Mediterranean Fleet for them to reinforce was another matter.

From the moment they received the news that Britain was at war with Italy, every sailor and airman (what few there were of the latter) in the Royal Navy's Mediterranean Fleet understood there was only one option: Cunningham was going to have to 'do a Nelson'. That was the expression buzzing around below the decks, referring to two great episodes in the history of the Royal Navy, the Battle of Copenhagen and the Battle of the Nile. In both encounters, Nelson used the element of surprise to attack enemy fleets whilst they were at anchor. Both ended in decisive victories for the Royal Navy and secured British domination for years to come.

The huge Italian fleet at the southern port of Taranto was asking for the same treatment. The only difference this time round was that it was not giant ships of the line, with a thousand guns between them, that were tasked to wreak the destruction.

It was a handful of cloth-covered biplanes that looked as if they had flown straight out of a Biggles adventure book.

There is a well-told story in the Fleet Air Arm of an officer from the US Navy boarding HMS *Illustrious* in 1940. He walks along the flight deck and, pointing at the strange-looking aircraft emerging from the lift hangar, exclaims: 'Oh My God! You don't actually fly those things, do you? They look more like four-poster beds than frontline airplanes.' There's no reason to doubt the truth of the story. Even seventy years on, you don't have to be an aviation expert to take one look at a Fairey Swordfish and wonder how its type had not been consigned to the scrapyard many years earlier. At a time when sleek, powerful Spitfires and Hurricanes were tearing up the skies with Me109s and Stuka divebombers, there's no getting away from the fact that the Swordfish looked like an aircraft better suited to a museum or a vintage airshow than a modern theatre of war. How that American naval officer would have been astonished to learn that not only would the Swordfish remain in frontline service until VE Day, but that it would account for sinking a greater tonnage of Axis shipping than any Allied aircraft in the war.

The Swordfish was conceived and went into production in the mid-1930s at a time when the rest of the world's aircraft manufacturers had begun to turn their creative minds to mono-planes, constructed from steel and toughened aluminium. The British designer Charles Fairey, founder of Fairey Aviation, believed there was still a role for an old-style biplane made from struts and wires and covered in linen cloth. At the behest of the Admiralty, it was designed as a maritime aircraft that, flying off carriers, could carry out antisubmarine patrols, reconnaissance and torpedo-dropping. Carrier aircraft, coming in at speed, needed to be extremely robust to withstand the heavy landings on deck and, operating far out at sea, often a long way from their targets, they also needed to have longer legs than most. The Swordfish had a range of 450 nautical miles, and that could be doubled by strapping on an extra fuel tank.

It was never imagined that the Swordfish would be able to hold its own against the speedy, powerful fighters of the Italian or German air forces. The Swordfish could reach 100 knots at a push, but nothing like that when laden with fuel and bombs or a torpedo. The Me109, the Luftwaffe's workhorse fighter, was four or five times faster; its armament of fixed machine guns and cannon immeasurably more powerful and accurate than anything the British biplane could put up. The Swordfish's only form of defence was a fixed forward-firing Vickers machine gun and a swivel-mounted Vickers or Lewis gun at the back of the open cockpit; these were so cumbersome and inaccurate that the gunner/wireless operator rarely bothered to use them and they were often removed altogether. A handheld pistol was seen as a more effective means of defence. Slow, defenceless and made from stretched cloth . . . the sight of a leisurely approaching Swordfish was unlikely to put the fear of god into its enemies. The hope was that they would rarely meet.

The Swordfish might not have been the most sophisticated

piece of kit to take to the air in the Second World War, but they didn't build 2,392 of them for the amusement of the Germans and Italians. Speak to the pilots of the Fleet Air Arm who flew her throughout the war, and you won't hear anything but affection and admiration for the aircraft. They will tell you that the Swordfish had three outstanding qualities: it was extremely manoeuvrable, highly adaptable and, in spite of its flimsy-looking cloth frame, it was as hard as nails.

Its aerobatic qualities certainly came in handy when being chased by German fighters in the Norwegian campaign a few months earlier. A number of Me109s, chasing Swordfishes up fjords, found it hard to lay a round on them as the biplanes twisted and turned. In the aerobatic tangle, the less manoeuvrable German fighters sometimes crashed into the steep rock faces of Norway's jagged coastline. The Swordfish was highly unlikely to shoot down an enemy fighter, but she could certainly give him the runaround. The aircraft's versatility earned it the nickname 'Stringbag'. The Swordfish was happy to drop anything: bombs, torpedoes, flares, depth charges, mines . . . Like a housewife's string shopping bag, the Swordfish could carry any number of items of equipment at a time. But above all, she could take a great deal of punishment, more than any other aircraft in operation at the time. Most rounds passed straight through her linen-covered fuselage and wings.

Since the emergence of military aircraft thirty years earlier, no strike from the air had ever been attempted on a heavily defended naval base anywhere in the world. This was in part down to the very sensible reasoning that such an operation could have only one outcome: disaster for the attacking force of aircraft. Taranto, like Portsmouth and Wilhelmshaven, was one of the world's great naval bases, protected by layer upon layer of defences. In addition to dozens of shore batteries, there were, of course, the countless guns of the ships themselves to see off any aircraft mad or brave enough to fly within their range. But Admiral Cunningham was not the only senior commander in the Med to believe that a surprise night attack on Taranto could be carried out. It was a happy coincidence that his air adviser, Rear Admiral Lyster, now in charge of carriers in the Mediterranean, had drawn up plans for an air attack on Taranto two years earlier when war loomed. When HMS *Illustrious*, Britain's only modern aircraft carrier, sailed through the Straits of Gibraltar in August 1940, his plans were immediately taken out of the filing cabinet and dusted down.

It has been well known to Britain's enemies down the centuries that the Royal Navy 'never refuses action'. Nor has it been in the habit of sitting back and waiting to react to its enemies' moves. The Royal Navy has always played on the front foot. Or as Admiral Nelson put it: 'Our country will, I believe, sooner forgive an officer for attacking an enemy than for letting it alone.' Cunningham was an aggressive commander in the mould of Nelson and, although at the start of the war he had no great enthusiasm for naval aviation, he was sharp enough to understand that the crews of the Fleet Air Arm represented his best, and probably his only, hope of delivering a decisive blow against the Italians. But when Cunningham, Lyster and Air Marshal

Longmore, the RAF Air Officer Commanding Middle East, sat down in Alexandria Harbour to draw up a plan for an air attack on Taranto, even those bright military minds could not have foreseen that they were devising one of the great raids in the history of warfare, and one that would have a major impact on the nature of naval warfare for many years to come.

When Rear Admiral Lyster submitted his plans for the raid they were met with an 'approval' by the Admiralty back in Whitehall that was so grudging it was almost a refusal. After giving 'Operation Judgement' a dim green light, Sir Dudley Pound, the First Sea Lord, couldn't resist a little dig. 'Only sailors who live in ships should attack other ships,' he wrote.

The broad outline of the plan was for two carriers, HMS *Illustrious* and HMS *Eagle*, to get as close to Taranto as possible without arousing Italian suspicions and launch a night attack on the Italian Fleet. The element of surprise was essential. The last thing they needed was every gunner in the Italian Navy at action stations on their arrival. The attack was to take place at night when there was no chance of being intercepted by the Regia Aeronautica, which had no nightfighters in its otherwise impressive air fleet. Although the first wave of Swordfish was tasked with dropping parachute flares to guide in the rest, the attack still needed a good 'moon period' to help light up the ships in the harbour. For that reason, and no doubt with a salute to Admiral Nelson too, 21 October – Trafalgar Day – was chosen as the date, only for it to be scrapped soon after a major fire broke out in

Illustrious's hangar. The additional fuel tanks were being attached when one of the aircraft burst into flames. The fire quickly spread, reducing one other Swordfish to a blackened wreck and seriously damaging five others. Much of the damage was caused by the sea water pumped in to douse the inferno. The aircraft that escaped the blaze had to be taken apart, washed in fresh water and re-assembled. The raid was postponed first to 31 October, and once more to the night of 11 November – Armistice Day – in order to exploit the light from a near-full moon.

There was a further setback shortly before the two carriers and their escort were due to set out from Alexandria. HMS *Eagle*, an ancient vessel already in her death throes, had to be withdrawn at the last minute after developing problems with her aviation fuel supply. Rather than delay the operation again, it was decided to leave her at Alexandria. Five Swordfishes and eight aircrew were transferred to *Illustrious*.

The Swordfish were to be launched in two flights of twelve aircraft with roughly one hour between each attack. Each flight was to comprise six aircraft carrying a mixture of 250-lb bombs and parachute flares, and six carrying torpedoes, which were expected to cause the greatest amount of damage. The orders were kept loose. It was left to the pilots to decide on their arrival at Taranto which was the best ship to target. The battleships were the main prizes, however, and the torpedo bombers, the heavy mob of the operation, were to go for them. It didn't matter which of the six they attacked because RAF reconnaissance images showed the Italians' capital ships were bunched so closely together that a torpedo, dropped in their general direction, stood a good chance of hitting one of them. The bombers' principal targets were the fleet's heavy and light cruisers and destroyers, but they were also to go for the seaplane base and the oil installations. The flying boats were the eyes of the Italian air force and the bane of the Mediterranean Fleet; the destruction of their operating centre would raise a loud cheer back in Alexandria.

Sitting on the instep of Italy's 'boot' in the heart of the Mediterranean, Taranto was the obvious location to house the Italian Fleet. It had two large harbours. The outer harbour, known as the Mar Grande, is shaped like a backward 'C' and is almost three miles in diameter. It was here that the six battleships were anchored, along with three heavy cruisers and eight destroyers. Behind it, in the land-locked inner harbour, known as Mar Piccolo, there was a bomber's feast of six cruisers, twenty-one destroyers, five torpedo boats, sixteen submarines and a variety of minor warships and support vessels. Not surprising, then, that Taranto was protected by a formidable network of defences designed to deter aircraft from attacking some of the most powerful warships afloat. Of the twenty-seven barrage balloons, sixteen were at the harbour entrance, protecting the battleships, and there would have been a further sixty had they not been wrecked in a recent storm. A shortage of hydrogen meant that they had yet to be replaced. With all the gaps between them, the balloons were expected to be more of a nuisance than a grave danger.

The battleships in the open expanse of the main outer harbour were vulnerable to torpedo attack and almost 14,000 metres of underwater netting were needed to protect them (were a torpedo ever to enter Taranto Harbour, it would come, the Italians believed, from a submarine, not an aircraft). On the night of the raid, a little over 4,000 metres of net had been installed – and even these could be avoided thanks to a new invention known as the Duplex pistol, which gave the torpedo two opportunities of detonating. It was fitted with a conventional contact pistol that detonated when the torpedo hit the target and also a magnetic one that went off when the torpedo passed underneath. All the propeller-powered torpedoes were set to run at twenty-seven knots at thirty-three feet, a depth great enough to slip under the protective nets.

It was more the vast array of anti-aircraft (AA) guns that the aircrews had to worry about. Strung out along the shore, as well as on the submerged breakwaters and the island of San Pietro at the mouth of the harbour, and on a series of floating pontoons, there were twenty-one batteries of 76-mm and greater calibre guns, eighty-four 17-mm and 20-mm guns and over 100 smaller weapons. There were also twenty-two searchlights to help the gunners pick out their targets. The guns of the ships doubled the weight of fire that could be brought to bear on unwanted visitors. How the crews of the lumbering Swordfish might expect to escape unscathed from the maelstrom of fire in so confined a space remained to be seen.

Illustrious was to leave Alexandria under cover of providing an escort for a number of convoys to reinforce Malta, Crete and the forces sent to assist the Greeks in their bitter struggle against the Italians. Alexandria was a port crawling with Axis spies and it was essential that *Illustrious*'s true objective should not be revealed. Were the Italians to pick up a whiff of suspicion that the aircraft carrier's true target was Taranto, then they would have promptly weighed anchor and moved the entire fleet to the sanctuary of more northerly ports beyond the range of the Swordfish. Rumours had been abounding below decks for weeks, but details of *Illustrious*'s mission were not confirmed to the aircrews until the naval force had slipped Alexandria on 6 November. The Fleet Air Arm crews were a highly experienced, tight group of young men who would all have flown with one another at some point. Each of them instantly understood the challenge of the historic task they had been handed. As was the strict custom, no one dreamt of airing their fears in the wardroom over a drink at the end of the day, but inwardly each one knew the odds were against them returning. As one of the pilots, John Wellham, noted: 'My feelings were mixed . . . Certainly, it was a boost to the ego to have been chosen but, on the other hand, it looked a pretty hairy operation, with less chance of returning in one piece than on earlier ventures . . . I had a drink and tried to look enthusiastic.'

The overall operation was given the code Mike Bravo Eight (MB8) and the total force involved practically every serviceable ship in the Mediterranean Fleet, consisting of five battleships, two aircraft carriers, eight cruisers, two AA cruisers, thirty destroyers and many smaller vessels. Once the convoys were considered secure, HMS *Illustrious* and her escort were to launch

Operation JUDGEMENT, while a diversionary attack was launched further along the Italian coast in the Straits of Otranto. Inevitably, it was not going to be long before a force of that size attracted the attentions of the Regia Aeronautica. Sure enough, seven Savoia-Marchetti SM79 bombers were soon on the scene but, attacked by three Fulmar fighters, two were sent spiralling into the sea and the rest ditched their bombs and turned tail.

In the countdown to the raid, the naval commanders requested daily sorties by the RAF's photographic reconnaissance aircraft to provide fresh information about the Italian Fleet and Taranto's defences. It was unfortunate that the rivalry between the Senior Service and its junior partner meant the relationship was not the healthiest at this time and the lack of cooperation threatened to jeopardise operational activity, including the raid on Taranto. To the undisguised annoyance of the Navy, the RAF regarded the images from their photographic recce flights as their property and they were unwilling to release them. The photos had to be flown from Malta to the RAF HQ in Cairo, where, incredibly, just one naval officer was allowed to look at them, and was refused permission to take them away.

The Navy might have enjoyed a good, clean fight with their enemy, but against their compatriots in the RAF they were forced to play an altogether dirtier game. On the eve of the attack, a young officer, Lieutenant David Pollock, was despatched to inspect the photos. When his RAF colleague was distracted, Pollock smuggled out the images. The following day the photographs were copied and then returned without the RAF ever realising they had been deceived. The copies shown to Admiral Lyster revealed that virtually the entire Italian Fleet, including all the battleships, was still at anchor in Taranto. But the good news was tempered by major alarm over the state of the Swordfish.

In the morning of 10 November, with less than thirty-six hours to go before the attack was launched, one of the Swordfish was on a routine recce patrol, about twenty miles from *Illustrious*, when the engine cut and the pilot was forced to ditch. Lt Clifford and his observer Lt Going managed to inflate their dinghy before the aircraft sank and, igniting their flame floats, were able to attract the attention of two Royal Navy cruisers. They were flown back to *Illustrious*. The following morning yet another aircraft was forced to ditch after the engine failed. Hasty examinations back on *Illustrious* revealed that the ship's aviation fuel tanks had been contaminated with sea water, probably during the efforts to put out the hangar fire in October. With the clock ticking down to takeoff time, the fitters raced to strip down all twenty-one aircraft earmarked for the operation, wash out their fuel systems, and then reassemble and refuel them.

The air crews on *Illustrious* had nothing but praise for the small army of riggers, fitters, mechanics and engineers of various description who kept their aircraft in immaculate working order. And it was thanks to their hard work and efficiency that, with barely an hour or so to spare, the attack was able to take place. Had they been forced to delay twenty-four hours, the Italians might well have suspected British intentions and moved the fleet to safer waters. *Illustrious* and her escort of four cruisers and four destroyers split from the main force and headed north. Admiral Cunningham signalled: 'Good luck then to your lads in their enterprise. Their success may well have a most important bearing on the course of the war in the Mediterranean.'

By 2000 hours *Illustrious* had reached Kabbo Point, the flying-off location situated 40 miles off the Greek island of Cephalonia, and 175 from Taranto. The first wave of Swordfish was ranged on deck poised to launch the most daring air raid in the history of warfare. The RAF had just given the Luftwaffe a sound thrashing in the skies over southeast England. Now was the moment for the pilots of the Royal Navy, facing equally daunting odds, to prove their skill and courage.

At 1900, scores of men filed out onto the flight deck to start ranging the twelve aircraft of the first striking force. One after another, the Swordfish emerged from the lift hangar and were wheeled into position at the aft end of the ship. The moon, three-quarters full, glowed brightly above a blanket of thick cloud at around 7,000 feet.

There were several reasons why, when the order was given, the deck crews endeavoured to get the aircraft off the ship as quickly as possible. To provide the heavily laden Swordfish with the necessary lift to get airborne, the carrier had to steam into the wind as fast as she could. Moving in a straight line made her an easier target for subs and bombers, so the sooner she could resume a zigzagging course, the better. What's more, as the deck was crowded with Swordfish, if an aircraft already airborne got into difficulties, it would be unable to land and would be forced to ditch. It also meant that, in the event of an air attack, the Fulmar fighters would not be able to take off and defend the ship. A rapid series of takeoffs also conserved fuel and extended the range of the strike force as less time was spent waiting for the rest of the aircraft to get airborne. On the night of 11/12 November there was an even more pressing incentive to get a move on: delays and dawdling risked jeopardising the element of surprise that was considered essential to a successful outcome. It was fortunate that in HMS *Illustrious*, the air crews had a well-drilled ship's company of the very highest efficiency and skill. While the men on deck went about securing and checking the aircraft, the forty-two pilots and observers of the two striking forces gathered in the wardroom for the final briefing. If all went to plan, they'd reconvene in the comfortable club-like surroundings in six hours' time to swap stories over a strong drink. It was probably just as well they didn't know that the planners were preparing for a 50 per cent casualty rate.

Having lost three aircraft to mechanical problems, the final total of aircraft available was just twenty-one, drawn from 813, 815, 819 and 824 Squadrons FAA (Fleet Air Arm). In order to accommodate the extra fuel tank, the gunner/wireless operator was jettisoned and crews were reduced to pilot and observer. There was no gun aboard, but that was hardly going to affect their chances of survival. A misfiring, ancient Vickers against the might of the Italian fleet's guns and shore defences were no more use than a teaspoon in a knife fight. W/T (Wireless/Telegraphy) silence was to be observed throughout and the removal of the heavy W/T equipment was of greater concern to the crews. Each crew would have to find its own way back to *Illustrious*. The aircraft carrier might have been over 740 feet long, but in the vast expanse of the Med at night, quite possibly in cloud and with a limited amount of fuel, trying to relocate her could be a nerve-racking challenge.

By 2015, with all twelve Swordfish on the flight deck, *Illustrious* and her escorts immediately began to increase their speed for the takeoff. As the bows of the ships cut into the calm surface of the sea, great sprays showered the foredecks and the gathering wind tugged hard at the clothes of all on deck. The wash from *Illustrious*'s giant propellors, or 'screws', churned up a seething froth of white foam below the quarterdeck at the stern of the boat. The pilots and their observers in their bulky flying suits and Mae Wests walked through the darkness to their aircraft, pulled themselves up into the cockpit, settled themselves on their parachutes and strapped themselves in. The riggers and fitters assigned to each aircraft slapped the backs of the air crew and offered cheery words of encouragement.

The luminous wand of the deck officer made circles in the darkness, telling the pilots to fire up their engines. The handlers inserted the handle to wind the inertia starter, filling the air with a high-pitched whining sound. Slowly the revs built, the pilots set the throttle, and twelve Pegasus engines, almost as one, coughed into life as clouds of smoke billowed from the exhausts. The pilots checked the gauges on the instrument panel and pushed the engine to full throttle, then back to tick-over, awaiting the summons forward. The ship was approaching maximum speed of almost thirty knots and the wind was now howling down the flight deck, offering as much lift as possible for the heavily burdened bombers. The crouching maintainers and handlers, buffeted by the gusts, dodged the whirling propellors as they slipped around the aircraft, ready to unfold and lock down the wings and remove the wooden chocks under the wheels. It was just before 2030 and some moonlight was visible through a break in the clouds.

A green light gave the signal for the first aircraft to fly off. The twelve aircraft, ranged on both sides at the rear of the flight deck, were to taxi out to launch their takeoff run, alternately from starboard and port. The silhouettes of 1,500-lb MkXII torpedoes were clearly visible under the fuselage of six of the aircraft and the 250-lb semi-armour-piercing bombs under the others. The first aircraft was flown by the leader of the striking force, Lt Commander Kenneth 'Hooch' Williamson, CO (Commanding Officer) of 815 Squadron. His observer was Lt Norman 'Blood' Scarlett. Moving out into the line running down the centre of the deck, Williamson held the brakes while the Swordfish's double wings were folded out and locked tight. On the signal, Williamson opened the throttle and released the brakes. The engine roared as the 3.5-tonne fully loaded biplane gathered speed along the 740-foot-long deck, dropped over the bow and then climbed into the night. The other eleven followed in rapid succession and, eight miles from *Illustrious*, still climbing and heading in a roughly northwesterly direction, the force formed up on Williamson's lead aircraft. Cruising at around eighty knots, the attack force were on course to reach Taranto shortly before 1100.

At around 7,500 feet, the twelve biplanes disappeared into thick cumulus cloud. When they emerged into the bright moon-light on the other side, the formation had been reduced to nine. Colliding in cloud could and did happen, but it was more likely that three other aircraft had become detached and were making their own way to the target area. All the aircrews later remarked on the extreme cold they suffered in the open cockpits. On arrival at the target area, the plan was for the twelve aircraft to split up. The two carrying the parachute flares were to drop them over the battleships as the torpedo-bombers negotiated the barrage balloons at the harbour entrance. The bombers were to head straight for the inner harbour to attack the cruisers and destroyers. The hope was that before the majority of the AA gunners had gone to action stations and opened up, the torpedo-bombers would be diving onto their targets. But, in the event, far from their arrival being a surprise to the defenders, virtually every gun in the Italian Navy was manned, loaded and waiting for the Royal Navy raiders. One of the aircraft that had become detached in the cloud, crewed by Lt Swayne and Sub-Lt Buscall, reached Taranto fifteen minutes before the others because it had flown at sea level. On realising they were the first to arrive, they had no choice but to fly around and wait for the rest of the attacking force. Inevitably, their presence was picked up by Italian listening devices and the alarm was raised.

Williamson and the others knew they were on the right navigational course when they were about ten minutes away. Hundreds of guns opened up and 'flaming onion' tracer shells erupted in the night sky. From that distance the skies above the harbour resembled a giant fireball. 'Taranto could be seen from a distance of fifty miles or more, because of the welcome awaiting us,' wrote Lt Charles Lamb, one of the flare-droppers, in his war memoir. 'The sky over the harbour looked like it sometimes does over Mount Etna, in Sicily, when the great volcano erupts. The darkness was being torn apart by a firework display which spat flame into the night to a height of nearly 5,000 feet.'

If the aircrews had been in any doubt about the risks they faced in the attack, they were dispelled in an instant by the scene ahead of them. Their survival would depend on the skill of each pilot and the famous manoeuvrability of the Swordfish. The torpedo-bombers' task of attacking the heavily gunned battleships was the most important and the most challenging. They would have to dive almost vertically through the wall of fire rising to meet them, straighten up a few feet over the surface of the harbour, line up a target, drop the torpedo and escape in a steep climb back through the barrage.

The formation reached Taranto at around 8,000 feet just before 11 o'clock. At 2256 the first flare-droppers, crewed by Kiggell and Janvrin, dropped their line of sixteen flares in rapid succession along the eastern side of the harbour. The flares, which would burn for three minutes, had delayed fuses, allowing the droppers to escape before they were lit up for the AA gunners.

The harbour, already illuminated by the defenders' fire, was soon bathed in a bright light, but there was so much smoke from the flak drifting through the air that some of the targets remained obscured. The barrage of the Italian gunners reached a feverish pitch as they concentrated their fire on the tiny flares slowly floating down from the heavens. In hindsight, they would have been better off focusing on the Swordfish. Kiggell's flares were burning so brightly and the ships were now so clearly visible that Lamb decided not to drop his, fearing they would be more help to the defenders than the attackers.

Sitting 5,000 feet above the harbour, Lamb had the best seat in the house from which to observe the unfolding drama below. 'For the last six months, almost without a break, we had attracted the enemy's fire for an average of at least an hour a week; but I had never imagined anything like this to be possible. Before the first Swordfish had dived to the attack, the full-throated roar from the guns of six battleships and the blast from the cruisers and destroyers made the harbour defences seem like a sideshow . . . into that inferno, one hour apart, two waves, of six and then five Swordfish . . . danced weaving arabesques of death and destruction with their torpedoes, flying into the harbour only a few feet above sea level – so low one or two of them touched the water with their wheels.'

The torpedo-bombers split into two subflights of three and launched their attack simultaneously. The first subflight attacked the northernmost battleships, while the second, led by Kemp, made for the southernmost. All six biplanes dived straight into the storm of fire. The first, led by Williamson and Scarlett, with the *Conte di Cavour* as their designated target, arrived on the scene bang on time, just as the first flares were adding their glare to the illuminations. Straightening up out of the dive, they passed unscathed through the barrage-balloon cables as they roared through the harbour entrance towards the line of battleships. Pointing straight at the massive silhouette of the *Cavour*, Williamson flicked the release button on his throttle lever. They were so low at this point that they felt the splash as the lethal 'fish' slapped into the water. The torpedo sunk below the surface and moments later an almighty explosion thundered across the harbour.

Almost instantaneously, the Swordfish slammed into the water.

The official reports suggest they had been hit by AA fire, which might have been the case, but the Swordfish might also have dipped a wing tip in the water as Williamson made to turn away. The flight commander, semi-delirious after cracking his head on impact, struggled to get out of the cockpit and he was under water when he finally managed to wrestle free from his parachute and harness. When he reached the surface, at first he thought it had started to rain until he realised he was swimming through machine-gun fire. 'Blood' Scarlett recalled: 'I just fell out of the back into the sea. We were only about twenty feet up. It wasn't very far to drop. I never tie myself in on these occasions. Then old Williamson came up a bit later and we hung about by the aircraft, which had its tail sticking out of the water. Chaps ashore were shooting at it.' For half an hour, the two men clung to the tail of the Swordfish and watched the rest of the raid unfold before they swam off to a floating dock 100 yards away and clambered into the clutches of some very angry dockworkers.

The two other aircraft in the subflight, piloted by Sub-Lts Julian Sparke and Douglas Macauley, survived the approach into the harbour, and managed to get their torpedoes away. But both narrowly missed the *Conte di Cavour* and exploded close to the *Andrea Doria*, without causing any damage.

The second subflight were assigned to attack the *Littorio*, which was anchored a mile to the north of the *Cavour*, closer to the town of Taranto and the entrance to the inner harbour. The first two, piloted by Kemp and Swayne, approached from the west and came under the heaviest fire yet as they swept down into the harbour. Having survived the barrage from the shore defences, they were at mast height when the cruisers lowered their guns and added their considerable weight to the fire. The guns were elevated so low that many of the rounds were seen to riddle some of the other ships in the harbour. Kemp dropped his torpedo about a thousand yards short of the *Littorio* and watched it streak towards the battleship. As always after dropping the 1,600-lb torpedo, the Swordfish bucked upwards, and Kemp corrected the attitude of the aircraft before climbing steeply back into the streams of AA fire.

Swayne had managed to drop his torpedo 400 yards short of the *Littorio*, a range so close that he almost careered into the battleship's rigging as he made his escape. There was a matter of seconds between the two explosions: Kemp's struck the starboard bow, Swayne's the port quarter. A column of smoke shooting out of the ship's smokestacks confirmed that *Littorio* had been struck a deadly blow. The third Swordfish, with Lt Michael Maund at the controls, was not so fortunate. He decided to attack the *Vittorio Veneto* anchored close by, but his torpedo ran aground in shallow water.

While the torpedo-bombers laid siege to the capital ships in the main harbour, the other six Swordfish swept towards the Mar Piccolo, the inner harbour where cruisers and destroyers were stacked up 'Mediterranean-style' in a neat row along the jetty. If the bombers could negotiate the flak, they could barely miss. Ollie Patch, the only Royal Marine in the attacking force, was the first to arrive over the harbour, but he could barely see the ships for all the smoke and flames from the AA fire. When he finally picked out a target through the haze, he dropped the nose of his Swordfish into a dive so steep he was virtually standing on the pedals. He released his six bombs and made his escape. He twisted and turned the aerobatic Swordfish so sharply to avoid the streaks of tracer heading their way that his observer Goodwin was lifted from his seat and was only saved from plunging to his death by the 'monkey's tail' wire that attached him to the aircraft.

In the space of ten minutes or so, the Italians had filled the air with thousands of rounds of various calibre and the smoke was so thick that when Sub-Lt Sarra dived from 8,000 to 1,500 feet over the Mar Piccolo, he was unable to identify clearly a single ship of the four dozen or so moored there. Dropping even lower to 500 feet, where the concentration of fire was even greater, he attacked the hangars and slipways of the seaplane base. All six bombs exploded and the hangars erupted in flames as he fled from the scene with AA flak and rounds of all description bursting around his tail and wings, shredding the cloth fabric as the biplane climbed as fast as it could to safety. Sarra and Sub-Lt Forde, who had only recently qualified as a pilot, were the most junior pilots of the twenty-one who took part in the Taranto raid and both showed remarkable courage and cool-headedness on the night. Forde, who had become split up from the rest of the bombers shortly before they went in, dived through murderous flak and dropped his bombs from 1,500 feet. Unsure whether all of his bombs had been released, he circled the harbour and plunged back into the firestorm again for a second attack. The last of the bombers, crewed by Murray and Paine, attacked the neat line of destroyers from 3,000 feet, dropping their bombs as they swept from east to west. One landed square on the destroyer *Libeccio* but, to their fury, it failed to detonate.

Having sensibly decided not to drop his flares, Lamb had circled the harbour, watching the inferno rage below. Keen to make his own contribution before leaving, he headed for the oil storage tanks, which had already been attacked by the other flare-droppers, Kiggell and Janvrin. His bombs found their target, but with no results observed; either the bombs had failed to go off or they had exploded deep inside the storage containers. Lamb's was the last of the Swordfish to leave the scene of the attack and, as he turned the aircraft back in the rough direction of Cephalonia, he was convinced that he and Grieve, his observer, were the only survivors of the attack. The raid had taken little more than five minutes, but for two and a half hours, the two young airmen flew through the darkness in gloomy silence.

At 2123, an hour after Williamson's force had set out, *Illustrious* was ploughing into the wind again when the first of nine aircraft in the second flight roared down the flight deck. The flight comprised five torpedo bombers, two bombers and two carrying a mixture of flares and bombs. There was certainly going to be no element of surprise in their attack. Taranto was already ablaze, the AA gunners now had their eye in and the early warning posts along the coast had alerted the Italian Fleet to the fact that a second wave of attackers was on its way. The pause between the two attacks also gave the defenders the opportunity to gather and reorganise themselves.

The second strike was led by the CO of 819 Squadron, Lt Commander 'Ginger' Hale, an excellent rugby player who had played for England before the war. Other notables in the second striking force included Lt Wellham, who had won a DSC for a daylight attack on Italian shipping at Bomba Bay in Libya, in which he had torpedoed and sunk an enemy supply ship. (The Royal Marine Ollie Patch sank a submarine in the same raid.) Wellham's observer, Lt Pat Humphreys, had been awarded the George Cross in 1937 (then called the Empire Gallantry Medal) during the Spanish Civil War. After his destroyer had struck a mine, he had helped rescue seriously injured men from a compartment flooded with water and oil.

The undisputed flying ace of the force, however, was a lanky Ulsterman, Lt Michael Torrens-Spence, the senior pilot, and second-in-command of 819 Squadron. Every memoir or account of Fleet Air Arm operations in the Second World War stresses his remarkable flying skills and courage. He pressed home his attacks with an almost suicidal disregard for his own safety.

Illustrious's aircraft had been bedevilled by problems from the moment plans for the raid were laid down, and it was no surprise when the second flight suffered a last-minute setback. The aircraft crewed by Clifford and Going – the same two who had been plucked from the sea the day before after ditching – was badly damaged when it was caught by another aircraft as it taxied across the flight deck. The cloth of the wings was badly torn and, worse still, several of the supporting ribs had snapped in half. There was no chance of it taking to the air in that state and she was taken down in the lift hangar. Clifford and Going were distraught at the prospect of missing the raid and ran straight to the island and begged Captain Boyd and Rear Admiral Lyster to let them catch up the rest of the force. Reluctantly, the commanders agreed. Working with incredible speed and skill, the riggers completed the extensive repairs; thirty minutes later, Clifford and Going climbed into the night and banked towards Taranto.

Passing them somewhere in the darkness were their colleagues, Lt Morford and Sub-Lt Green, who were returning to *Illustrious* after developing serious problems of their own. Their long-range fuel tank had fallen off and, in the process, damaged some fittings, which were now smashing against the fuselage. They had already turned back when the engine suddenly cut and the Swordfish began losing height. Morford managed to restart the engine, but the danger hadn't passed. Observing the strict W/T silence that had been ordered, they were unable to inform *Illustrious* they were arriving and, as they approached the ship, the gunners on the carrier and the escorting cruiser *Berwick* opened fire. Green quickly fired the two-star identification signal of the day, the firing ceased at once, *Illustrious* turned back into the wind and they landed on.

The cloud had lifted as the formation of seven Swordfish slowly climbed to 8,000 feet. Shortly after 1100, still more than fifty miles from Taranto, the observers/navigators in the rear cockpits were able to stow their clipboards of navigational charts. The first wave had just launched their attack, turning the skies over the harbour into a ball of fire that acted like a homing beacon, growing bigger and brighter as they rumbled towards it. At five minutes to midnight, a few miles short of the coast, the two flare-droppers, piloted by Lts Hamilton and Skelton, peeled off from the main attacking force. Coming in from the south, they released twenty-four parachutes in rapid succession before turning their attentions to the oil depot a mile inland from the southern end of the Mar Grande.

In this attack, all the torpedo-bombers flew into the north of the harbour, avoiding the gun emplacements on San Pietro Island and the floating batteries at the harbour entrance, but the reception from the Italian gunners, now on full alert, was even more ferocious than that which greeted the first wave. One Swordfish, crewed by Lts Bayley and Slaughter, swooped to torpedo the heavy cruiser *Gorizia*, but was caught up in the intense volleys of flak, burst into flames and careered into the harbour. Both young officers were killed. The torpedo that was found floating near the crash location the following morning was thought to have been theirs. Its striking head had been crushed but had failed to detonate, suggesting they had managed to hit their target.

Simultaneously, Flight Leader Hale and Lt Torrens-Spence both dived into the intense flak to attack the *Littorio*, Italy's newest battleship, whose beleaguered crew were busy trying to contain the damage sustained in the first assault. The Swordfish screeched and strained violently as they fell out of the sky almost vertically before their pilots pulled them hard out of the dive. When they levelled up to make their final approach, they were so low that the undercarriages were almost touching the water. Both pilots flicked the release buttons on the throttle at the same time, roughly 700 yards from the 40,000-ton warship. Both torpedoes found their target on the starboard side and yet another booming explosion added to the already deafening uproar. The other torpedo failed to go off having slapped into the muddy seabed directly below the ship.

Seconds away from smashing straight into the severely wounded battleship, Hale banked sharply, missing a barrage balloon cable by just a few yards before disappearing into the night as fast as his lumbering biplane would allow. Torrens-Spence was flying so low that, as he fled the scene of destruction, the wheels of his aircraft actually dipped into the water. With less skilled aviators at the controls, the Swordfish would have cartwheeled on impact, but in that split second Torrens-Spence showed why he had come to be regarded as one of the best in the Fleet Air Arm. By immediately pulling back on the controls, the Ulsterman saved himself and his observer Lt Alfie Sutton from certain death.

Lt Lea, meanwhile, had his sights on the *Caio Duilio*, moored at the northernmost end of the main harbour. Dropping beneath the AA barrage, he flew within 600 yards of his target before releasing his torpedo. From that range, he could barely miss the 550-foot-long battleship and, sure enough, seconds later the warhead tore a huge hole in its starboard side beneath one of its main turrets. With his observer, Sub-Lt Jones, clinging on in the back, unable to do anything but watch and pray, Lea also experienced a hazardous escape from the harbour. Flying just above the water, he had escaped colliding with a fishing boat by a matter of feet when he came under heavy fire from the two cruisers *Zara* and *Fiume* before struggling clear and heading back out to sea.

Lt Wellham, too, had to show excellent airmanship to emerge from the maelstrom unscathed. In the thundering, blinding chaos of the battle, Wellham had become detached from the other torpedo-bombers but, spotting a gap in the flak, he began his dive. He was gaining speed, pushing 170 knots as the multicoloured streaks of tracer flashed past, when a barrage balloon that had broken free from its mooring loomed into his path. With a less skilled pilot at the controls of a less manoeuvrable and robust aircraft, that would have marked the end for men and machine alike, but Wellham swerved out of the way at the last possible moment. The Swordfish rocked violently as one of the wings caught the balloon's trailing cable. The wing was badly damaged and Wellham battled with all his strength to rescue the stricken biplane. 'There was a tremendous jar, the whole aircraft juddered and the stick flew out of my hand . . . We were completely out of control . . . We were diving almost vertically into the centre of the City of Taranto! I hauled the stick back into my stomach.' Others might have chosen to remove their wounded aircraft from harm's way, but Wellham pressed on. 'I was determined to aim at something after carrying the bloody thing all that way and having a rather hairy dive – I'd be damned if I didn't do something with it.' Struggling to keep the Swordfish on an even approach – the aircraft needed to be level when the torpedo was dropped – Wellham was 500 yards short of the *Vittorio Veneto* when he released his 'fish'. The flagship of the Italian Fleet was leading a charmed existence that night and once again it escaped potentially catastrophic destruction. Given the difficulties that Wellham was having in preventing his Swordfish from crashing, it was not surprising that his effort narrowly missed its mark. (It was subsequently discovered that the ailerons of Wellham's port wing had been wrecked and a giant hole had been torn in the fuselage.)

Clifford and Going, meanwhile, having made good time in their patched-up aircraft, arrived while the attack was in full cry. A hellish scene played out below. Through the billowing smoke, trails of tracer and explosions of flak, they could see vast slicks of oil stretching out across the main harbour. Clifford, piloting the only out-and-out bomber, circled the Mar Piccolo several times waiting for his chance to swoop. As soon as he spotted a gap in the flak, he put the nose down and tail up, and dropped the three-and-a-half-ton biplane towards the long line of cruisers and destroyers, whose gunners responded with a murderous barrage of fire. At 2,500 feet, he levelled off and turned towards two cruisers, dropping a stick of six bombs as he surged through the flak. Five of the bombs narrowly missed their targets; one scored a direct hit on the *Trento*, but failed to go off. Not for the first time that night, the bravery and skill of the bomber crews was let down by the shoddy design of the bombs they dropped. Had every bomb exploded as they should have done, then the destruction at Taranto would have been at least twice as great. Most of the bombs had missed their targets by so little that the explosions would still have caused significant damage to the lightly armoured cruisers and destroyers. Clifford banked to the north and disappeared over the coast into the darkness, leaving behind a scene of smouldering devastation. But not until an RAF reconnaissance aircraft photographed the harbour would the Swordfish crews discover if their heroic efforts had succeeded in inflicting any significant damage on the Italian Fleet.

Back on *Illustrious*, Rear Admiral Lyster, Captain Boyd and the rest of the ship's company were growing increasingly anxious. The W/T silence that had been ordered so as not to give away the ship's location was allowed to be broken just once. Williamson was to contact the ship with one short, sharp message to alert them of their imminent return, but he was now a prisoner of war. The time set for the return of the first wave had passed and the men back on *Illustrious* were beginning to fear the worst for the Swordfish crews when the radar officer picked up a formation of aircraft on his set. Not long afterwards, the dimmed navigation lights of the first Swordfish were visible on the horizon and Boyd turned the giant carrier into the wind for them to land on. To the mounting relief of all aboard, one after another the wheels of the sturdy biplanes thumped onto the flight deck. Each aircraft came to a violent halt as the hook at the tail of the Swordfish caught one of the arrestor wires strung out across the deck before taxiing to the end of the ship where their wings were folded and they disappeared back into the sanctuary of the hangar. By three o'clock all but two of the twenty-one aircraft to set out for Taranto were back in the hangar. Those piloted by Williamson and Bayley would never return. The ship turned southwards to rejoin the rest of the Fleet and head back to Alexandria.

While the observers heaved their weary, frozen bodies from the cockpits and hurried stiffly into the ship's island to be debriefed, the exhausted pilots went below to inspect the damage to their battle-torn biplanes. Almost every Swordfish had been punctured and perforated, their cloth fabric shredded and singed by the shells and machine guns of the Italian defenders. Sarra's aircraft alone had seventeen shell holes along its fuselage and wings, while Wellham's was so badly damaged that the riggers and fitters were astonished he'd been able to keep it aloft, let alone fly it two and a half hours back to the ship. Had the Swordfish been made from metal, it is doubtful whether more than one or two of them would have survived to tell their tale of what the Italians still call *La Notte Di Taranto* – 'Taranto Night'.

Most of the aircrews were convinced that the raid had been a failure. The bombs had failed to detonate, that much was sure, and it was impossible to know if the torpedoes, striking far below the surface, had caused any damage or even hit their targets. Neither striking force was going to hang around in the umbrella of flak over Taranto to inspect the results of their night's work. But the opinion expressed by one of their number in the wardroom that night – that they had made 'a complete cock of it' – summed up the general mood of despondency, a mood that was deepened when the news filtered through that they were going to be asked to launch a further attack. On hearing the speculation, one wit was heard to wisecrack: 'Bloody hell, even the Light Brigade was only asked to do it once!'

The exhausted pilots and observers who took part in the Taranto raid had been living on their nerves for months, and few of them attempted to disguise their delight when it was announced the following day that Admiral Lyster had decided against a third strike. His decision is often put down to worsening weather conditions, but there was a more weighing factor. At first light, the three Italian battleships that had not been targeted by the Swordfish torpedo-bombers slipped harbour and steamed as quickly as possible for the safety of Naples. With the major prey gone, there was little point in Lyster risking his precious aircrews and aircraft in the pursuit of the smaller warships that were now even less likely to venture out of port and risk action against the Royal Navy.

At the same time that the Italian battleships were weighing anchor and the dumbfounded authorities of the Regia Marina began inspecting the destruction in the oil-choked harbour, *Illustrious* was joining up with the rest of the Mediterranean Fleet off the south coast of the Peloponnese mainland. If the Commander-in-Chief of the Mediterranean Fleet, Admiral Cunningham, was impressed by the efforts of his Fleet Air Arm, he had a peculiar way of expressing it. As *Illustrious* steamed within view, flags were hoisted aboard his flagship, HMS *Warspite*, spelling out a message from the Admiral which read: '*Illustrious* manoeuvre well executed'. The signal has since become a famous footnote in naval history, and Cunningham, as already noted, no great fan of naval aviation, was roundly barracked in some quarters for his lukewarm congratulations.

In mitigation, two points need to be made. Firstly, Cunningham was of the old naval school and believed no man should receive special praise for doing his duty and carrying out the job he was trained to do. More relevant, however, was the fact that it was early in the morning and the RAF reconnaissance aircraft was yet to produce its post-raid images of Taranto. Cunningham had no idea of the scale of the damage the Swordfish had inflicted. Had he known that the clumsy-looking, obsolete biplanes had effectively knocked the Italian Fleet out of the war and given him almost total control of the Med, then no doubt even he would have overcome his natural reserve and offered more effusive praise for their efforts. And, to his credit, soon afterwards he tacitly admitted that he had failed to acknowledge the airmen's achievements: 'Admirably planned and most gallantly executed in the face of intense anti-aircraft fire, Operation Judgement was a great success,' he wrote in a report four months later.

While *Illustrious* steamed eastwards to Egypt, as soon as there was sufficient light, three Cantieri flying boats were dispatched to pinpoint her location so that Italian bombers might deliver immediate revenge. All three were shot out of the sky by *Illustrious*'s Fulmar fighters and the carrier was spared the efforts of a fighting retreat. Lt Cdr Williamson and Lt Scarlett, meanwhile, were getting used to life as prisoners of war. Their crewmates back on *Illustrious* had no idea whether they were dead or alive, but the widespread assumption was that they had perished in the crash. After clambering ashore into the clutches of an angry mob of dockyard workers, they were roughly treated at first – perhaps understandably given the destruction being wrought all around them. Their clothes were torn from their backs and they were bundled into a hut. But their captors soon calmed down and gave them a blanket and some cigarettes. They were taken for questioning to the destroyer *Fulmine*, whose gunners were firing at them when they were downed. Their interrogation could not have been more civilised. They were handed glasses of cognac and issued with clean clothes, and then given a hot meal, beer and a comfortable bed for the night.

'In fact,' recalled Williamson, 'we were almost popular heroes. Two nights after our raid the RAF came over and we were put into an air-raid shelter full of seamen. They all pressed cigarettes on us and towards the end of the raid about twenty of them sang "Tipperary" for our benefit.' After a short spell in a prisoner-of-war camp at Sulmona, they were transferred to Germany where they saw out the war in less hospitable and comfortable circumstances. In 1945 Scarlett was mentioned in dispatches for organising a bid to escape from his Stalag. The other crew not to return from Taranto were not so fortunate. The body of the observer Lt Slaughter was never found. Lt Bayley is buried in the Imperial War Graves Cemetery at Bari.

As the sun rose over Taranto, thousands of sailors and dockyard workers were working furiously to salvage their crippled ships. The full details of the damage would not be known for a further twenty-four hours but, as he surveyed the scene, Admiral Riccardi, the Chief of the Italian Naval Staff, did not need a team of engineering experts to tell him that his fleet had suffered a catastrophic blow. As an expert in air warfare, he might even have privately admired the skill of the British raiders. In the Mar Grande, the battleships *Littorio*, *Caio Duilio* and *Cavour* were either sunk or beached to prevent them sinking. Three cruisers and two destroyers and two fleet auxiliaries suffered significant damage, mainly from near-misses by the bombs, while the seaplane hangar had been gutted by fire and two aircraft destroyed. The oil depot had also been damaged; it was only the faulty mechanisms of the bombs that had prevented its total destruction.

Between them, the Swordfish dropped eleven torpedoes and over forty 250-lb bombs. The Italian shore defences alone had fired over 13,000 regular flak rounds as well as 1,750 rounds of four-inch and 7,000 rounds of three-inch shells. There are no records of the ammunition expended by the fleet's gunners, but the aircrews reported that the volume of fire from the warships was even greater than that from the fixed-gun emplacements. Many of these rounds hit the merchant vessels, the dock installations and the city itself, adding considerably to the scale of the damage. Italian casualties, however, were remarkably light: twenty-three killed aboard *Littorio*, sixteen in the *Conte di Cavour*, and just one on *Caio Duilio*.

The *Littorio* had been hit by three torpedoes, two to starboard and one to port, each one tearing huge chunks out of her thick armoured hull. Kemp's strike had blown a hole forty-nine by thirty-two feet in the first strike, but it was the follow-up blow delivered in the second strike by either Hale or Torrens-Spence that completed the job. It was a credit to her designers and builders that the damage suffered did not prove fatal. She was left to rest on the bottom of the harbour shallows while repairs took place. The work was complicated by the danger of the unexploded torpedo beneath her keel which, it transpired, had hit her but failed to explode. It was six months before she was refloated and made seaworthy again.

The *Conte di Cavour* suffered the heaviest damage. Williamson's torpedo had blown a hole roughly forty feet by twenty-five feet close to the forward ammunition magazine, and she was on the bottom with water over her main decks by the morning. She never returned to service.

The *Caio Duilio* suffered damage from Lt Lea's torpedo which ripped a hole of about thirty-five by twenty-five feet in the starboard, right between two ammunition magazines. She was immediately beached to prevent sinking. Two months later she was refloated and sent to the dry dock at Genoa for repairs. It was six months before she was able to return to service. Had Lea's warhead struck a yard or two to the left or right and hit a store of explosive shells, she would have been blown to smithereens.

According to the Italians, a mere handful of the forty or so bombs dropped by the Swordfish exploded. The crews of the bombers who braved the storm of flak were especially annoyed to hear that their courageous efforts had brought no reward. With the destroyers and cruisers moored so closely together in the Mar Piccolo inner harbour, there would surely have been destruction on a terrifying scale had just half a dozen of the bombs managed to detonate. Had the first striking force managed to retain the element of surprise and arrive unannounced, before the gunners had taken their stations, then the damage might have been that much greater again.

It took almost two days for an accurate assessment of the damage to be constructed from intelligence reports and images from the RAF's Photographic Reconnaissance Unit. After month upon month of announcing setback after setback, defeat after defeat, Churchill could barely hide his smile when he stood up to address the House of Commons on 13 November. 'I have some news for the House. It is good news. The Royal Navy has struck a crippling blow at the Italian Fleet.' When the cheering had died down, he continued: 'The total strength of the Italian Battle Fleet was six battleships, two of them of the "*Littorio*" class, which have just been put into service and are, of course, among the most powerful vessels in the world, and four of the recently reconstructed "*Cavour*" class. This fleet was, to be sure, considerably more powerful on paper than our Mediterranean Fleet, but it had consistently refused to accept battle. On the night of the 11/12 November, when the main units of the Italian fleet were lying behind their shore defences in their naval base at Taranto, our aircraft of the Fleet Air Arm attacked them in their stronghold . . . I felt it my duty to bring this glorious episode to the immediate notice of the House. As the result of a determined and highly successful attack, which reflects the greatest honour on the Fleet Air Arm, only three Italian battleships remain effective.'

To a layman listening to the Prime Minister, the crippling of three battleships might not have sounded such a mighty blow, but a navy man would have instantly understood the significance. Although carriers would soon overtake them as the capital ships of a fleet, battleships were the heavy brigade of the sea, and no navy in the world could hope to compete with the Royal Navy if they didn't possess a superior complement. Mussolini's 'Mare Nostrum' had become 'Cunningham's Pond', thanks to two attacks lasting no more than fifteen minutes between them carried out by twenty biplanes from a bygone era. Taranto represented not just a major shift in naval power in the Mediterranean, it heralded a major shift in naval strategy. Events in southern Italy didn't go unnoticed by the Admirals in the Imperial Japanese Navy. Although the Japanese had already started planning their carrier-borne air attack on the US Pacific Fleet in Pearl Harbor, Taranto proved it could be done.

Praise for the *Illustrious* and the men of the Fleet Air Arm came from every quarter. In a letter to Admiral Cunningham, King George VI wrote: 'The recent successful operations of the Fleet under your command have been a source of pride and gratification to all at home. Please convey my warm congratulations to the Mediterranean Fleet and, in particular, to Fleet Air Arm on their brilliant exploit against the Italian warships at Taranto.' The First Sea Lord Admiral Pound, who had been so disdainful about the unchivalrous notion of aircraft attacking ships, wrote to his successor in the Med: 'Just before the news of Taranto the Cabinet were rather down in the dumps; but Taranto had a most amazing effect on them.' Indeed, news of the attack, trumpeted across the front page of *The Times* and other newspapers, gave the whole country an enormous lift, not least in London and the other major cities that were suffering the full force of the Luftwaffe's Blitz at the time.

The mood was less buoyant in Rome and Berlin. The Italian Foreign Minister Count Ciano, Mussolini's son-in-law, made the following entry in his diary for 12 November 1940: 'A black day. The British, without warning, have attacked the Italian Fleet at anchor in Taranto, and have sunk the Dreadnought *Cavour* and seriously damaged the battleships *Littorio* and *Duilio*. These ships will remain out of the fight for many months. I thought I would find Il Duce downhearted. Instead he took the blows quite well and does not, at this moment, seem to have fully realised its gravity.'

The price of neutering the Italian Navy was a high one. Mussolini might not have understood – or wanted to understand – that the Taranto raid had changed the balance of power in the Med overnight, but Hitler and his staff certainly did, and they knew that it had been brought about by the efforts of just one ship. Soon afterwards the Luftwaffe was dispatched to the Med to take over from the Regio Aeronautica, partly to assist the Italian invasion of Greece and the Balkans, but also to support Rommel's campaign in North Africa by attacking Allied convoys and protecting their own. They arrived in huge numbers and among them was an entire Fliegerkorps of 300 aircraft, most of them Junker Ju87 Stuka divebombers, based on Sicily, just a short flight from Malta. The rocky little British colony, the key to the Mediterranean, was the principal objective of the German bombers, but there was one other target high on their list of priorities: HMS *Illustrious*.

On 7 January 1941, *Illustrious* accompanied the Mediterranean Fleet on Operation Excess to escort large merchant convoys to and from Malta and Crete. Once that task was completed, Admiral Cunningham wanted to make the most of the Fleet's presence to seek out and attack enemy shipping along the Italian coast. Rear Admiral Lyster and Captain Boyd implored their Commander-in-Chief not to place *Illustrious* within range of the Stukas based on Sicily. With only five or six Fulmar fighters fit for action after a series of losses to the squadron, the carrier was as good as defenceless against hundreds of German divebombers. But Cunningham rebuffed their pleas, insisting she was needed for the morale of the rest of the fleet. As events soon proved, it was a fateful decision.

The morning of 10 January was a bright one and Lts Lamb and Torrens-Spence were leaning on the rail of *Illustrious*'s quarterdeck enjoying a post-breakfast cigarette. Beneath them, the surf seethed and frothed under the force of the carrier's giant propellers. The force was close to the island of Pantelleria, 60 miles southwest of Sicily and 150 miles west of Malta. They were watching the escorting destroyer, HMS *Gallant*, cutting through the surf, when a huge explosion tore off her bow. She had struck a mine that had detonated her forward magazine, killing sixty-five men. The rest of the ship's company were rescued and *Gallant* was towed into Malta but it was a bad omen for the watching airmen. Much worse was to follow.

Torrens-Spence, the senior pilot of 819 Squadron, had been briefed about the Stuka threat. He turned to Lamb and said: 'This is a day you will never forget. You can thank your lucky stars that you are flying this morning and not sitting in the hangar at action stations.'

It was almost 1230 and Lamb was returning to the carrier after a morning hunting submarines. Getting low on fuel, he was circling the carrier waiting for her to turn into the wind so that the next wave of aircraft could take off and he could land on. Back on board, the radar officer looked on his screen in horror: a swarm of aircraft was bearing down on the carrier. Lamb banked, levelled out, and had begun to make his approach when he watched the first screeching Stuka dive from on high and drop its 1,000-lb bomb. Every gun on the *Illustrious* opened with a furious barrage, but there was little they could do to prevent the thirty-three divebombers from hitting such a large target, falling vertically upon her and dropping their deadly loads from a mere 500 feet. In the chaos of the minutes that followed, the Stukas scored six direct hits with their enormous bombs; the three-inch-thick armour on the flight deck of Britain's most modern carrier and the reinforced fire curtains of the hangar were no defence against the assault. One of the bombs dropped straight into an open hangar lift-well, and the force of the explosion was so great that it picked up the lift platform and dumped it on the flight deck. From the bridge of his flagship, Admiral Cunningham watched in awe as the *Illustrious* battled for her life. 'We opened up with every AA gun we had as one by one the Stukas peeled off into their dives, concentrating almost the whole venom of their attack upon *Illustrious*,' he recalled in his memoir. 'At times she became almost completely hidden in a forest of great bomb splashes . . . We could not but admire the skill and precision of it all. The attacks were pressed home to point-blank range, and as they pulled out of their dives, some of them were seen to fly along the flight deck of *Illustrious* below the level of the funnel.'

They certainly weren't admiring the skill and precision of it all down in *Illustrious*'s hangar, which had become a scene of utter horror. For reasons that no airman could ever fathom, the drill was that whenever the carrier came under attack and action stations were called, they were to head down to the hangar where they were to remain, closed down, listening to the boom of the falling bombs and the ceaseless crack of the AA guns until the danger had passed. But the hangar was probably the most dangerous place on board, being packed with aircraft, tons of aviation fuel, tens of thousands of rounds of ammunition and dozens of torpedoes, bombs and depth charges. The state-of-the-art flight deck could take only so much punishment against the 1,000-lb fully armour-piercing bombs of the Stukas – and even when a smaller 500-lb arrived through the open lift shaft, the result was carnage below deck.

Many aircrew officers took themselves to the wardroom during an attack, figuring that, as there was nothing they could do, they might as well have a gin and tonic and read the paper until they were given the all-clear. On this occasion the wardroom took a direct hit. The effects of a blast can be extremely random and in this instance, while the thick metal supporting columns of the wardroom were bent into crazy shapes by the explosion, an RAF officer, on board as an observer, was found sitting in an armchair, holding a copy of *The Times*, but with his head nowhere to be seen and the clock still ticking on the wall behind him. Torrens-Spence was one of only three officers in the room to survive.

But it was the men caught in the hangar who suffered the worst horrors. The disintegrated bodies of men, talking and walking just a moment earlier, lay scattered across the deck and the bulkheads. The first deaths were caused by the blasts themselves and a storm of red-hot metal shards measuring up to four feet long, decapitating and dismembering anybody caught in their dreadful path. All the aircraft quickly caught fire, setting off their ammunition. Thousands of rounds bounced around the metallic interior, and anyone lucky enough to survive the maelstrom soon perished in the intense heat and thick, acrid smoke that followed. Within a matter of seconds the ship's insides had become unrecognisable, her decks twisted and buckled and filled with the screams of the dying and the injured, suffering from the most hideous wounds imaginable. Neil Kemp, whose torpedo had sunk the *Littorio*, was one of six Taranto raiders to die that awful day. The young Lieutenant, whom many had tipped to make it to Admiral, was talking to his new CO, Lt Cdr Jackie Jago, when the first bomb struck the hangar. When Jago turned back, Kemp was still standing there but without his head. The England rugby player William Luddington was among the many who lost their lives in the hangar.

Meanwhile, Lamb was fighting for his life in the skies above *Illustrious*. In theory, a Swordfish stood no chance against a Stuka in a dogfight, but it remains a source of great pride in the Fleet Air Arm that not one of their biplanes was ever shot down by the powerful German divebomber in the course of the war. Lamb succeeded in leading his attacker a violent, twisting dance before the German finally conceded defeat and returned to Sicily. Once again, the incredible manoeuvrability and durability of the

Swordfish, and the great skill of its pilot, had carried the day against its state-of-the-art predator. The wings and frames of Lamb's Swordfish had been shredded by the Stuka's machine guns and, more alarmingly, his fuel tank had been riddled and was spilling rapidly. With a matter of seconds before the engine cut on him, Lamb managed to ditch the Swordfish alongside the destroyer HMS *Juno* and was rescued.

Eighty-three men were killed and over 100 wounded, 60 of them gravely, during the 10-minute attack, but had it not been for the ferocious defence put up by her gunners, the casualty list would very probably have been a great deal higher and *Illustrious* might well have ended the day on the bottom. Incredibly, she lived to fight another day. (The German pilots were dumbfounded to learn that she had survived their pounding.) Working amidst the horrific conditions below deck, the ship's company toiled heroically to douse the flames and save the ship while the medics tended to the many injured. It was a testament to the designers and dockyard workers at Vickers Armstrong in Barrow-in-Furness, Cumbria that, instead of slipping beneath the waves as most of the world's other carriers would have done, *Illustrious* steamed to Malta at a stately twenty knots, in spite of the heavy damage to her steering. It was the sturdiness of her construction that saved her. The inferno raged below deck for some time but neither the magazines containing the torpedoes and bombs nor the giant fuel tanks caught light. Had they done so, *Illustrious* would have been blown out of the water and the death toll would have been closer to 2,000. One of the most stirring moments of the day was the sight of the ship's Fulmars, which had been unable to land on, returning to the scene to protect their mother ship after refuelling in Malta. They succeeded in shooting down half a dozen Stukas before the Germans turned back to Sicily. It was at a quarter to ten that night, her flight deck still steaming from the heat below, that *Illustrious*, bent and bruised but not broken or bowed, slipped into Malta's Grand Harbour. It was now that the grisly, traumatic task of collecting the bodies and limbs of friends and crewmates began. Some were never found.

The fact that the other ships of the fleet were left virtually unscathed by the Stuka attack provided the physical evidence that the Germans had come for one reason and one reason alone: to exact revenge for Taranto by sinking *Illustrious*. But they had failed and three days later they were back. This time, supported by Junker 88 bombers and Messerschmitt Me111 fighters, not to mention dozens of bombers and fighters from the Regia Aeronautica, the Stukas were determined not to give *Illustrious* a second chance. For much of the time, repairs continued below deck while air-raid sirens wailed and the gunners above tried to beat off the attacks. For two weeks, the Luftwaffe came in wave after wave but, heroically defended by the RAF Hurricane and Fulmar squadrons on the island and the gunners of the harbour defences, *Illustrious* refused to die. Two huge bombs succeeded in hitting her and three near-misses lifted her out of the water and smashed her against the wharf, damaging her hull. With losses mounting by the day and the RAF growing dangerously short of pilots, Lt Julian Sparke, who had taken part in the Taranto raid, volunteered to fly Hurricanes to help in the island's increasingly desperate defence. He died ramming a German bomber. On 24 January 1941, following a fortnight of round-the-clock repair work, much of it while under attack, Captain Boyd stood on the carrier's bridge, *Illustrious* slipped the Grand Harbour and steamed for Alexandria at twenty-six knots. On arrival, the carrier and her company were given a hero's salute by every ship in harbour.

In the eight months since she had been launched, the *Illustrious* had certainly led a colourful existence. It was from her flight deck that the first-ever attack on a fleet at anchor had been launched. That bold action, by half a hangar of antiquated biplanes, had swung the balance of power in the Mediterranean and undoubtedly helped Britain hang on to Malta and the Suez Canal, as well as beat Rommel in North Africa. Her efforts were applauded by Churchill and Roosevelt and hailed around the free world. The Battle of Taranto had truly been one of Britain's finest hours . . . and yet. And yet, when the gallantry medals were announced in the immediate aftermath of the attack, just two Distinguished Service Orders (to the two flight leaders) and four Distinguished Service Crosses were awarded. The fury below decks – chiefly amongst the sailors and deck crews – was uncontained. When the notice announcing the awards was pinned up on board, it was torn down by a disgusted sailor. No one had forgotten his 'manoeuvre well executed' signal the morning after the raid, and at first many suspected it was the cold hand of Admiral Cunningham grudgingly handing out the gongs. But subsequent investigations suggested that the meanness belonged to Whitehall mandarins, not the Admiral.

The matter was raised by Sir Murray Sueter MP in Parliament in May. As a retired Rear Admiral, he was disgusted by the lack of recognition and he suggested to the First Lord of the Admiralty that honours should be awarded to all forty men who took part in the raid. Medals were subsequently awarded to every one of them, but by the time they were announced a quarter of them were dead.

Almost half of the Swordfish crewmen who took part in the Taranto raid did not survive to see the war's end. But they did at least have the satisfaction of knowing before they went to their deaths that they had played a part in one of the boldest raids ever undertaken; an action that, even in the illustrious history of the Royal Navy, will be remembered as one of its more glorious episodes. Captain Boyd of *Illustrious*, addressing his ship's company after the raid, was speaking the truth when he said: 'In one night the ship's aircraft had achieved a greater amount of damage to the enemy than Nelson had achieved in the Battle of Trafalgar, and nearly twice the amount that the entire British Fleet achieved in the Battle of Jutland in the First World War.'

Operation Archery

0739 27 December 1941

The icy rooftops glistened in the moonlight as the sleepy fishing port of Vaagso slowly stirred into life. It was one of the shortest days of the year and it would be two and a half hours before the sun finally appeared. Fishermen were heading down to the quays to prepare their boats, mothers were busy laying the breakfast table and replenishing the fires and stoves to keep out the perishing cold. Sleeping off the festive celebrations, most of the 250 German troops stationed in and around the little Norwegian town were still in their barracks and billets. There was little reason to rise early. On the fringes of the Arctic Circle, far from the frontline of the European war, once again the biggest challenge of their day would be to beat off the boredom. Fifty of the troops, a crack unit sent to the area to rest up after months of hard fighting, could at least look forward to a day of lazing around and drinking.

Four miles offshore, Rear Admiral Burrough stood on the bridge of the cruiser HMS *Kenya* and checked the clock on the wall. They were a minute later – not bad considering the earlier weather and the distance the force had covered. At the mouth of the Vaagsfjord, the submarine HMS *Tuna* quietly rose from the depths of the Norwegian Sea and broke the surface of the ice-cold water. There was relief at both ends when the two vessels made contact. Everything was going to plan. Five hundred and fifty Commandos, the new elite fighting force in the British Army, fingered their weapons, ammo pouches and Mills bombs, fastened their haversacks and helmets and clanked their way up from the lower decks of the two troopships and lined up in silence by the landing craft waiting for the signal to embark. No one spoke. Surprise was essential.

The seven ships of the naval force reduced speed and slowly crept towards the harbour mouth. The coastal gun batteries were not to be roused. A Norwegian pilot on the bridge of the *Kenya*, familiar with the hidden hazards of the fjord, guided the ships towards land. Navigation in Norwegian waters is a perilous affair at the best of times. The rock formations below the surface are as sheer as those in the landscape that tower over the water like giant walls. One moment, a ship has fifty fathoms below it, the next it might be impaling itself on the peak of an underwater mountain. Only the most astute observer would have noticed the slight increase in surf, from the wake of the vessels, rolling towards the steep, craggy coast. It was probably as well that none of the 2,000 souls ashore had the first inkling of the fate that was about to befall their sleepy, picturesque community of red wooden houses, huts and warehouses stretched out along the waterfront. The clock was running down to the launch of Operation ARCHERY, one of the most audacious and significant raids undertaken in World War Two, with consequences far beyond those intended or imagined by its planners at Combined Operations HQ in Whitehall. By the time the first major raid by British Commandos was over, a subtle shift had taken place in the European conflict – and the very nature of warfare had been changed forever.

Within days of the evacuation of Dunkirk in May 1940, Churchill had sent a memorandum to his Chiefs of Staff asking how they might bring down a 'reign of terror' on German forces in occupied territories. Aware that it would be many years before the UK was ready to launch a full-scale fightback in Nazi-occupied Europe, the Prime Minister was eager to maintain an aggressive strategy. 'The completely defensive habit of mind which has ruined the French must not be allowed to ruin all our initiative. It is of the highest consequence to keep the largest numbers of German forces all along the coasts of the countries they have conquered, and we should immediately set to work to organise raiding forces on these coasts where the populations are friendly. Such forces might be composed of self-contained, thoroughly equipped units . . . How wonderful it would be if the Germans could be made to wonder where they were going to be struck next instead of forcing us to try to wall in the Island and roof it over!'

Churchill called these proposed elite units 'striking companies', and his Chiefs of Staff gave his impassioned suggestion a cautious welcome. Some of them were old enough to recall the Boer War forty years earlier – no doubt with some discomfort – when bands of a few dozen irregulars succeeded in tying down thousands of British troops. Churchill certainly remembered the Boer guerrillas well. As a war correspondent, he was captured by them in an ambush and held as a POW before managing to escape. When the draft proposal from his planners landed on his desk, containing the words 'Kommando-style', Churchill had no hesitation in rubber-stamping it. Knowing that Britain was unable to launch an invasion on his Western flank, Hitler concentrated his resources on the eastern and southern fronts of his rapidly expanding empire. The defences along the west coasts of Europe were barely upgraded and it was this weakness that the Commandos looked to exploit.

Work to raise the new Commando units within a 'Special Service Brigade' under the command of Combined Operations began almost immediately. The highly regarded Brigadier Joseph Charles Haydon, who a few months earlier had organised a special mission to evacuate the Dutch royal family, was handed the task of overseeing the creation of a new elite force within the British Army. He handpicked eleven commanders and left it to them to choose their junior officers and NCOs so that each unit would have its own distinct identity and stamp of its commander's personality.

Overeagerness to put Commandos into action at the earliest possible date led to the failure of two pinprick raids on Boulogne and Guernsey. Hastily planned and poorly executed by troops lacking sufficient training and suitable equipment, the Commando initiative hardly got off to a flying start. The general feeling back in Whitehall was that if that was the best our elite forces could manage, then Hitler could laugh himself to sleep at night. The almost comic shortcomings and mishaps of the raids demonstrated the need for much harder training, higher fitness levels, superior weapons and kit and improved means of transporting the units to and from the target site.

In March 1941, Operation CLAYMORE, the first large-scale Commando raid, was launched. The aim of the raid was to destroy the fish oil factories on the Lofoten Islands in northern Norway. Fish oil was an important commodity for the Germans: it provided Vitamin A which was vital for the health of their U-boat crews who were causing such havoc among Allied shipping out in the Atlantic. The crews went weeks without seeing daylight, and fish oil was the perfect substitute. The oil was also important for the production of nitro-glycerine in the manufacturing of explosives. Much planning went into the assault that involved two full Commandos – roughly 1,000 men – and seven

Royal Navy vessels. The Commandos stormed ashore, but to widespread disappointment, they met no resistance. The operation was a success of sorts. They destroyed their targets, suffered no casualties, sunk 18,000 tons of shipping, captured 200 German prisoners and gathered 300 volunteers to join the Free Norwegian Forces. But to sceptics of the Commando enterprise, the returns did not justify the huge logistical effort and the deployment of scarce resources and elite troops. (Operation CLAYMORE proved to be a more important moment in the war than it seemed at the time. A set of rotor wheels for an Enigma cypher machine and its code books were seized from the German armed trawler *Krebs*, which helped the scientists at Bletchley Park to break German naval codes.)

Unaware of this crucial development, the top brass of the three services looked upon CLAYMORE as a waste of scarce resources. Each service had its own sound reasons for not wanting to commit to the Commando cause: the Army resented the release of some of its best officers and men, the Navy was reluctant to free warships from other more pressing tasks and the RAF was eager to concentrate on hitting targets they considered to be of greater importance. Another problem with the Commando experiment was Admiral Keyes, the director of Combined Operations, an abrasive character who clashed regularly with the Chiefs of Staff. Though a close personal friend, Churchill knew he had to replace him. His choice of successor was a bold gamble. Lord Louis Mountbatten, a cousin of the King, was well-regarded within the Royal Navy but he was only a Captain, and would be taking his seat around a table of Generals, Admirals and Air Marshals. In the event, it proved to be an inspirational move by Churchill. A character of great charm, energy and daring, Mountbatten's arrival at Combined Operations HQ led to smoother cooperation between the three services and a significant ramping-up of operational activity.

Encouraged by the qualified success of CLAYMORE, large-scale raids that would cause significant damage to enemy operations became the priority at COHQ. Planners pored over maps of Europe's Western coastline from Spain to the Arctic, searching for a target that met all the criteria laid down. The target had to be a) vital to the German war effort, b) no more than a mile from the sea, c) offer good coastline for the amphibious landing of troops, d) present good intelligence of enemy numbers and defences and e) located away from areas with heavy concentrations of troops.

One location stood out from the list: Vaagso. At first glance, a small fishing community on an open-ended fjord halfway up the Norwegian coast towards the Arctic Circle might not appear to be the most urgent objective in the middle of a world war, but Vaagso fitted the bill on all counts. As Norway's main processing centre of fish oil, it was a vital asset. It also had the added attraction of being within reach of RAF bases in Scotland, which could give air cover to the raiding party and the naval force. The main objective of the operation was to destroy the processing factories, but to do that the force would first have to destroy the enemy's main defences. The most important of these were four coastal gun batteries on the island of Maaloy, 500 yards from the town, guarding the mouth of the fjord. Two other coastal batteries and a torpedo station also required elimination.

The official intention of Operation ARCHERY as stated in the planning documents was 'to carry out a raid on military and economic objectives in the vicinity of Vaagso island with the object of harassing the coastal defences of S.W. Norway and diverting the attention of the enemy Naval and Air Forces from Operation ANKLET.' This simultaneous operation was considered to be the more important of the two. Comprising a much larger force of twenty vessels, one Commando plus a contingent of Norwegian troops, its objective was the Lofoten Islands, 100 miles north of the Arctic Circle. The plan was for it to remain there for several weeks; it was to cut off German sea lanes, sweep the coastline, harassing convoys, and interrupt shipments of iron ore, another natural resource vital to the enemy war effort. A twin operation, it was hoped, would divide enemy resources and give each a greater chance of success. The plans were received enthusiastically at the Admiralty, which wanted to put on a show of strength in Norwegian waters to rattle the German High Command. The jagged coastline of Norway, with its myriad inlets, fjords and islands, allowed German shipping to move around largely unmolested, and provided an ideal base for harassing Allied convoys carrying vital supplies to Russia around the northern Cape through the perilous waters of the Arctic.

On 6 December, Rear Admiral Harold Burrough was appointed to take charge of naval forces responsible for the deployment of ships and bombardment of coastal defences during ARCHERY. Brigadier Haydon, the Military Forces Commander, was to oversee the operation on land. They had just three weeks before the scheduled date for the raid to finalise their plans. For his principal assault force, Haydon chose 3 Commando, led by Lt Colonel John Durnford-Slater, officially the very first Commando. Two troops from 1st Norwegian Independent Company, commanded by Captain Martin Linge, would also be deployed, while two troops from 2 Commando were to be held as a floating reserve. Detachments from the Royal Engineers and Royal Army Medical Corps would team up with the assault troops. In total, the raiding party amounted to 51 officers and 525 other ranks. The naval force comprised seven ships and a submarine. The Colony-class cruiser HMS *Kenya* was to be the headquarters of the operation as well as the principal bombardment ship. With a main armament of twelve 6-inch guns and a battery of smaller guns, it packed a formidable punch. The rest of the force was made up of four destroyers, HMS *Onslow*, HMS *Oribi*, HMS *Offa* and HMS *Chiddingfold*, the T-Class submarine HMS *Tuna* and two ships' transporters, HMS *Prince Leopold* and HMS *Prince Charles*. The destroyers were to engage enemy ships and vessels and positions ashore and provide anti-aircraft fire. *Tuna* was tasked with guiding the force into the fjord.

With the raid taking place in broad daylight and with little room to manoeuvre in the tight confines of the fjord, the ships were going to be vulnerable to air attack. Anti-aircraft fire alone would not be enough to see off the threat of divebombers. They were as good as sitting ducks for the Luftwaffe pilots. Air cover was essential, the RAF role crucial to the outcome. The two nearest bases in Scotland, Sumburgh on Shetland and Wick on the mainland, were 250 and 400 miles away respectively. Fuel was a major issue and the margins were extremely fine. The plan was to rotate four squadrons of Beaufighter and Blenheim fighters, each arriving to a strict timetable so that the naval force was exposed for the shortest period of time possible. In addition, ten Hampden bombers were assigned to attack enemy gun installations, six Stirling bombers were to hit Luftwaffe airfields at Herdla and Stavanger, and nineteen Blenheim bombers were to attack airfields and coastal shipping to draw off Luftwaffe resources and prevent them from attacking the assault force at Vaagso.

The Commandos were split into five groups with Group 2 handed the toughest task of leading the raid into the town of South Vaagso itself. In the final plans, the objects of ARCHERY are stated as:

(a) To destroy or capture enemy troops and equipment
(b) To destroy enemy industrial plants
(c) To seize documents, codes and instruments
(d) To arrest Quislings (collaborators known as Quislings after Vidkun Quisling, Hitler's puppet ruler in Norway)
(e) To withdraw Norwegian volunteers for the Free Forces

With only five hours between sunrise and sunset, timing would be critical. The Commandos were to carry ashore all the weapons and ammo they would need for a day's hard fighting. Most of the men carried the standard infantry Lee Enfield rifle with long bayonet (and 100 rounds), but a handful were issued Thompson 'Tommy' machine guns. All men carried Mills bomb hand grenades and the Fairbanks-Sykes Commando dagger. Bren gun crews and mortar detachments provided the heavy firepower on the ground. There was no chance of resupply during the action. All men were to help carry ashore the Bren magazines and mortars during the landings.

III Commando had been in intensive training for months at their camp at Largs on the West Coast of Scotland, concentrating specifically on amphibious landing operations. The men knew a major operation was in the offing but they had no idea where or when it would take place. Rumours swept through the wooden barracks when the daily exercise programme was suddenly intensified in the first half of December. Speculation turned to near-certainty when the 500-strong unit embarked in two troopships on the Clyde and steamed for Scapa Flow in the Orkneys, the base of the Royal Navy's Home Fleet during the war. Two full-blown rehearsals involving all three services took place before Brigadier Haydon summoned his officers and NCOs and unveiled details of the operation. After months of hard training and a mounting hunger for action, there was a palpable buzz of excitement below deck when the news reached the men.

The planners at COHQ had built a full-scale, minutely detailed model of South Vaagso based on recce photos and intelligence. Every building, street, alley and natural landmark was featured.

While the companies of the seven ships refuelled, loaded the magazines with shells and stored away the final shipments of provisions, each of the five Commando groups took it in turns to pore over the intricate model and run through the tasks they had been assigned. What they saw was a miniature version of a hilly island, eight miles long by four wide, situated on the west coast of Norway and facing onto the North Sea at the mouth of a fjord known as Vaagsfjord. Roughly 250 miles from the capital Oslo and 500 miles from the northernmost tip of mainland Scotland, it is one of thousands of islands along the coast, surrounded by a maze of waterways and inlets. It is separated from the mainland by a narrow stretch of water known as the Ulvesund that runs for five miles between the north and south exits to the North Sea.

Most of the island's 2,500-strong population lived in South Vaagso, the main town and home to the fish-processing factories concentrated on quays along the waterfront. The main street, running parallel to the coast for almost a mile, formed the spine of the community with a few smaller streets and lanes branching out towards the steeply rising hills of the interior. A few hundred yards to the east of Vaagso lies the much smaller island of Maaloy, where the Germans had built the gun batteries to guard the southern entrance of the Ulvesund. The area was defended by troops of the German 181st Division, amounting to around 250 men as well as 50 sailors.

On 22 December the large force detailed for Operation ANKLET set sail from Scapa into an ominously gathering sea for the longer passage to the Lofotens. The men of 3 Commando completed their last rehearsal and ran through their final checks for the first-ever large-scale operation involving all three services undertaken by the British armed forces. Operation ARCHERY was also Britain's first major incursion into Nazi-occupied Europe since Dunkirk eighteen months earlier, the first step in a gruelling fightback against the most powerful military force the world had ever seen. In one respect, ARCHERY was just a sideshow next to the titanic struggles of the Eastern Front, the North Africa campaign and the Atlantic convoys, but a great deal was riding on its outcome: the lives of 2,000 servicemen, the future of Combined Operations, the reputation of the newly formed Commandos and the morale of a battered, despondent British public reeling under the hellish bombardment of the Blitz. Failure was not an option.

It was an inauspicious start to the operation. When the seven ships of the raiding force slipped the sheltered sanctuary of Scapa Flow at 2215 on Christmas Eve, they steamed out into the teeth of a Force 8 gale. Heading for Sullom Voe, an anchorage 150 miles to the northeast in Shetland, the flotilla was battered by crashing waves and roaring winds. It was a particularly difficult passage for the two troopships, *Prince Leopold* and *Prince Charles*, which were tossed around in the churning seas like corks. Below deck, Commandos heaved and vomited and clung on as the ships lurched from side to side, up and down. No one slept a wink. There was no let-up in the storm for twelve hours. By the time they reached the calmer waters of Shetland at noon on Christmas Day, both ships had each taken on over 120 tons of water, most of it in the forward compartments where the flooding reached 14 feet. Both former North Sea Ferries had been damaged and needed emergency repairs. Rear Admiral Burrough had no choice but to postpone the operation by twenty-four hours. Christmas dinner was eaten at anchor, not on the open sea as planned.

When all repairs were completed by 1400 the following day, the winds had begun to drop and, to the relief of the commanders, the weather forecast they received was far more promising. Burrough gave the order to move out at 1600. Operation ARCHERY would launch at dawn, 27 December 1941. Before setting out, the assault force received a surprise visitor. Mountbatten was piped aboard *Kenya* where he delivered a short but inspirational address. Conscious that most of the men before him had never experienced combat, he warned them not to be too soft on their opponents, recalling the day his ship, HMS *Kelly*, was sunk off Crete, when the Germans machine-gunned his men in the water. 'There's absolutely no need to treat them gently on my account,' he said.

The weather was still fairly lively at the start of their passage across the North Sea, but it improved rapidly and by the time they closed on the Norwegian coast, conditions were excellent. Having made contact with HMS *Tuna*, Burrough lined up his ships as planned and, still shrouded in darkness, the force edged towards the southern end of Vaagso. But for the odd word on the bridge of the ships and whispered words of encouragement below deck on the troopships, the 2,000 men slid quietly towards their target. The one sound that the commanders wanted to hear was that of approaching RAF aircraft. Sure enough, bang on time, the distinctive hum of Hampden bombers began to fill the still, wintry air. Their target was the giant gun emplacement on the island of Rugsundo, eight miles to the east up Nordfjord, one of Norway's most beautiful and famous fjords. The AA guns stayed silent. The British presence had so far passed unnoticed.

Or so Burrough thought. In fact, the ships had been spotted by a lookout who immediately telegraphed the harbourmaster at South Vaagso to raise the alarm. The sleepy harbourmaster brushed aside the eager lookout's anxieties. 'Relax, it's nothing,' he told him, 'a convoy is expected this morning.' The idea of a squadron of Royal Navy ships having the audacity to slip into the narrow waterways of the well-defended coastline verged on madness . . . But dim flashes soon lit up the northern horizon and the thud of explosions from the bombing raid at Rugsundo echoed down the water. Ack-ack tracer streaked skywards, crisscrossing the dark sky. In their barracks and billets, the German troops were either asleep or slowly starting to wash and dress. At this time of year, the sun did not rise till ten o'clock. The fleet edged into the fjord, dwarfed by the steepling snow-blanketed cliffs and mountains. Brigadier Haydon said later that he felt as if he could stretch out his arms and touch the walls of the narrow waterway. Others said it was like entering a dark tunnel. Tense with anticipation, the silence was unnerving for the Commandos as they stood on deck by their landing crafts, breathing steam into their cupped hands and moving from foot to foot to counter the bitter cold. They all knew that within minutes the peace was going to be shattered in the most spectacular fashion.

Burrough checked the time again and announced: 'Hoist the battle Ensign!' Splitting off from the rest of the force, HMS *Chiddingfold* escorted the two troopships to the bay south of South Vaagso, out of sight of the main gun emplacement on Maaloy Island, half a mile or so around the corner. *Kenya* and the other destroyers crept forward to take up position.

The Commandos climbed into the Higgins landing craft suspended over the sides of the *Prince Leopold* and *Prince Charles* and the crews quickly loaded on the heavier equipment including ammunition magazines, Bren guns, mortars – and 250 kitbags full of Christmas stockings for the children of Vaagso. Embarkation was completed on time by 0835. For four minutes the men sat silently in the swaying craft, fidgeting with their weapons, focusing on the tasks ahead, praying for a safe return to the ship. At 0839 the landing craft began to descend. Chains clanked and jangled, pulleys whined and screeched, the boats splashed into the icy water as one and the formation moved off into the gently rolling water of the fjord's mouth. Within five minutes, as planned, No. 1 Group was ashore at Halnoesvik, the southernmost tip of the island, scrambling over the rocks towards the gun battery. Groups 2 and 3, the largest of the assault units, continued towards the main targets of South Vaagso and Maaloy.

The gap between the two islands was now clearly visible in the moonlight as they rounded the headland. The gunners aboard *Kenya* and the destroyers *Offa*, *Oribi* and *Onslow* braced themselves for the first salvos of the bombardment.

The first dim stirrings of dawn had lightened the sky above the Norwegian mainland only a little when the unflappable Burrough calmly gave the order: 'Open the line of fire!' It was 0848. The bridge-talker immediately passed on the command to the fire control department. Seconds later, a barrage of star shells burst over Maaloy, lighting up the snow-covered outcrop like a giant overhead lamp. Battle had commenced. And some battle it was to be.

Moving slowly between the two islands, *Kenya* immediately opened up with her two forward turrets, firing six-inch shells, before the captain turned her side-on to the island and opened up with a mighty barrage from all four turrets, fore and aft. Almost instantaneously, twelve shells, each weighing roughly half a ton, slammed into the German batteries. A cloud of flame and smoke burst into the sky. *Offa* and *Onslow* joined in the bombardment with their own broadsides. There was no return fire. They had caught the Germans by surprise, just as they had hoped. The gun crews were still in barracks when the first wave of the bombardment crashed down on the island. For the next nine minutes, the three warships pounded an area the size of a village green with between 400 and 500 shells. It was saturation shelling, and the mighty concussion of the guns reverberated along the coastline. When his landing craft were within 100 yards of the shoreline, Durnford-Slater took out his Verey pistol and fired 10 red flares in rapid succession, the 'cease bombardment' signal. As he and the men of Group 2 prepared to beach at South Vaagso, behind him plumes of smoke hung over Maaloy and the stench of cordite drifted across the short stretch of water.

The roar of the guns was immediately replaced by the re-assuring roar of aircraft overhead. Having attacked the Rugsundo battery to the east, diverting the attention of the AA batteries away from the approaching ships, the Hampdens dropped low and turned back to assist the landing parties on South Vaagso and Maaloy. Unfortunately, the best-fortified of the Rugsundo guns had survived the aerial bombardment and, moments after the last British aircraft had banked away, it opened up on HMS *Kenya*. The firing was erratic, but it was a nuisance that couldn't be ignored. A lucky shot could have had catastrophic conse-quences. *Kenya* swivelled its guns eastward and opened up. Royal Navy gunnery skills soon persuaded the enemy guns that silence was the more sensible option.

The turnaround in the weather had come as a huge relief to the RAF. Twenty-four hours earlier their airfields had been buried in snow, visibility was poor and winds battered the coastline. Now it was bright, clear, the wind was negligible and they had had time to clear the runways and scrape the snow and ice off the aircraft. Thirty seconds after the naval bombardment, right on schedule, seven Hampden aircraft, 'showing great skill and dash', according to the official report of the operation, swooped low over the water and dropped their smoke bombs over Maaloy Island on a 250-yard front at the landing site. Drifting down on their mini-parachutes, the phosphorus bombs fizzed and billowed in the windless atmosphere, creating a thick wall of white smoke.

At the same time, the landing craft of Group 3 advanced into the shallows with the men crouched out of sight. The group, led by Major John 'Mad Jack' Churchill, had been given the vital task of seizing the four coastal gun positions. Failure to put the guns out of action would doom the raid and present a grave threat to the warships. Even after the huge naval bombardment, the heavily fortified positions still needed to be silenced by men on the ground. A large garrison was known to be stationed on the island and a fierce engagement was predicted. Churchill (no relation to the PM), an eccentric, fearless character, was the obvious choice to lead the assault. Also known as 'Fighting Jack', Churchill liked to go into battle wearing a kilt and brandishing a claymore sword and, sometimes, a longbow. 'Any officer who goes into battle without his sword is improperly dressed,' he was fond of saying. He had won a Military Cross in France two years earlier and was said to have taken down a German with his bow and arrow.

On this occasion, he was no less flamboyant as his party burst ashore on Maaloy. Standing at the front of the landing craft, he played 'March of the Cameron Men' on the bagpipes as the boats ground onto the shingle before streaking into the smoke, waving his sword and bellowing at the top of his voice. In the event, there was little cause for his stirring actions. Resistance was minimal. Those Germans who did put up a fight were quickly cut down. The rest had been so stunned – quite literally – by the naval bombardment that they surrendered without complaint. The sappers set about demolishing the gun batteries, ammo dumps, barracks and the two oil factories. Barely twenty minutes after landing, Maaloy was engulfed in flames, all targets had been destroyed and the enemy had either been eliminated or captured. At 0924 Churchill signalled to the bridge on *Kenya* that the whole island was under British control. Safe from the Maaloy guns, the destroyers *Oribi*, carrying Group 5, and *Onslow* slipped through the thinning smoke into Ulvesund. At the same time, the Rugsundo battery, eight miles to the east, dared once again to try its luck against *Kenya,* firing blindly into the smoke-screen laid down by *Chiddingfold*. This time it received both barrels from the British cruiser, or at least two turrets' worth of sustained pounding.

If the assault on Maaloy had been a walkover for Churchill's group, South Vaagso was a different matter altogether. The problems began as the men prepared to disembark from the landing craft. One of the Hampdens was hit by AA flak or by fire from the German patrol boat *Fohn*, which had appeared from around the point along the coastline. The pilot had lost control but still tried to get away his smoke bomb before plummeting into the fjord, killing three of the four crew. Unfortunately, the smoke bomb fell right on top of the landing craft carrying a troop section. The commander, Lieutenant Komrower, saw the bomb at the last moment and shouted to his men as he jumped clear, but it was too late. It exploded in their midst and caused injuries, mostly from burns, to all twenty men on board. Two died outright, several others later of their hideous wounds. The craft caught fire, setting off ammo and flares in all directions. Engulfed in flames, it beached itself, crushing Komrower's legs beneath it. Prompt action from the Norwegian commander Linge saved Komrower from a painful end. Ignoring the flames and exploding ammo, he rocked the boat until Komrower was able to free himself and crawl ashore. The rest of the section scrambled to get clear of the inferno, dragging injured comrades as best they could.

Despite the accident, the smoke bombs enabled the rest of Group 3 troops to get ashore with light casualties from the sporadic fire of automatic weapons that greeted their arrival. Durnford-Slater's uniform caught light from sparks from another smoke bomb, but he was able to beat out the flames and set about establishing his HQ, close to the landing place, once the area below the southern end of the town had been secured. A temporary ammunition store was established nearby for a small mountain of demolition materials, which included 300 lb of plastic explosives, 150 incendiary bombs, half a ton of gun cotton and 500 yards of fuse. Group 2 headed straight into town, scrambling over the crags, under cover of the smokescreen, onto the road leading north into Vaagso. To the left the hills rose steeply above them, to their right lay the warships and Maaloy, smouldering from its naval shelling. Led by Captain John Giles,

3rd Troop raced to its first target, a German bunker and AA position. A short, brutal engagement ended with the British killing two officers and several others to take the position.

As the Commandos advanced into the town, nervous and bemused locals, appearing at doorways and windows, were ordered to stay indoors and keep their heads down. It wasn't long before the Germans had overcome the initial shock of the assault and organised their defences. Within minutes a bitter street-fight had erupted among the snow-covered streets, with isolated engagements flaring up across town, each of them fought with incredible ferocity by both sides. The Commandos were forced to work their way up the town, building by building, on two main fronts: up the main street and side roads and along the waterfront. The demolition teams of the Royal Engineers were forced to wait at the rear until the buildings were cleared and the line of confrontation moved northwards. Time and time again, a shot rang out and a Commando fell to the ground. In the frenzied confusion of the scene – clouds of smoke drifting through the gloom, the boom of explosions and crackle of small-arms fire filling the air – it was difficult to tell where the fire was coming from. The hills? Windows? Rooftops?

What was perfectly clear to the raiders – most of them seeing action for the first time – was that a hard day's fighting lay ahead and that a great number of them were unlikely to be still standing when the guns finally fell silent. Led by the fifty-strong unit of veterans sent to Vaagso for Christmas leave, the Germans put up a formidable defence. The post-operation dispatch to the

Admiralty, written by Haydon and Burrough, stated: 'Group 2, from the start, encountered very stiff opposition, both from Germany Infantry who fought to the last man in the buildings in which they were established, and from snipers, armed often with automatic rifles, who took up positions on the hillside west of the town where they were very difficult to locate owing to the excellent natural cover . . . By 1030 hours house-to-house fighting in the centre and northern end of the town had become bitter, resulting in severe casualties, especially in officers and senior N.C.O.s.'

The first wave of RAF fighters arrived over Vaagso at 0928 as the fighting began to intensify into a full-scale confrontation on land, sea and in the air. For the rest of the day, protection over the assault force was provided by the Blenheims and Beaufighters of 404, 254, 235, 236 and 248 RAF squadrons. They were by no means the most sophisticated aircraft in operation, and not a patch on the Spitfire or Hurricane, but they were flown by highly skilled, courageous crews and, with resources stretched to breaking point, the sight of any friendly aircraft was welcomed by the forces below. The German air base at Herdla – 100 miles to the south, or 30 minutes' flight away – was in a state of high operational readiness, but it was first thing in the morning and the nine Me109s based there still needed to be de-iced. It was almost ninety minutes after the raid had begun that the first enemy aircraft appeared at the scene. Two Me109s swept in and homed in on the slower, less manoeuvrable Blenheims. Communications were proving to be a major problem between the many units involved in the operation – as it was for British forces everywhere in the first half of the war – and the men on the ships could only watch as one of the German fighters, attacking from below, took the Blenheim unawares and sent it plunging into the sea.

Two days before the force had set sail, to the exasperation of ARCHERY's commanders, Bomber Command cancelled its plans for the Stirling bombers to launch an early morning bombing raid on the airfields at Herdla and Stavanger, where a total of eighteen Me109 fighters were based. (There were a further nine at Trondheim to the north but they would all have to use Herdla as an advanced refuelling base.) The Stirlings were reassigned to what was seen as a more urgent priority, and this left the fighters free to operate all morning until a subsequent bombing run by Blenheims scheduled for noon. For two hours, during the critical early phase of the assault, the force was susceptible to attacks from the air. At the very least, the attentions of the Luftwaffe were a distraction the raiders could have done without.

As activity in the air increased and the battle for Vaagso intensified, fighting erupted at sea. Once the smokescreen for the landing parties had cleared, the destroyers passed through the narrows between the two islands and began seeking out enemy shipping. Small-arms fire from the town peppered the hulls of the ships and three minor casualties were sustained aboard *Oribi*, but the destroyers arrived at a timely moment. Four German vessels – three commandeered steamers and the armed trawler *Fohn* – had taken one look at the opposition and turned tail for the northern exit of the Ulvesund. They were no match for the

Royal Navy destroyers in speed or firepower. But like their compatriots on land, they made it clear from the outset of the engagement that they weren't going down without a fight. The *Fohn* immediately opened fire on the *Onslow* with her Oerlikon AA 20-mm guns and punched a few holes in her armoured side before the destroyer returned fire and killed half the crew. The other half rushed ashore and continued to fight back with small-arms fire, but a shell from *Onslow*'s main armament quickly put an end to their brave if futile resistance. At the same time, two Me109s attacked the destroyers with cannon fire but failed to hit their targets. In his official report, Captain Armstrong of *Onslow* quipped: 'At one moment we were sinking a merchant vessel with the after 4.7, covering the military with the foremost 4.7, engaging aircraft with a 4" and the close-range weapons were covering the landing party against German snipers. Unfortunately, there was no torpedo target.'

Two of the steamers, SS *Reimar Edzard Fritzen* and SS *Normar*, followed the *Fohn*'s example and beached themselves in a small bay to the north of the town. Shots were fired across their bows and their upper decks swept with Oerlikon fire but it failed to deter the crews who leapt overboard and scrambled ashore. The third, SS *Eismeer*, was left on the open water as its crew abandoned ship. While *Onslow* dealt with the *Fohn*, and sent boarding parties aboard the two beached steamers, *Oribi* steamed up the Ulvesund and landed a party of Commandos, Group 5, just south of the village of North Vaagso. Here the Commandos encountered only light resistance and they quickly rounded up the crews of the beached vessels as well as the town's chief collaborator. Their detachment of sappers cratered the coast road connecting South Vaagso and wrecked the telephone exchange.

Out on the Ulvesund, *Onslow* and *Oribi* had just finished sinking the steamers and the armed trawler when a German merchant ship, the *Anita L. M. Russ*, accompanied by a tug, appeared from the north. By the time they realised their blunder, the guns of the destroyers were already lined up. Seconds later, both vessels had been holed and were sinking fast. In a matter of minutes, the destroyers had eliminated 15,000 tons of enemy shipping. Their tasks completed, Group 5 withdrew to the landing site to re-embark the *Oribi*, harassed by a platoon of German infantry all the way to the shoreline. Seeing the threat to the Commandos, the captains of *Onslow* and *Oribi* turned all their guns towards land and opened up on the enemy, which allowed the men to clamber aboard without taking casualties.

The Norwegian troops under Captain Linge, back in their homeland, were desperate to get into the fight. In addition to their assault role, they were tasked with rounding up collabora-tors and seizing documents from the HQ. Working close to 4th Troop, led by Captain Forrester, they made their way along the buildings on the waterfront towards the German HQ in the Ulversund Hotel in the middle of the main street. The HQ had become a strongpoint of German resistance, commanded by the naval harbourmaster who had earlier ignored the lookout who had raised the alarm about the approaching naval force. Speed was of the essence if they were to take the HQ before the Germans had a chance to destroy the paperwork – but progress was hard. Fourth Troop had already lost two officers – Komrower, crushed beneath the flaming landing craft, and another taken out by a sniper bullet to the neck. The fighting was confused and intense. Gunfire crackled across the town, and the air was filled with the shrieks and groans of injured and dying soldiers and petrified civilians against a backdrop of exploding grenades, mortars and naval shells. The Commandos poured fire from their Tommy guns and Bren guns into windows and doorways, shattering glass, splintering wood, and kicking up puffs of ice and snow. The difficulty of the assault was made worse by having to ensure that Norwegian residents cowering in their homes did not end up as collateral casualties. Bursting in and out of houses and rooms, the Commandos had a split second to decide whether to open fire. Before lobbing a hand grenade through a window they had to make sure it was a German and not a local in there.

It was a similar story on the inland side of the main street where 3rd Troop were edging forward through a withering hail of fire coming from all angles. They were led from the front by Captain Giles, an outstanding athlete and the heavyweight boxing champion of Southern Command, worshipped by his men. The defence on this side of town was concentrated in a large stone house, and no amount of fire was able to dislodge the Germans. Eager to maintain some momentum to their advance, Giles decided to go for broke. Followed by his men, he raced across the open ground and crashed through the entrance. Bursting into every door, the Commandos tossed grenades and sprayed the rooms with machine-gun fire. Those who survived the onslaught fled through the back door, chased by Giles. But as the burly young captain emerged in the open, he was shot in the stomach by a wounded German on the ground. He died where he fell. Almost immediately, his second-in-command, Lieutenant Hall, was cut down by a sniper bullet, and the two men who went to his rescue suffered the same fate. Command automatically passed to Giles's younger brother, Bruce, but he was so shaken by the sight of John's death that the attack stalled and the troop was left without effective command.

Two hundred yards away, 4th Troop had fought their way up to the Ulversund Hotel. Unaware that the hotel was bristling with enemy, Captain Algy Forrester led a frontal assault on the building, his NCOs firing Tommy guns from the hip as they charged. Sprinting towards the main entrance, Forrester was a few yards short when he pulled the pin on his grenade and was shaping to hurl it when he was cut down by enemy fire and slumped on top of his grenade which, to the horror of his men, exploded beneath him. Two others were hit and the troop withdrew to consider their options. At that moment, Linge and his Norwegians arrived on the scene and immediately took command of the leaderless troop. Ever eager to take the fight to the enemy, Linge ordered another direct assault, in spite of the misgivings of some of the troops. Having gathered his men behind an adjacent building, leading from the front he gave the order to charge, but he had barely appeared in the open when an enemy bullet thumped into his chest. He dropped like a stone. His sergeant tried to pull him clear but another bullet smacked into Linge's body and the men were again forced to withdraw. Two assaults, two commanders dead. (Linge is still honoured in the Norwegian Army, which named a Commando Company after him. A large statue stands where he fell.)

From intelligence sources, the assault group knew there was a tank inside the garage next to the hotel. It was an outdated model, captured during the Fall of France, but in close-quarters fighting against lightly armed troops it had the capacity to cause havoc if its crew managed to bring it onto the streets. As planned, after Forrester's 4th Troop had cleared the area around it, two sappers, Sergeant Cork and Trooper Dowling, dashed into the building and laid a string of charges around the armoured vehicle. Dowling had just crawled out of the door when Cork lit the fuses. Usually, the fuses are cut to a length to burn just long enough for the demolition team to scramble to safety but, inexplicably, on this occasion the explosion was instantaneous. Cork never stood a chance and, such was the force of the blast, men over 200 yards away were hit by flying shrapnel. Incredibly, Dowling escaped without a scratch.

With all British officers and senior NCOs in 4th Troop and the Norwegian contingent either dead or injured, command fell to Corporal White. Distraught at the death of their leaders, whose bloodstained bodies lay scattered in the snow all about them, the men of both units were baying to storm the hotel and exact revenge. Aware that a change of tactics and more firepower were required to crack the German stronghold, White beckoned over a mortar unit crouched in the shadows of a neighbouring building. Minutes later, ten 3-inch bombs, fired by a Sergeant Ramsey, rained down on the hotel. As the upper floor burst into flames, White gave the order to charge. Several dozen men rushed along the street, guns blazing, before hurling themselves at the foot of the front wall. Each man reached for his Mills bombs, the distinctive iron-cast 'pineapples' that the British Army had been using as hand grenades since the First World War. Pulling the pins, they counted 'One, two . . .' then stood up and hurled them through the windows and into the entrance. '. . . Three, four!' A succession of explosions rocked the building. Glass shattered and clouds of dust, plaster and smoke filled the interior as White and his men, hollering, burst inside. Within minutes the hotel, the largest public building in town and the fulcrum of the German resistance, was cleared, and White's casualty-ravaged unit reassembled to the rear of the hotel.

Casualties were mounting so fast that Durnford-Slater called for all spare troops to be brought forward. The clock was ticking, and if the demolition teams were to complete all their scheduled tasks, the Commandos had to secure the northern end of the town first. As it was, the assault party was still pinned down at the southern end and had advanced only a few hundred yards from the landing site. Churchill, who had completed his work on Maaloy, sent over half of No. 6 Troop, commanded by Captain Peter Young, a highly talented young officer destined for high rank. The floating reserve was brought ashore and the reserve unit at Durnford-Slater's HQ was also sent into action. This was the critical juncture of the action and every available body was committed to the fight.

As Durnford-Slater reinforced and reorganised his men, thirteen Blenheims from 114 Squadron, each carrying four 250-lb bombs and a batch of incendiaries, arrived over the Norwegian coast 100 miles to the south shortly before midday. Dropping to a height of 250 feet, the squadron lined up and swept towards the Luftwaffe aerodrome at Herdla, the wooden collection of huts and timber runways clearly visible in the snow-bound landscape. Air-raid sirens wailed and puffs of flak filled the air as one after another the Blenheims went in and dropped their devastating payload. Explosions tore up the earth, splintered the runways into kindling, and one Me109, which had been taxiing into position, flipped onto its back under the force of an explosion. Flames and smoke poured from the buildings. Hit by flak, one Blenheim lost control and veered violently off course, straight into the path of another as it pulled up and turned for home. The aircraft were so low the crews had no chance to bale out, and both plunged into the water. The raid was all over in seconds and by the time the last aircraft pulled up steeply and banked away, the runway had been turned into a mess of mud and scattered wood. Images from the Photographic Reconnaissance Unit taken immediately after the attack revealed over twenty craters. Operation ARCHERY could now proceed without significant interference from the air. Only aircraft making the long trip from Trondheim, and the last detail to have left for Vaagso, could trouble them now.

The action was intensifying on land, sea and in the air. Back at Vaagso, HMS *Offa,* protecting the naval force from the west, reported a merchant ship, the SS *Anhalt*, and an armed trawler escort named *Donner*, proceeding to Vaagsfjord from the north. It was just after noon and the last of the RAF bombs were falling on Herdla, 100 miles along the coast. Unable to hear or see the fighting on the other side of the mountain, the two vessels realised their error as soon as they rounded the point and saw the Royal Navy warships strung out before them. Ordered to capture the vessels, *Offa* chased the *Donner* as it made a dash for the open sea. It was a race the converted fishing boat was never going to win. *Offa* could make thirty knots to her ten and she quickly closed on her prey with her guns at the ready. *Offa* fired a warning shot, but still the trawler refused to stop. *Offa* fired again, this time with deadly intent, and after securing a number of hits, the crew abandoned ship. *Offa* went alongside the trawler and picked up the survivors. Unfortunately, the *Donner* had insufficient fuel for the return passage to Scotland under a prize crew, and was promptly sunk.

While *Offa* dealt with the trawler, *Chiddingfold* went after the *Anhalt*, which had turned hard and was steaming as fast as it could for the shore. She succeeded in beaching herself in shallow water and the crew were clambering into their rowing boats when the captain of the *Chiddingfold*, using the loud hailer, ordered the oarsmen, in German, to bring their boats alongside, warning that they would be fired upon if they disobeyed. The oarsmen kept pulling, *Chiddingfold* opened fire, sinking one boat and damaging the other. At that moment, enemy aircraft appeared overhead and, as the *Chiddingfold*'s guns were elevated to deal with the threat, the survivors of the second boat were able to scramble to safety – for the time being at least.

On his arrival at Durnford-Slater's command post, a few hundred yards away from the naval engagements taking place, Young was informed that only one officer was left amongst the original force troops fighting their way through the town. Up the road lay a scene of hellish devastation. Much of the waterfront was ablaze, and clouds of smoke rose into the bright morning sky; casualties were being carried or helped back to the shoreline for treatment. Men crouched behind walls and the corner of buildings. The attack had ground to a halt. The new plan was for Young's men to sweep along the waterfront, clearing the enemy from the wharfs and warehouses while the men of the floating reserve were to advance down the main street. From the outset, both parties were met by very stiff resistance, but sheer weight of numbers and firepower helped the British raiders regain the initiative and build some momentum. Houses and buildings were flushed of the enemy or set ablaze as the forces nosed northwards. Snipers once again were the greatest threat to progress. When three of Young's men dropped in rapid succession, hit by a sniper in the upper window of a building to their rear, the rest scrambled into a small woodshed close to the water. As more enemy guns opened up, thirty men, including Young and Durnford-Slater, crowded inside the small structure, attracting increasingly heavy fire. Bullets tore splinters from the piles of logs and timber and the men crouched behind any cover they could find. It was obvious to all that they could not survive there for much longer, but it was the same problem that had dogged the force all morning – they had no idea where the fire was coming from.

While Durnford-Slater and Young pondered their next move, the wider battle raged outside. Several formations of Heinkel 111 bombers, working in details of two or three, appeared overhead and tried their luck against the naval force. One was shot down and the rest were driven off by ferocious AA fire having dropped their bombs wide. Shortly afterwards, the Ragsundo gun battery, which had remained silent for three and a half hours and was thought to have been knocked out, suddenly returned to life and caught the *Kenya* off guard. All morning the largest warship in the force and the communications hub of the operation had fired the odd salvo at the battery, partly to check its guns' range but also to warn off the emplacement from attempting another attack on the force. It came as a shock when, just after one o'clock, a perfect shot from eight miles away punched a large hole in the side of the cruiser about ten feet above the waterline. Another round struck the armour belt and a near miss close to the port torpedo tubes slightly wounded one rating. *Kenya* immediately responded with a furious, sustained barrage that silenced the emplacement once and for all. At exactly the same time, more German aircraft had appeared overhead and the air was filled with puffs of smoke from the AA guns of *Kenya* and the four destroyers. The squadron of Beaufighters, circling the scene, helped to chase them away. On the ground, the demolition teams added to the din as one building after another along the waterfront was blown to pieces. Six Blenheims from 110 Squadron, based at Lossiemouth, had meanwhile arrived over the Norwegian coast to the south, with the aim of attacking enemy shipping and drawing Luftwaffe fighters away from Vaagso. Spotting a convoy, four of them dived to attack, but were immediately set upon by Me109s. None of them returned to Scotland.

Meanwhile, the sniper hampering the progress of Young's men was spotted in the top window of an adjacent building. On the signal, a dozen British guns opened up as one and the enemy marksman slumped forward over the windowsill. The Commandos were able to move on . . . or so they thought. The struggle for control of the town was by no means over. No sooner had they eliminated one source of heavy fire, when another started up, this time from a red wooden warehouse fifty yards ahead of them. One end of the building was a stable and the men could hear the horses stamping their hooves and whinnying with fear. Wide, open space lay between raider and defender. There was not so much as a solitary lamppost for cover to protect their advance. If the assault was not to peter out, the Commandos had no option but to run the gauntlet against accurate and heavy German fire.

The problem was solved by Lieutenant Denis O'Flaherty and the men of Group 1's 2nd Troop. They had been the very first troops ashore and silenced the gun battery at Halnoesvik on the southern tip of the island in a series of sharp skirmishes. Carrying two injuries and almost demented with fury, O'Flaherty had had enough of German stubbornness for one day. The young firebrand burst forward and dashed through the main entrance followed by a trooper. Instinctively, Captain Young followed them into the gloomy interior. They were met by a wall of fire and the first two men were cut down instantly. A bullet shattered O'Flaherty's jaw, holing the plate of his mouth and taking out an eye. Young fired into the darkness and withdrew. Perhaps sympathetic to the badly wounded officer, or too busy concentrating on the threat outside, the two Germans inside made no attempt to stop the wounded Britons as they dragged themselves out into the open. As the casualties were led away to the aid post close to the landing site, Young and his men set about devising a plan to flush out the Germans hindering their progress. Storming the building with a frontal assault was not an experience Young thought wise to repeat. He had a better idea: they would firebomb the building.

He ordered a contingent of men to work their way around to the stable end of the warehouse and lead out the horses. As the last of the animals cantered away, no doubt to find a quieter corner of town, the troop sergeant threw a bucket of petrol through a window and followed it with a grenade. A dull thud shook the wooden frame and moments later the building was engulfed by an inferno. The fleeing Germans were scythed down in a burst of Bren gunfire. With progress being made elsewhere in the town, the enemy gun boats and batteries silenced, the balance of the battle had tipped decisively in the raiders' favour.

Young's men pressed on to the northern end of the town, clearing out the pockets of resistance in small groups rushing from one building to the next. Durnford-Slater gave orders to seal off the town against enemy reinforcements arriving from the north so that the demolition teams were able to finish off the last of the factories and wharfs. The sun had long since begun its descent behind the mountainous interior of the island. Time was running out to complete all the tasks. Armed only with a pistol, the commanding officer had been a highly visible presence throughout the day's action, directing operations across town and providing a boost to morale for his embattled men. He was lucky not to have joined the mounting casualty list. The last of several close shaves occurred as the final explosives were being laid and he was making his way up to the front line to oversee the final stages. As he walked past a doorway, accompanied by a handful of minders and messengers, a stick grenade was lobbed at their feet. The grenade exploded almost immediately, severely wounding two of his men, but the Lieutenant-Colonel was able to get to his feet with nothing worse than a few abrasions and some ringing in his ears.

Unwelcome though it was, the quality and courage of the German resistance, which continued until the last man had re-embarked, impressed the raiding force. No doubt Durnford-Slater's thoughts were sought by Admiral Burrough and Brigadier Haydon for their official report of the raid which summed up the action in the town. 'It must be emphasised that the opposition in South Vaagso was severe in degree and skilful in quality,' the report reads. 'It appears from the interrogation of prisoners that the garrison had been fortuitously augmented by a detachment who had been moved into the town for Christmas but, however that may be, there is no doubt that the fighting spirit, marksmanship and efficiency of the enemy in this area was of a high order.'

At 1230 Durnford-Slater contacted the Force HQ on the bridge of HMS *Kenya* to inform them that resistance was nearly overcome and that final demolitions were in progress. The landing craft were making their way to and from the stony shore at the southern end of the town, ferrying dozens of wounded men and German and Quisling prisoners as well as a large contingent of locals. Among them were elderly men and women and mothers with babies and small children, but mainly they were young volunteers, who had been gathering all day by the landing site, eager to join the Norwegian Free Forces based in the UK. At 1250 hours, the commanders ordered full re-embarkation and the last of the Commandos, covering their withdrawal, started making their way back to the landing site. Young's men held the area but there was no opposition on the ground now.

The Heinkel bombers that had recently appeared overhead the fjord tried their luck against the ships, but were beaten off each time by RAF fighters and some fierce fire from the Navy gunners. Against a backdrop of raging fires and billowing clouds of smoke, faces bloodied and blackened, uniforms torn, the men filed through the devastated town, with the evidence of a bloody day's work all about them. Dead Germans littered the ground, ruined buildings smoked and steamed, charred timber and debris choked the shoreline. Some of the buildings were still burning so hot that the men had to divert from the main street and walk along the foot of the hill. In his war memoir, Young recalled the grisly scenes of their withdrawal to the landing craft: 'As I went I counted the enemy dead. I saw about 15 lying in the open, but of course most of their casualties had been inside buildings . . . As we passed the German headquarters, the Ulvesund Hotel, I took an epaulette with yellow piping from one of the casualties. Here the dead lay thicker, some of them horribly burned.'

Young and his men were gathering up stocks of mortar bombs they had left earlier when a breathless messenger appeared to inform them that the last demolition was about to take place – the largest of a day that had already seen some massive explosions. They had three minutes to find cover from the moment that the sapper laying the fuses emerged from the 'Firda' factory and blew his whistle. The men were lying down close to the shore when a deafening blast filled the air and shook the ground. A mountain of black smoke rose quickly into the darkening sky and debris crashed over the town, splashing into the water before what was left of the structure collapsed in on itself.

With all his troops safely re-embarked, Durnford-Slater strode aboard the last landing craft at 1408, just as the sun began slipping over the horizon of the North Sea. Twenty-five minutes later all the craft had been hoisted and the force began its withdrawal. Behind them, plumes of dark smoke climbed as high as the snow-peaked hills above the once sleepy fishing community and pockets of orange flame burnt bright against the snow-covered slopes. The destroyers formed a protective screen for the assault craft, and *Kenya*, the last to leave the fjord, stopped briefly to fire fifteen rounds of 6-inch shells, at point-blank range, into the beached *Anhalt,* leaving her burning severely. It was almost completely dark by the time the naval force were clear of the fjord, out in the open sea, and the landing craft were raised out of the water and the men climbed wearily out onto the decks. As they did so, a formation of Heinkel bombers swept out of the gloom, but the gunners of all five warships were on high alert and beat them off with an intense barrage of flak. Streaks of tracer and bright bursts of explosive lit up the dark winter sky. The bombs came up short, the formation split and the Heinkels disappeared over the mountains. Their crews were wise enough not to return for a second attempt.

As the force made smoke for Scapa, aboard the two troopships surgeons and orderlies (assisted by the ships' cooks, still at their action stations) tended to the seventy-one wounded men, including a number of Germans. Intelligence officers went straight to work interrogating the prisoners, most of whom had been locked in the toilets of the two ships. News of the raid's outcome was signalled to the respective High Commands of Germany and Britain, prompting very different reactions. In London, there was jubilation; in Berlin fury and incredulity. Details of the raid were made public and were headline news in papers throughout Britain and the Commonwealth. After two and a half years of almost unrelenting setbacks, here finally was some good news. The message was clear: Britain's fightback against Nazi Germany had begun in earnest.

As the exhausted Commandos sat in the lower decks smoking their cigarettes and reflecting on the day's furious events and the loss of their comrades, little could they have known that they were now the trailblazers of a new and very potent form of warfare – one that in a few years' time, on a much larger scale, would eventually decide the outcome of Europe's most savage conflict on the beaches of northern France. Nor could they have known that the first raid of its kind would go down as one of the great *coup de main* operations of that war.

The force entered Scapa Flow almost exactly twenty-four hours after they had cleared Vaagsfjord and, as a hospital ship came alongside and took on the seriously wounded, Durnford-Slater went below to address his men. After congratulating them, he issued a warning: maintain the highest standards of discipline and fitness on leave or go back to your regular units. 'Have all the fun that's going – drinking, gambling, chasing the girls and so on – if it appeals to you,' he said. 'But if these things interfere with your work they must be put aside . . . You must always behave and look like super soldiers. If you cannot then there is no place for you in Number 3 Commando.'

One hundred and two prisoners were captured in the raid, comprising seven officers, ninety-one ratings and other ranks (forty Army, fifteen Navy and thirty-six merchant seamen) and four Norwegian Quislings. In addition seventy-seven Norwegian volunteers were embarked. It is estimated that at least 150 Germans were killed in South Vaagso and Maaloy in the course of the operation. The cost for 3 Commando was seventeen officers and men killed or died of wounds, and fifty-four wounded. Navy casualties included two fatalities and six wounded. The Norwegians lost one man, Linge, plus two wounded. The RAF suffered the heaviest casualties, losing thirty-one men and eleven aircraft: two Hampdens, two Beaufighters and seven Blenheims.

All planned tasks were completed. On Maaloy, four coastal gun emplacements, one anti-aircraft battery, searchlight and generator were blown up, fuel and ammunition dumps set ablaze, the German barracks and HQ were demolished in the naval bombardment. On Vaagso, every single fish-processing factory was destroyed by fire or explosives, and every German office, billet, barracks or hut was burnt out or demolished. Other targets destroyed included the W/T Station and mast, the transport depot, a beach mine store, a telephone cable hut, the Ulvesund Hotel (the German strongpoint) and the operating mechanism of the main lighthouse. The road was cratered between North and South Vaagso and the apparatus in the telephone exchange at a neighbouring hamlet was smashed beyond repair.

The raid gave hundreds of elite troops vital combat experience and the experience gained there was absorbed into future Commando training instruction. The success also provided a welcome boost to the morale of the army as a whole as it rebuilt itself after Dunkirk. The Navy had carried out its tasks with barely an error, safely transporting men to and from the objective and protecting the area during the assault. The RAF were equally impressive, arriving bang on time and maintaining constant air cover throughout, seeing off the enemy, laying smoke-screens, drawing off the Luftwaffe and bombing Herdla airfield into disuse. Above all, the three services had proved they could work together to pull off an audacious and highly effective assault on enemy territory. In short, the raiders had carried out exactly what the planners had tasked them to do and hoped to achieve. It was a major coup for Mountbatten and Combined Operations, proving that a complex but clear plan could be carried out to near-perfection if freedom and flexibility was granted to the men on the ground.

Ten days after the force returned to Scapa, the following dispatch, introducing the official summary of the operation, was submitted to the Admiralty by Sir John Tovey (aka 'Splashguts'), Commander-in-Chief, Home Fleet. 'The operation was well conceived, planned and rehearsed with skill and thoroughness, and executed with great efficiency, precision and boldness. Though a minor operation, it affords a fine example of smooth and effective cooperation between the three Services and reflects great credit on Rear-Admiral H. M. Burrough, C.B., Brigadier J. C. Haydon, D.S.O., O.B.E., and all officers, ratings and ranks taking part. The cooperation of the aircraft of Coastal and Bomber Commands was most effective. The operation could not have proceeded without it.'

Impressive enough though they are, the statistics, bare facts and official reports that you can read in the National Archives at Kew do not reveal the true significance of the intense, six-hour running battle in a remote corner of the Norwegian coast. In the wider context of the world war, Vaagso was a minor operation, a mere butcher-and-bolt skirmish on the northern fringes of a massive conflict. It would be months before the raid's greater significance began to emerge and years before its impact was fully understood and appreciated. Ultimately, its consequences were wildly disproportionate to the original aims.

The short-term strategic gains were impressive enough. News of the raid set alarm bells ringing in the corridors of German High Command. Intercepted intelligence reports revealed bitter recriminations between Berlin and the German HQ in Oslo. The British had intended the raid to be no more than a harassing operation to divert German resources from ANKLET, the larger operation to the north (which ended in failure, and prematurely, much to Churchill's fury). No one had imagined for a minute that it was ARCHERY, not ANKLET, that would cause the greatest consternation in Berlin. And cause not mere unease, but pure panic. For Hitler, Operation ARCHERY confirmed his long-held suspicion that it was in Norway that the Allies would one day launch their inevitable invasion of the mainland. Rich in natural resources, it was a country vital to his war effort and had to be safeguarded at all costs. To that end, Hitler insisted 30,000 troops be immediately dispatched there and ordered the renovation of Norway's coastal defences. By mid-1944, over 370,000 German troops were stationed in Norway, effectively sitting on their helmets at a time when they were desperately needed to shore up Germany's crumbling fronts in eastern and southern Europe. From then on, Hitler also began concentrating most of his naval forces in Norwegian waters, where the Royal Navy and RAF were able to keep them penned in for the rest of the war, picking them off one by one and preventing them from breaking out into the Atlantic to attack convoys. By the end of the war, most of Germany's major warships had been eliminated.

The first amphibious assault on an enemy coastline involving soldiers, sailors and airmen might not have been one of the key points in world history, but it certainly led to one. The men who carried it out were the pioneers of a form of warfare that revolutionised military thinking. The first steps of the D-Day landings in Normandy were taken in Vaagso.

Operation Biting

27 February 1942

By Thursday, the troops had all but given up hope. For three days, they lay on their beds in full battledress waiting for the order to climb aboard the twelve Whitley bombers lined up on the runway outside. But every afternoon, the staff officer arrived at the airfield to announce that the operation had been postponed and the air was filled with the sound of 120 men cursing and groaning as one. Three conditions had to be satisfied. They needed a full moon, or as good as full; they needed a rising tide and a calm sea for the landing craft so that the Navy could get them off the beach as quickly as possible once the task was completed;

and they needed no more than a light wind so that they didn't take casualties when they went in. But it was late February and the weather was playing havoc with the plans – and their nerves.

If the raid didn't go ahead on Thursday, it would be back to the mud and monotony of Tilshead barracks for another month of training until the next full-moon period – and the men had had quite enough of Tilshead and quite enough of training. But on this occasion, there was a difference to the familiar routine. When the staff car swept past Thruxton's guardroom and up to the wooden troop huts, it wasn't the staff officer who stepped out of the back, but Major General 'Boy' Browning himself, Commander of 1st Airborne Division. The weather was clear. They were to take off that night, he told them.

Major John Frost, the commander of the raiding force, was as pleased as anyone to be seeing some action at last, and there was a bounce in his step as he made a final tour around the airfield huts to visit his men. He found them in high spirits. Some were busily fitting their parachutes and checking their weapons; others sat around, smoking and drinking mugs of tea and chatting excitedly. In one of the huts, the men were singing at the top of their voices.

After two months of exercises and rehearsals, it was now that Frost was able to reveal the object and destination of the mission. Until then, Operation BITING had been veiled in secrecy. Its details were known to the Prime Minister and his War Cabinet and a handful of scientists, but no one else. Not even the four other officers who were to take part in the raid. Now he could put them out of their mounting curiosity and finally tell them where they were going and why.

There was a beautiful, clear sky above them, strewn with stars, when the men of 'C' Company formed up and marched around the perimeter of the airfield. The piper played the regimental marches of Scotland as the twelve sticks of men filed out to the twelve Whitleys of No. 51 Squadron RAF. Frost was enjoying a last cigarette and a flask of tea fortified with rum when he was called to the telephone. It was Group Captain Sir Nigel Norman, the man who planned the air element of the operation. The French coast, the RAF man warned, had taken a dumping of snow and returning crews had reported that the anti-aircraft flak in the area around Le Havre was a little 'lively' that night.

Frost swore under his breath as he hurried out to his aircraft. It was too late to swap their khaki uniforms for the white smocks issued for winter warfare. As he prepared to climb aboard the twin-engined bomber, the familiar figure of Wing Commander Charles Pickard, the squadron leader on the night, approached him. Pickard, the hero of innumerable bombing raids and a name known throughout Britain's households, made no effort to hide his unease about the raid as Frost passed him his flask of tea and rum. 'I feel like a bloody murderer,' he said. It was not an auspicious start to the first major operation carried out by British paratroopers.

No element of the British armed forces lost a greater percentage of its men during World War Two than Bomber Command and, at the start of the conflict, a good number of those losses could be attributed to Germany's night-time detection system. The eminent scientist R. V. Jones, Britain's first Scientific Intelligence Officer, who had been working on radar technology for many years, was convinced that Germany was using some form of night-time early warning radar system to alert them to the imminent approach of British bombers. Bomber Command's losses had increased steadily throughout 1941 and the crews who survived the raids into the continent backed up Jones's suspicions. Flying sorties every night the weather allowed, and losing men and aircraft at an alarming rate, Bomber Command was desperate for any help they could get from their shadowy colleagues in the top-secret Intelligence Section of Britain's Air Ministry. No one was more eager to help them, or better qualified, than the brilliant physicist Reginald Victor Jones.

Images from the RAF's Photographic Reconnaissance Unit (PRU) were the key to cracking Germany's radar system. Stripped of their armament to reduce weight and increase speed, Supermarine Spitfires, fitted with cameras, were dispatched on lightning sorties over occupied Europe to spy on German developments and activities. Using the PRU images in conjunction with other intelligence sources, Jones soon discovered that high-frequency radio signals were being transmitted across Britain from a directional radar system somewhere across the Channel. It was known as 'Freya', but how it worked, Jones had very little idea. These were the very early days of radar and little was known about a system which would revolutionise war in the air and at sea by VE Day. In the autumn of 1941, an RAF photographic unit returned from a mission to Cap d'Antifer near Le Havre with a fresh batch of images, revealing a suspicious installation at a private property. Flight Lieutenant Tony Hill, one of the unit's most skilled and daring pilots, went to investigate it more closely. He overflew the site in his Spitfire on 5 December and, within twenty-four hours, Jones was running over the images with his magnifying glass.

As always the pictures were brilliantly clear and precise and Jones's eye was immediately drawn to a dish-like object, roughly ten feet in diameter, sitting in the front garden of an ostentatious villa on a 400-foot cliff above a beach near the village of Bruneval. Jones was convinced he had found the missing element he had been so desperately looking for. The vertically standing dish, shaped like a saucer, was known as a Würzburg and it worked in combination with Freya. Further RAF images soon revealed a whole chain of radar apparatus strung out along the shores of western Europe facing Britain. Before he and his fellow scientists could devise a way of confounding or even defeating the German early warning system, Jones needed to know how it worked. There was only one way to find out.

Knowing Churchill's enthusiasm for any form of offensive action, Jones immediately suggested a raid to capture the Würzburg at Bruneval. His idea was sent up to Combined Operations Headquarters in Whitehall, where Lord Mountbatten and his staff were only too happy to lay on the suitable arrangements. Plans were immediately set in motion to mount the raid at the earliest possible opportunity. The 1st Airborne Division was the obvious choice to execute the raid. Unlike a large amphibious landing force, paratroopers could be inserted quickly and remain undetected in the crucial early stages, allowing them to capture and hold the objective while the engineers set about their work. The operation was given the go-ahead in early January and scheduled for mid-to late February.

The force handed the task was C Company of the 2nd Parachute Battalion, plus some sappers from the Royal Engineers and a handful of men from B Company to make up the numbers. When they arrived at the training base at Tilshead in Wiltshire at the end of January ('a miserable sort of place with mud everywhere', he noted), Frost still had no idea about the nature of the mission he had been assigned. He found it difficult to disguise his disappointment when he was informed by the liaison officer from divisional headquarters that he and his men had been chosen to carry out a parachuting demonstration for the benefit of the War Cabinet somewhere on the Dover coast or Isle of Wight. The liaison officer held out the prospect that C Company would almost certainly be chosen to carry out a raid in enemy territory at some time in the future, but that was little consolation. When the young officer began to tell Frost how he was to organise his men, Frost's moustache began to twitch with barely disguised fury.

The following day, the liaison officer returned to Tilshead and, binding him to the strictest secrecy, he told Frost the truth. The demonstration was just a cover story, he explained. The raid was to take place within the month. 'I had no further objection to raise,' wrote Frost.

When training for the operation began, the men had only just completed their parachute jumping course and only a few of them had leapt from a moving aircraft more than five times. At this stage of the war, only a small handful of British service personnel had qualified to parachute. In the months to come, thousands of fully trained paratroopers would be available to jump from aircraft all over Europe, but the 1st Airborne had only just been founded and equipment, including aircraft, was extremely hard to come by. Such was the strain on resources in rebuilding the army after Dunkirk that the small, fledgling airborne force barely had a parachute between them or an aircraft to jump out of, let alone qualified instructors to show them how to do it. Major Frost recalled that when he joined the Paras, 'a damaged parachute and jumping-helmet captured from the Germans were the only models available and for aircraft . . . four Whitley Mark IIs were seldom simultaneously serviceable.' But once Mountbatten's Combined Operations HQ and the War Cabinet became involved, every resource and item of equipment Frost needed to carry out the raid were made available to them.

The training, which took place mainly on Salisbury Plain, was intensive and exhausting. Neither time nor the weather was on their side. All the equipment they had been promised soon began to arrive by the crate-load at Tilshead, providing further evidence for the men that they were about to be sent on a major operation. The item of equipment arousing the greatest amount of interest was the recently invented Sten submachine gun, a fully automatic rifle/pistol hybrid that made their bolt-action Lee Enfield .303 rifles look distinctly old-fashioned.

In the second week of February, the raiding party took the train to the west coast of Scotland to carry out training exercises with the Navy. They were quartered near Inveraray, aboard the *Prince Albert*, the parent ship of their landing craft which, all going to plan, would provide their means of escape from France after the attack. The freezing cold waters of Loch Fyne might not have been the most popular of training areas for the men, but the exercises did at least focus the minds on the challenges they faced. Embarking 120 men, with equipment, casualties and prisoners, in the dark and under fire, was, they soon realised, by no means a straightforward procedure. 'The possibility of being left stranded on the coast of France after we had done our job was unpleasant,' Frost recalled. 'And in the end we went on the raid without having had one really successful evacuation.' The high point of the training in Scotland was a visit from Combined Ops chief Lord Mountbatten who, without giving away details of the raid, made a stirring address to all ranks, naval and military.

Back at Tilshead, they carried out a practice drop with the Whitley bombers detailed to take them in on the night. It was the first time that No. 51 Squadron had ever dropped parachute troops but, unlike every other element of the training, the exercise passed off successfully. The cold ground was rock solid and there were a few sprains and bruises, but no serious injuries.

The raiding party consisted of 120 all ranks, divided into three groups with the code names *Drake*, *Hardy*, *Jellicoe*, *Nelson* and *Rodney*, who were each given separate tasks to carry out on the night. Major-General Browning chose the names as a salute to the Royal Navy, whose men and vessels would, if all went to plan, evacuate the raiders and their top-secret prize and return them safely to Portsmouth. BITING was to be a combined operation in the purest sense. The RAF was to deliver the Army to the target by air, the Army would execute their tasks on the ground, and the Navy would transport them from France by sea.

For security reasons, it was not possible for Jones or any other leading scientist in possession of highly confidential information to join the raiding force. Were they to fall into enemy hands, they would be subjected to the Gestapo's most extreme forms of interrogation to extract their invaluable store of secrets. And yet, it was important that an engineer with more than basic knowledge of radio technology joined the sappers tasked with dismantling the Würzburg. Were they unable to remove the apparatus, the engineer would at least be able to photograph it and scrutinise its parts at the scene. Any information whatsoever was to be welcomed by Jones and his colleagues down at the Telecommunications Research Establishment at Worth Matravers, near Swanage, on the Dorset coast.

A request for volunteers to take part in a 'special mission' was put out in the appropriate circles. One of the first to put his name forward was RAF Flight Sergeant Charles Cox, a former cinema projectionist who had never been in an aircraft, let alone jumped out of one. Nor had he ever been on a ship – and his wife had given birth just a few weeks earlier. It was only when he arrived at Adastral House on Kingsway, the London home of the Air Ministry, that Cox, an expert radio mechanic, was made to understand quite how 'special' the mission was going to be. Without revealing the precise objective of the mission, Cox was left in no doubt about the hazards involved – an impression reinforced when he was dispatched to Ringway, the parachute centre near Manchester, to learn how to jump. But Cox was not just bright and patriotic, he was brave too, and he took to the training with the same degree of commitment as the dedicated paratroopers.

All the key figures involved in the raid were men of the highest standing or greatest promise. Major Frost, who had been commissioned in the Cameronians, a Scottish infantry regiment, was a tough, resourceful leader, destined for fame in the grim battle at Arnhem. His men were mainly Commandos drawn from Scottish regiments. The Company Sergeant Major, Strachan, of the Black Watch, was almost a stereotype of his rank: a no-nonsense, highly efficient, experienced man, who had the huge respect of men and officers alike. If you wanted something done, you went to Strachan. During the training, a young German Jew, Peter Nagel, who had fled Germany before the war, was added to the party. He was to act as interpreter and his name was changed to Private Newman.

The air element was commanded by Pickard, whose fearless

exploits had already earned him a Distinguished Flying Cross. Frost needed only a short meeting with the dashing, handsome airman and his men to know his troops were in good hands. 'They belonged to a crack bomber squadron . . . We were left in no doubt as to their efficiency, and we felt that if anybody was going to put us down in the right place, they were the people to do it.'

The naval force assigned to take the raiders back to England was under the command of Commander F. N. Cook of the Royal Australian Navy. He was one of 400 (out of 1,250 men) who survived when the battleship HMS *Royal Oak* was sunk by a torpedo from a German U-boat while at anchor in Scapa Flow. His force, escorted by two destroyers, consisted of half a dozen Motor Gun Boats, the same number of assault landing craft, and two support landing craft, manned by thirty-two officers and men of the Royal Fusiliers and the South Wales Borderers. They were to provide covering fire while the raiding party was embarked.

The last week of the training was spent rehearsing the evacuation in the landing craft, but there was little improvement on their poor performances in Scotland. Much of each day was spent in the back of troop trucks, slowly winding through Dorset lanes to get to the stretch of coast where the exercises took place. When they finally arrived, foul weather prevented them from taking to the water. It was highly frustrating and Frost, not a man to flap in a crisis, was starting to get worried. The last rehearsal 'could not have been a more dismal failure', he wrote.

The equipment containers landed in the wrong place, the landing craft went to the wrong beach and the paratroopers ended up ten miles from the target site . . . in a minefield.

The raid was scheduled to take place forty-eight hours later, on the night of Sunday 23 February, but the Navy were insisting that a further rehearsal should be carried out. Fortunately, the weather that had been causing so many problems forced a postponement to the following night, and a final rehearsal was performed near Southampton. It wasn't perfect, but it was a great improvement on the shambles that had gone before.

By the eve of the raid, Frost's men knew every last detail of the German position at and near to the villa. They knew every strongpoint, pillbox, light machine gun position, every roll of barbed wire; they knew the location and exact strength of the local billets and barracks and the weapons at their disposal. They even knew the names of some of the troops. For this remarkable intelligence, they had the French Resistance to thank, and three men in particular.

The man in overall command of reconnaissance and intelligence gathering was Gilbert Renault, known to the British Intelligence Services as 'Colonel Rémy', one of the most famous secret agents of the war. After a short stay in England following the collapse of France, Rémy returned to his homeland to recruit and train underground intelligence operatives. It was to one of his best men, Roger Dumont (codename 'Pol'), that he entrusted the task of reconnoitring the Bruneval site. Assisted by Charles Chauvenau, aka 'Charlemagne', a garage mechanic from Le

Havre, Pol quickly began gathering remarkably detailed information about the objective. By chatting to one of the guards near the villa, they made the crucial discovery that, in spite of the warning signs along the cliff, the beach below was not mined. The RAF's photographic unit, meanwhile, continued to provide first-class images of the coast from which a very detailed model of the objective was constructed.

A considerable number of German troops were stationed in the area immediately around Bruneval, comfortably outnumbering Frost's force. At the large, modern villa, guarding the Würzburg apparatus to the front, was a garrison of between 30 and 40 men. Most of these were thought to be from the signalling corps and a few of them were likely to be in the house when the paratroopers arrived. Many others would be operating or guarding the Würzburg dish or the Freya installation 750 yards to the north. The major threat was likely to come from the 100-strong garrison, stationed at Le Presbytère, a complex of farm buildings 200 yards to the north of the villa, set within a rectangle of woodland, housing coastal defence troops and off-duty signallers. There were also three or four dozen troops billeted in Bruneval village, less than half a mile from the beach along the main lane. These were believed to be the personnel who manned the defensive positions on the top of the cliffs and down at the beach. The operational orders, shown to Frost, refer to eleven light machine gun positions around the villa, cliff and beach, as well as a pillbox halfway up the steep slope leading from the shore to the villa. They also refer to enemy infantry reinforcements based six miles away, and a reconnaissance battalion fifteen miles away.

Diversion raids by Bomber Command started on the night of February 17/18. Flying to targets in the Paris area, the bombing force were ordered to cross the French coast at low level between Le Havre, ten miles to the south, and the Somme estuary, eighty miles to the north, in order to get the enemy in the Bruneval area accustomed to the approach of low-flying aircraft by night.

The plan was to split C Company into three groups and drop them in a ten-minute period between 0015 and 0025, roughly half a mile to the east of the villa. 'Drake', the first and largest section, led by Frost, was to be the first to jump. After forming up, they were to head towards the cliff and capture the Würzburg. Their primary task was to enable Flight Sergeant Cox and the sappers, under Captain Denis Vernon, to dismantle the radar dish. The aim was to bring back the entire apparatus, but what couldn't be removed was to be photographed. There were fifty men in Drake, split into two groups. One under Lieutenant Peter Young, who had played a key role in Operation ARCHERY in Norway two months earlier, had orders to assault and hold the Würzburg while Cox went to work. The other, under Frost, was to clear out and secure the villa. Among the orders issued to Frost were the following instructions: 'No prisoners will be taken other than officers and technical personnel . . . It is imperative that the scientist (Cox) should run no risk of capture.'

The second group (known as 'Nelson'), under the command of Lieutenant Euen Charteris, was to capture the beach and hold it. The third ('Rodney'), under Lieutenant Timothy, was to act as reserve and/or fight off German counterattacks at the radar position or the beach.

Every man of Frost's party was to be in position by the time he blew his whistle to signal for the battle to begin. Speed and precise timing were to be essential. The raiders were not to remain on French soil for a minute longer than necessary. It would not be long before the enemy arrived at the scene in significant numbers, some armed with weapons considerably more powerful than Sten guns and Mills bombs. Good timing and a swift execution of the raid's objectives were essential for the evacuation as well. The Navy, strict timekeepers, would be waiting off shore. Whether it was the right shore was another matter.

It was 2230 when the first of the twelve Whitleys roared down the runway at Thruxton and climbed into the clear night sky above Hampshire and banked southeastwards towards the Channel. Pickard was at the controls and, behind him, Frost sat uncomfortably on the ribbed aluminium floor of the draughty fuselage, squeezed in amongst his men. To keep out the intense cold, some sat with blankets over their legs, others climbed into sleeping bags.

The noise of the bombers' huge engines and the heavy vibrations made talking impossible, but playing cards and singing helped break the tedium and distract minds from the challenges ahead. When the paratroopers had run through their favourite tunes, Flight Sergeant Cox added to the entertainment with a solo rendition of 'The Rose of Tralee'. The men had drunk so many mugs of tea during the countdown to takeoff that, an hour into the flight, many of them, including Frost, were desperate to piss. Unfortunately, the lavatories had been removed from all the aircraft in order to free up space and they had to squirm where they sat.

The twelve bombers formed up over Selsey Bill, south of Chichester, and left England behind them. As they approached France, a diversion bombing raid was taking place at Le Havre a few miles to the south. Two bombers attacked an aerodrome and marshalling yard. The paratroopers, their faces blackened with tar, had been in the air for almost two hours when the hole cover in each Whitley was removed and a freezing blast of air surged through the fuselage. Below, the flat surface of the Channel glistened in the moonlight and, as the aircraft levelled out at about 550 feet, they could see the snow-draped coast of France. Moments later, the long beams of coastal searchlights began to scour the heavens and the AA gunners opened up. The shells burst around the slow-moving bombers, three of which were hit but suffered only minor damage. The pilots threw the lumbering bombers around the sky to dodge the stream of shells and tracer streaking towards them. Two aircraft, carrying Lt Charteris and half his men from the 'Nelson' group, were forced to take evasive action and veered away from the approach path they had plotted. All twelve aircraft headed a few miles inland before turning back towards the coast to drop their human cargo.

The cry of 'Action stations!' told the men that the time of

reckoning had arrived. Pickard throttled back to fly as slowly as possible without stalling, but the Whitley was still travelling at just over 100 miles an hour. Frost, who was the first to jump, sat with his legs at the edge of the hole. The red warning light gave way to green. Frost took a deep breath and dropped out. He felt his legs pulled out horizontally by the slipstream and for a brief moment he was lying parallel with the ground. Dropping in sticks of ten, the other 120 men followed in rapid succession, with the aim of landing in as small an area as possible. A second or two after jumping, each paratrooper felt the jerk from the line pulling out the parachute from the bag on his back. Almost instantly, the plummeting fall towards earth was checked as the canopy of the parachute burst into its full twenty-eight-foot diameter above his head and he began to float towards the earth. It felt gentle, but they all knew from the shock of the landings in their practice jumps that they were falling much faster than they thought.

The landscape, illuminated by the bright moon, looked exactly as it had been represented by the model they had been shown. One by one, the 120 men hit the ground with a thud, rolled over and immediately cast off his parachute harness. Falling at speed, it is very difficult for a parachutist to calculate exactly when he is going to touch down, and the shock of a landing has been compared with that of jumping blindfold from a height of about six to eight feet. On this occasion the jolt was softened only a little by the carpet of snow that lay over the area.

The Commandos of No. 11 SAS Battalion, who were dropped

in to blow up an Italian aqueduct in February 1941, can claim the honour of carrying out the first ever paratrooper operation by British forces. Technically, the Bruneval raid was the second, but it was a far bigger and infinitely more important and hazardous enterprise. It was also the first carried out by the 1st Airborne Division, the country's first dedicated force of paratroopers, created on Churchill's insistence. It was half an hour after midnight on 28 February 1942 when the boots of the first British paratroopers thumped onto Nazi-occupied French soil.

The 120 men of C Company, 2 Para had under an hour to prove their worth to Britain's war effort. The best-case scenario envisaged by the Combined Operations planners was a successful removal of the radar dish, a light casualty toll, an orderly evacuation and safe passage back to the UK. The worst case? Slaughter on the beaches or capture and 'interrogation' by the Gestapo.

It was an unpromising start to the raid. The two aircraft that had diverted to avoid the flak barrage dropped their 'sticks' over two miles south of the intended dropping zone. As soon as he hit the ground, Lt Charteris realised that he and the twenty other men from the Nelson group had landed in the wrong place. They had been handed the crucial task of capturing the beach and holding it so that the landing craft could come ashore. Without Nelson, Lt Timothy's reserve of thirty men was not strong enough to hold their other positions and simultaneously attack the German pillbox and all the machine-gun positions covering the beach.

Aware that catastrophe loomed without them, Charteris quickly assembled his men, and using the distant beacon of the lighthouse at Cap d'Antifer north of the villa to guide him, they set off in single file at a fast trot. Within minutes, they had stumbled into the enemy and the first bursts of a short but brutal firefight cut through the still night air.

The intended dropping zone was a large area of open ground 600 yards east of the villa to the north of the Bruneval ravine, through which the road trailed from the village to the embark-ation beach. Several inches of snow lay on the ground and, under the bright moon, 100 British paratroopers were clearly visible as they quickly gathered up the nylon canopies. The only sounds were the rustle of parachutes and the humming engines of the bombers as they disappeared back across the Channel. The tension that every man must have been feeling at this moment was suspended by a brief, comic scene when several dozen of them, including Frost, unzipped their trousers and relieved them-selves of several pints of processed tea. 'It was not good drill,' the Major conceded, 'for now was the time when a stick of parachutists are most vulnerable and one's first concern should be to make for the weapon containers.'

But there was no sign of the enemy and, within ten minutes, Frost's group ('Drake') had located all the containers, gathered their weapons and equipment and formed up in the copse at the bottom of a shallow gorge, according to plan. On Frost's signal, the fifty men began jogging the short distance back towards the coast in a silence broken only by the crunch of boots on snow.

The going was slightly harder as they came up the slope, especially for the radio engineer Cox, Lt Vernon and the rest of the sappers as they dragged their wheeled canvas trolleys and equipment for the Würzburg over the icy ground and through a maze of barbed wire. While the engineers laid up below a ridge waiting to be called forward, Lt Young and his men split off towards the Würzburg installation close to the cliff's edge, while Frost and his men took up position around the house. Flanked by four men, Frost walked to the front door as calmly as a postman and blew on his whistle. Immediately, the sound of explosions, machine gunfire and shouting shattered the eerie calm. Bursting upstairs, Frost's men silenced the only German inside the house, who had opened up on Young's men from a first-floor window.

Leaving two of his men to secure the villa, Frost and the others raced the 200 yards over the frozen lawn to assist Young, only to discover that the Germans manning the Würzburg had been quickly overwhelmed. Those that hadn't been killed were taken prisoner. Seized by terror when the assault began, one of them had fled and leapt over the 400-ft-high cliff. It was his good fortune that he landed on a ridge about ten feet below. After he was dragged back up, Private Newman set about interrogating him, but like the others he questioned, the man was virtually dumb with shock.

Sergeant Cox and the sappers arrived on the scene at the same

Operation Judgement: The Swordfish biplane, considered obsolete, sunk more enemy ships (by tonnage) than any other aircraft in the war.

Operation Judgement: A Swordfish drops its 1,500lb torpedo. At Taranto, the bi-planes dived almost vertically before pulling up at the last moment.

Operation Judgement: A Swordfish bi-plane on the deck of HMS *Illustrious*. The attack on the Italian Fleet by two squadrons of Swordfish swung the balance of power in the Mediterranean.

Operation Judgement: Luftwaffe dive bomber pilots were amazed to learn that HMS *Illustrious* survived their savage attack to avenge the Taranto raid.

Operation Archery: A wounded Commando is helped back to a landing craft
in the Norwegian fishing town of Vaagso.

Operation Archery: The Combined Operations' dawn raid at Vaagso
caused widespread devastation.

Operation Archery: A British Bren gunner
takes aim during bitter fighting.

Operation Biting
The Paras arrive at
Portsmouth Harbour
the morning after the
Bruneval raid. Major
John Frost, the C.O.
of the assault force
is on the bridge
second from left

Operation Biting:
An aerial picture
of the Würzburg radar
the Paras were tasked
with commandeering.
Frost's men landed
undetected in the
snow to the right
of the picture.

time and immediately pulled their tools from the trolleys and
set about dismantling the dish. The apparatus, they soon discovered, had been installed very securely, and the engineers were
having difficulty in taking it apart. When they began to come
under heavy fire, Cox admitted, 'We proceeded to rip the rest
of the stuff out by sheer force.'

The fire was emanating from the direction of Le Presbytère
farm in the woods to the north where the main German garrison
was stationed. It was only a matter of time before they were
roused into action, but Frost's men, in position and waiting for
the counterattack, brought heavy fire to bear on the position.
Two rounds rang on the metal dish a few inches from Cox's
hands, but the RAF Sergeant was uncowed and continued with
his work.

Slowly the fire from Le Presbytère intensified and enemy vehicles were observed manoeuvring through the trees. Whether
they were reinforcements or resident troops looking to move into
a flanking position, Frost could not tell. Worried about the threat
from mortar units, which would have caused carnage among his
men, he snapped at the engineers to hurry up. Vernon and Cox
had managed to remove the entire structure from its base as well
as most of its component parts and they quickly loaded the final
items into the trolleys. They had dismantled the entire structure
in under twenty minutes. Leaving half his men behind to cover
the withdrawal, the engineers and the rest headed towards the
beach. They had just begun to descend the steep slope when they
came under raking fire from the pillbox that Charteris's group

had been assigned to capture. A number of men went down in the hail of machine-gun fire, including Company Sergeant Major Strachan, who took three bullets to the stomach. Bleeding profusely, he was dragged to cover and administered morphine.

Frost was confused. The beach was meant to have been secured and all German defences neutralised. With his signallers unable to operate the faulty wireless sets, he was unable to contact Charteris, Timothy's reserve group or his second-in-command, Captain John Ross. He couldn't send out a runner because every time they moved, the gunners in the pillbox opened up on them.

They had been lying up for about ten minutes when a voice further down the slope shouted: 'Come on down! Everything is all right, the boats are here.' In all likelihood, this was a German trying to lure them into the open because almost immediately Captain Ross, who was close to the beach, yelled at them to stay where they were. Frost was not a man to panic, even in the direst emergency, but he was becoming concerned. 'Obviously something was seriously wrong,' he recalled. His anxiety increased when one of his men appeared at his shoulder to inform him that the Germans had retaken the villa, regrouped and were preparing to advance. Frost immediately took a group of men back up the slope and sent the Germans running for cover.

When he returned, he was surprised to discover that the pillbox had been silenced and the sappers were on the move again. They had been sliding so much in the icy conditions that they decided to abandon the trolleys and carry the bulky radar equipment down to the beach instead. Sergeant Major Strachan, barely conscious now, was being helped down with the rest of the party, barking incoherent orders at his men.

The three groups of the assault party, Drake, Nelson and Rodney, converged on the beach almost simultaneously, and Charteris was able to explain to Frost why the beach had not been secured. The young Lieutenant, as it turned out, had done well to lead his men back to the area in such good time. After a running battle with an enemy patrol near Bruneval village, he had followed the sound of the guns and arrived on the scene at the critical moment. Frost's men and the sappers were pinned down and the beach was still in enemy hands. (In the darkness of the woods and the confusion of the running fight, a German soldier had attached himself to Charteris's men in the mistaken belief they were his comrades. On being discovered in their midst, he was promptly dispatched.)

The two sections of Charteris's four that had been dropped in the right place and arrived at the original assembly point as intended had waited for over an hour for the rest to arrive. Fearing the worst, Sergeant Sharp, the senior NCO, had decided to launch an attack. Under the original plan, Sharp's men were to have provided the covering fire while Charteris attacked, and he realised the seriousness of the situation if the beach was not taken. The two sections had just begun moving out to their designated objectives when, to their relief, they heard an ear-splitting yell of '*Cabar Feedh!*', the war-cry of the Seaforth Highlanders. That could mean only one thing: Charteris and the other half of the group had arrived and gone straight in on the attack. Supported by Timothy and the reserve group, Charteris and his men stormed the beach, quickly clearing out the guardroom and silencing the strongpoint. The offending pillbox on the cliff was put out of action and, in a matter of minutes, the enemy's dogged resistance was overcome and the beach and cliff area were soon securely under British control – but it had come at a cost. Two men were killed and six lay wounded, half of them seriously.

It was past two o'clock in the morning when the assault party began to assemble on the small beach at the mouth of the Bruneval ravine. The raid might not have gone completely to plan, but the paratroopers had achieved what they had intended: to reach the objective, subdue the enemy and remove the radar equipment. The apparatus now lay in the sand alongside the six wounded, all of whom had now been treated with morphine. The white chalk cliffs towered above them, almost luminous in the bright moonlight. The odd crackle of gunfire broke the stillness as the covering troops took up defensive positions to hold the area for the evacuation. There was one problem: there was no sign of the Navy.

The signallers attempted to contact the ships but without success. They flashed signals from a lamp but still the sea offered nothing but darkness and silence, save for the gentle lapping of the waves on the beach. A thin mist sat over the water and it was impossible to see more than a few hundred yards. As a last resort, it had been agreed that Frost would fire red flares from a Very gun, one to the north and one to the south of the beach. He did this several times, but still nothing. Following the repeated disasters in training, Frost had always feared that the evacuation would be the most challenging element of the operation. 'With a sinking heart,' Frost noted, 'I moved off the beach with my officers to rearrange our defences.'

The men had just taken up their positions and were braced for the countermeasures of the German reinforcements when one of the men shouted to him: 'Sir, the boats are here! God bless the ruddy Navy, sir!' Indeed they were. As if to make up for their late arrival, the support landing craft, carrying the Royal Fusiliers and South Wales Borderers, emerged from the mist firing every gun in their possession at the cliffs. This had been their order, but with many of Frost's men now back up above the beach, their heavy fire was no longer welcome. The entire raiding party yelled at the top of their voices for them to stop, and the guns quickly fell silent. Mercifully, no one was wounded.

The plan had envisaged six landing craft arriving in pairs, but reality had rudely punctured any hopes of an orderly evacuation. They were well behind the strict timings laid out in the schedule, the sea was running high and German reinforcements were certain to be pouring into the area. All six of the landing craft arrived at once. The six wounded men and the Würzburg equipment were the priority and, once they were safely loaded into the first landing craft, the rest of the troops waded out up to their chests to scramble aboard the other five. As they did so, the Germans appeared at the top of the cliff and started throwing grenades and firing mortar bombs onto the beach. It was a noisy and confused scene and there was no time to count heads. Frost watched the disorderly scramble with dismay, but there was no alternative now. The landing craft chugged out to the waiting Motor Gun Boats at a stately twelve knots, their maximum speed. Once the troops had climbed aboard the larger, faster vessels, the landing craft were hooked to the stern to be towed back to England.

The bodies of the two men killed in the raid had been left behind deliberately, but shortly after boarding Frost learned that six men, who had become lost, had arrived at the beach a minute after the last landing craft had pulled away. Frost hid his distress but knew there was nothing they could do for them now. There could be no turning back. He could only hope that the men would be treated well by their captors.

While the crews of the gun boats handed out blankets and generous tots of rum to the sodden paratroopers, they explained why their arrival had been delayed so long. The force had been lying offshore, as planned, waiting to launch the landing craft, when a German destroyer and two torpedo boats passed within a mile of them and the wireless operators had been unable to respond to the signallers' promptings. It was most probably the light mist that saved them from being detected, but it had been a close shave. Had the German ships passed any closer or spotted Frost's Very flares, the evacuation force would have been attacked and the paratroopers would have been stranded ashore.

Fifteen miles out from the French coast, a squadron of Spitfires arrived to escort them back home. German divebombers had been expected to stalk the flotilla from daybreak, but no attack materialised. Destroyers came out to join the escort and it was the afternoon by the time they steamed past the Isle of Wight and into Portsmouth. Once in the harbour, the destroyers saluted the raiding force, 'Rule Britannia' rang out from Tannoy speakers and the Spitfires swept down low in tribute before disappearing back to their bases.

In the early evening, the raiders boarded the troopship *Prince Albert* to be welcomed by Wing Commander Pickard and his crews. A throng of photographers and reporters were there in numbers to report on the success of the highly daring raid, the first significant operation by a new breed of soldier. 'The limelight was strange after weeks of secrecy and stealth,' said Frost. 'All we really wanted was dry clothes, bed and oblivion; but before that there was some serious drinking to be done.'

The following day a Hurricane was sent over the Channel on a reconnaissance flight to Bruneval. A group of German officers was standing round the foundations where the Würzburg had been operating twelve hours earlier. The sight was too tempting for the pilot and, turning back, he swooped on the gathering and opened fire with his four wing-mounted cannons. Before climbing out of the dive, he had the pleasure of watching the grey-coated Germans diving into the shallow hole.

That night C Company returned to Tilshead and Frost was climbing into a hot bath, looking forward to a quiet evening and a good night's sleep, when he was called to the telephone and instructed that he was to be in London for a meeting at nine o'clock. A staff car, he was told, was on its way to pick him up. Driving through the blacked-out streets of London, he was taken to a building on Birdcage Walk, between Buckingham Palace and Westminster, and led below to an underground bunker. Dressed in his Cameronians uniform, he was met by Deputy Prime Minister Clement Attlee; the replica of Bruneval stood on a table in the centre of the room.

Soon the room began to fill up with the most important figures in the British administration of the day: Foreign Secretary Anthony Eden, Secretary of State For War Sir James Grigg, First Lord of the Admiralty 'AV' Alexander, First Sea Lord Sir Dudley Pound, Chief of the Imperial General Staff General Sir Alan Brooke and Chief of the Air Staff Air Chief Marshal Sir Charles Portal. Frost felt increasingly anxious about the prospect of addressing the War Cabinet about details of the raid and he was relieved to see the more familiar face of Commodore Lord Mountbatten, the Combined Operations chief.

'Suddenly the Prime Minister was there, siren-suited and with outsize cigar,' recalled Frost. And Churchill approached him, saying: 'Bravo, Frost, bravo, and now we must hear all about it.' To the young Major's relief, Mountbatten as Chief of Combined Operations laid out the details of the raid.

The six wounded men all made full recoveries, although the life of Company Sergeant Major Strachan hung in the balance for several days. Within a few months he was back in uniform and promoted to Regimental Sergeant Major. The six men left behind became prisoners of war. French Resistance chief Colonel Rémy survived the war but 'Pol'(Roger Dumont) was exposed by the signal sent from England congratulating him for his work on Bruneval. He was shot by a German firing squad. Many of the paratroopers who took part in Bruneval were killed in subsequent operations.

Four weeks after Bruneval, Private Newman, the German-Jewish interpreter, was captured during the Combined Operations assault on the dockyard at St Nazaire, in what has since been dubbed the 'greatest raid'. Fortunately his true identity was never revealed and after the war he settled in England for good. Pickard was not so lucky. Three times he was admitted to the Distinguished Service Order before meeting his death two years after Bruneval when he led the low-level Mosquito bombing raid on a prison at Amiens to free the hundreds of French Resistance men held there.

Major Frost and Lt Charteris were awarded the Military Cross, and Flight Sergeant Cox and two sergeants received the Military Medal for their roles in Bruneval. Company Sergeant Major Strachan was later awarded the Croix de Guerre, Lt Young was Mentioned in Dispatches and the scientist R. V. Jones was given a CBE. For Frost, Bruneval turned out to be little more than a light diversion and skirmish compared to the actions and operations in which he subsequently became involved. He saw heavy fighting in the bloody campaigns in Tunisia, Sicily and Italy, but it was for his leadership and gallantry at Arnhem, immortalised in the film *A Bridge Too Far*, that he was to be best remembered. Badly injured and captured at Arnhem, he saw out the war in a POW camp. He retired from the army as a Major General in 1968 and became a farmer in West Sussex.

'So what did we get out of all this?' This was the question that Churchill barked across the table at his Cabinet Ministers and Chiefs of Staff when Frost had joined them in their bunker. Radio technology is a complex subject and this is the wrong place to explain its finer details, but in brief, the capture of the Würzburg was a significant breakthrough for the British. As a result, Britain was able to improve its own radar network, and, in the words of R. V. Jones, the man leading the scientific fight against the Nazis, the Würzburg provided, 'A first-hand knowledge of the state of German radar technology, in the form in which it was almost certainly being applied in our principal objective, the German nightfighter control system . . . it had provided us with the equivalent of a navigational "fix" in confirming the "dead reckoning" in our intelligence voyage into the German defences.'

But these were not the only happy consequences of the Bruneval venture. Soon after the raid, the German authorities issued orders that all radar installations were to be protected by barbed wire – to the delight of the RAF's Photographic Reconnaissance Unit. The smallest details in an image were often the key to revealing the true nature of an object or location being photographed. Barbed wire was too thin to be detected from the air, but its presence was revealed by the grass which grew longer and darker underneath it as well as from the debris that became caught in it. Subsequently, Jones and his colleagues were able to identify several more sites of interest to them.

The British scientists and military planners were not the only ones to appreciate the quality of the Bruneval raid. The official German report recorded that 'the British displayed exemplary discipline when under fire. Although attacked by German soldiers they concentrated entirely on their primary task.'

The success of the raid boosted the status of Combined Operations and secured the future of British airborne troops. Bruneval is the first battle honour awarded to what today is known as the Parachute Regiment or, more often, 'the Paras'. The War Office immediately expanded the fledgling force and, by the war's end, thousands of paratroopers had served with great distinction and courage in all major theatres of the war. More often than not, they were the first troops in.

In the wider scheme of the war, Bruneval was a very minor affair. The name was spoken over breakfast tables and in pubs around Britain in the days following the raid, but it was soon overtaken by events elsewhere and forgotten. One place where it hasn't been forgotten – outside of the Parachute Regiment – is Bruneval itself. If you drive around the little village today you will pass along the Avenue du Colonel Rémy, Rue Lord Louis Mountbatten, Rue Roger Dumont and Rue Major Frost, but you won't find the villa where Frost blew his whistle to launch the assault. The Germans knocked it down soon after the raid in the mistaken belief its presence had given away the Würzburg. The Rue Major Frost will lead you to the tree-lined rectangle of Le Presbytère farm and continues up to the site of the villa. The foundations of the building are still clearly visible and if you walk out towards the cliff you will come to a scruffy dirt circle. It was there that Flight Sergeant Cox and the sappers wrenched the Würzburg from its base while under heavy fire. And it was there, it can be said, that the glorious tradition of the Paras was born.

Operation Gunnerside

16 February 1943

It was 2320 when, in rapid succession, five British-trained Commandos leapt from a Halifax bomber over the frozen wilderness of the Hardanger Vidda in the Telemark region of central southern Norway. Jumping from just 700 feet, their chutes billowed open and floated in a neat diagonal line through the moonlight towards the vast white expanse stretching out to all horizons. Somewhere in that frozen wilderness were four comrades who, for three months, had battled starvation and some of the harshest conditions on the planet as they waited and waited and waited . . . Finally, the raid was on. The saboteurs knew from the huge risks they had been asked to take that their objective was of great importance – an impression underlined by their carefully worded orders. What they didn't know was that Prime Minister Churchill in London and President Roosevelt in Washington were anxiously monitoring their mission. Operation GUNNERSIDE was one of the most important raids of the Second World War. It wasn't until after the conflict that they learned quite how important.

At the outbreak of the war, Albert Einstein was one of a very small handful of people in the world who understood the terrible potential of atomic power. To most scientists, even very eminent ones, the notion that a single bomb could annihilate an entire city was absurd. Churchill was extremely sceptical too, but it wasn't long before he was persuaded of the dire threat it posed. London, the intelligence suggested, was the first target on Hitler's list. The reasoning was obvious: destroy the British capital and the war was won. Britain would surrender and the United States would be unable to help launch an invasion of Europe.

A great number of Germany's leading physicists – many of them Jews – had fled the Nazis for Britain and the United States, bringing with them warnings of the rapid advances being made to build an atomic weapon. So began frantic efforts by the Allies to beat Germany to the bomb. In the US the atomic research programme was known as 'The Manhattan Project' and no expenses were spared in its development. To their advantage, the Americans did now have many of the world's leading experts in their field, following their flight from the Nazis, but they were months off the pace, years even, and it was going to take a lot of time, effort and resources to overhaul their German counterparts. For fear of causing widespread panic, strict secrecy blanketed this apocalyptic arms race. No more than a few dozen scientists, military chiefs and senior politicians were aware of its existence.

German scientists had been working on three different approaches to developing nuclear energy. At the start of the war, the one considered most likely to succeed involved the production of a liquid known as deuterium oxide or 'heavy water'. The fluid was used as a moderator to slow the nuclear chain reaction in unenriched uranium. This was a laborious, costly process and the entire world's stocks of the fluid could be found in a few canisters inside a heavily protected hydroelectric plant known as Vemork in an ice-bound valley deep in the interior of Nazi-occupied Norway. But minute by minute, splash after splash, the stock of this potentially deadly liquid was increasing and Germany was inching that bit nearer to building the most powerful weapon in the history of warfare.

In May 1941, intelligence sources signalled that Germany had demanded a ten-times increase in Vemork's heavy water production to 3,000 lb per year. By January 1942, production was ramped up to 10,000 lb per year. Churchill didn't need the code-crackers at Bletchley Park to decipher the significance of the updates: Hitler was demanding rapid acceleration in the race to build the first atomic weapon. In June 1942, Churchill flew to New York to meet Roosevelt. Nuclear energy was high on the agenda of priority topics. The two leaders of the free world agreed that every effort should be made to thwart Germany's bid to build the world's first 'super-explosive'. After the war, Churchill wrote: 'We both felt painfully the dangers of doing nothing.'

Destroying the stocks of heavy water at Vemork was considered the most effective way of retarding Germany's nuclear energy programme, but that was a great deal easier said than done.

An inside job was implausible. At that stage of the war, the Norwegian Resistance was no more than a fledgling operation with limited resources and very little offensive capability. There was also the problem of Vemork's remote location. Roughly 150 miles from the coast, accessible only by one winding road, it sat on a steep, rocky slope of a narrow valley at the foot of the Hardanger Vidda, a beautiful but forbidding wilderness – the highest plateau in western Europe – where only the most experienced outdoorsman could survive for any significant length of time. The 3,500 square miles of terrain features barren, treeless, undulating moorland punctuated by hundreds of peaks, lakes, rivers, streams and marsh. In the summer, the Hardanger is a magnet for hillwalkers and nature lovers. In the winter, only the hardiest and most intrepid venture into its wind-blasted and frozen interior. When the Germans invaded Norway, they went around the Hardanger and they never advanced more than half a day's march into it, for fear of being caught out by the volatile weather.

Bombing the plant was rejected on a number of grounds. Innocent lives were very likely to be lost and the hydroelectric plant, the principal centre of economic activity in the region, would be put out of action. What's more, it was thought unlikely that an air raid would succeed in destroying the heavy water, which was stored under several storeys in the basement of the solidly constructed plant. But such was the urgency of the situation that there were even discussions about blowing the Møsvatn Dam at the head of the valley – a course of action that would have led to the deaths of hundreds, possibly thousands of civilians, with no cast-iron guarantee that the heavy water stocks would be put beyond use. After endless series of meetings and streams of interdepartment 'Top Secret' memos, the planners reached the conclusion that the only plausible option was a '*coup de main*' raid carried out by elite Commandos in a joint mission involving the Special Operations Executive (SOE) and Combined Operations.

Established on Churchill's order in the summer of 1940, SOE's purpose was to wage guerrilla warfare behind enemy lines, to train and assist local resistance groups and carry out espionage and sabotage tasks – or, in Churchill's words, the clandestine unit of highly trained irregulars was 'to set Europe ablaze'. Many of the SOE operatives were refugees from the Nazi-occupied countries who, after completing their training, were reinserted into their homelands on specific missions. The work was amongst the most dangerous in the war.

In the early days, the organisation was not highly regarded

within Whitehall. The 'Ministry of Ungentlemanly Warfare', as it was dubbed, was thought to cause more trouble than its achievements were worth. Existing intelligence and espionage services, local resistance groups and governments-in-exile all had cause to complain about its activities. When SOE was first approached about plans for an attack on the Vemork hydro-electric plant, it saw an opportunity to establish its credentials and silence its many critics.

The rough plan was for an advance party of SOE-trained Norwegians to be dropped by parachute onto the Hardanger. They would live in the wild and act as a reconnaissance unit and reception committee for a force of British glider-borne Commandos. Their task was to find a suitable dropping zone in the rugged terrain, guide in the aircraft, lead the British troops to the plant and help them escape. Airborne operations were best undertaken under cover of darkness, which ruled out any missions in the summer months when there was near-permanent daylight. During the summer of 1942, the instructors of SOE's Norwegian unit were ordered to pick a handful of exceptional recruits with the aim of dropping them into Norway as soon as the RAF considered the nights long enough for them to operate in relative safety.

Operation GROUSE was the name given to the advance party and it was to be led by Jens Anton Poulsson, a pipe-smoking, Norwegian Army cadet and expert mountaineer who grew up in the town of Rjukan, a mile or so from the Vemork plant. The three men he put forward to make up the team, Claus Helberg,

Knut Haugland and Arne Kjelstrup, were also born in Rjukan. Helberg, a brilliant skier and man of adventure, had sat next to Poulsson in school. The families still lived there but their sons were under strict instructions not to make contact with them. Haugland, one of the best underground W/T operators of the war, had worked with the embryonic Norwegian Resistance but escaped to Britain after being arrested on several occasions. Kjelstrup, a plumber, was born in Rjukan but raised in the suburbs of Oslo. Short and powerful, he had shown during Germany's Blitzkrieg invasion that he was not a man to shy away from a fight, even in the face of overwhelming odds. The four men would set up an operating base in one of the small wooden huts dotted over the Hardanger used by walkers, hunters, fishermen and skiers.

The men were SOE recruits of the Norwegian Independent Company who had passed through a number of top-secret Special Training Schools (STS) across Britain, learning the dark arts of irregular warfare. (The unit was also known as the Linge Company after Martin Linge, the Commando leader killed in Operation ARCHERY.) By the time they had completed the intensive and gruelling series of courses, they had become masters in close combat, demolition and sabotage, silent killing, wireless operation, intelligence gathering, propaganda and training local resistance militia. At the Norwegians' main base in the Highlands of Scotland, the men underwent training in outdoor survival in extreme conditions . . . but their instructors soon realised that there was not a great deal they could teach the Norsemen. The great majority of them were first-class outdoorsmen who since childhood had learned how to survive in the most exacting conditions nature can present.

Surviving in the wild was one challenge, but overcoming German defences and destroying the heavy water supplies was quite another. Einar Skinnarland, SOE's agent in the Rjukan area with contacts inside Vemork, had cabled London to report that there were 20 German soldiers stationed at Vemork, 35 billeted in a nearby school, 100 more a ten-minute drive down the road at Rjukan and a further 20 in billets near his family home at the Møsvatn Dam at the head of the narrow, winding valley.

Skinnarland was told he would learn of GROUSE's arrival through a concealed message on the BBC Norwegian Service on the night they were to be dropped in. The announcer would say 'This is the latest news from London' rather than the customary 'This is the news from London.'

By the end of the summer, the GROUSE party were put on standby to depart. They had completed the advanced courses of the SOE training, received their orders and reached a peak of physical fitness. Having packed and repacked their equipment over and over, they waited to be summoned to Wick Airfield. As always in parachute operations, they were at the mercy of the weather. If it was too cloudy or windy, the RAF couldn't drop them. On two separate occasions in a month, they pulled on their parachutes and boarded the aircraft, the adrenalin pumping hard as they flew over the coast of their homeland and stood over the hatch in the floor poised to leap, only to be told the drop had been cancelled. On the first occasion, thick cloud meant that they were unable to locate the drop zone; on the second, engine trouble and heavy anti-aircraft fire over the coast combined to thwart them. The intense frustration felt by the four men is evident from Poulsson's blunt comments in his operational notes.

A third attempt was made at nightfall on 10 October 1942. Once again, the four young Norwegians stood in line as the RAF dispatcher pulled open the hatch and the freezing wind rushed through the floor. Below, the snowbound plateau glistened under the bright moon. At 2318, the dispatcher hurled out half a dozen containers of supplies and equipment. There was no turning back this time. The young Norwegians were going home. Poulsson was the first to leap, followed barely a heartbeat later by Haugland, Kjelstrup and Helberg. Moving at 200 miles an hour, it was important not to hesitate; a few seconds delay could mean separation from the rest of the group by hundreds of yards. The dispatcher tossed out the final two containers and slammed shut the hatch. The rear-gunner counted the silk chutes drifting in perfect symmetry towards the frozen landscape.

The four men suffered heavy landings on very rough terrain. The RAF had dropped them in the wrong place, ten miles from the prearranged landing zone. 'It was fortunate that none of us was severely hurt when we landed,' Poulsson recorded in his log. 'The ground was just a mass of stones.' The four immediately tore off their parachutes for fear that a strong rush of wind would drag them over the rocky, broken land. The wind had scattered the eight containers over a very wide area and after four hours of searching they decided to start again the following morning. Had they been able to find the container with their skis and poles, they would have completed the search in a matter of minutes, but wading through heavy, wet snow in the dark they made little progress. They passed the rest of the night in sleeping bags, sheltered from the biting wind in the lee of a large outcrop of rocks. At first light, they resumed the search for the remaining containers, but without success. The rocky, hilly terrain and deep snow combined to frustrate the men for two full days. By the time they found the container with the skis, they were completely shattered.

The mountainside on which they had been mistakenly dropped lay ten miles to the west of where they wanted to be and roughly twenty miles from Vemork. Poulsson chose to head for a hut known as Sandvatn at Grasfjell, which he knew from his childhood and was situated in an ideal location. It was three miles from the designated landing zone for the gliders bringing in the Commandos and its remoteness made it highly unlikely that German patrols would discover them. What's more, the area around it was largely flat, making it excellent country for wireless communication.

Ordinarily, a ten-mile cross-country journey was a distance that expert skiers could take in their stride, but the GROUSE team were burdened by equipment weighing a third of a ton, including food provisions to last a month, bulky radio equipment, clothing, spare ski equipment, first-aid materials, weaponry and ammunition. Poulsson decided to take all their rations but bury roughly 150 pounds of the nonessentials to collect after the raid. The difficulties of the march were compounded by damage sustained to their Primus stove during the parachute drop. Heat for cooking and drying out clothes was essential in Arctic-type conditions and, without any available, the party were forced to drop their plan of walking in a roughly straight line over the mountains. Instead, they would stay lower down, close to the lakes, where there were a number of huts they could use.

The weather had been kind to them but the day after they finally set out for Sandvatn, 21 October, a savage snowstorm burst over the Hardanger. Unable to find a hut, they spent the first night in snowholes, but the storm continued to rage the following day. Even without equipment the march would have been a slog, but with 500 pounds of kit it was a back-breaking experience. Dividing their kit into eight loads of thirty kilos, the four men made the same journey twice a day to bring up all the equipment to the next overnight location, skiing through deep, wet snow. Whenever they veered from their tracks, they sank up to their waists and soaked their clothing. Long-distance Nordic skiing is an exhausting business in any event, but in the teeth of a powerful storm, pushing through wet snow and blizzard conditions when already exhausted, it pushes men to the limits of their endurance. It is little wonder that the Norwegian explorer Roald Amundsen and his fellow adventurers trained on Hardanger. The temperatures, which can sink below minus

30 Celsius, coupled with the raging winds, were ideal preparation for polar expeditions – and even Amundsen experienced problems there.

GROUSE's route was elongated further because the lakes and rivers were too treacherous to cross. The early winter ice hadn't hardened sufficiently and so they had no choice but to march round them. Their rations were nowhere near adequate to give their bodies the energy required to cope with the combination of cold and physical exertion. Each man's daily quota consisted of a quarter of a slab of pemmican (dried meat mixed with fat and fruits), half a cup of groats, a few biscuits, a handful of flour, small quantities of butter, sugar and chocolate. No one complained, however. Quoting an old Norwegian saying, Poulsson wrote in his log: 'A man who is a man goes on till he can do no more, and then he goes twice as far.' On some days, the storm was so fierce that they could advance no more than a mile or two. Poulsson's predicament was made worse when he broke one of his ski sticks and found he had left his map behind. Their only respite was provided by the warmth and shelter of the huts they found.

Back in London, the SOE planners, having heard nothing from Skinnarland or Haugland, had begun to fear the worst when finally, fifteen days after they had set out from the drop zone, the shattered advance party finally arrived at the Sandvatn hut.

'In good weather it would have taken us a couple of days but because the snow was wet, the ground wasn't frozen, the streams and lakes were open (free of ice), it took us one hell of a long time with all that equipment,' recalled Poulsson. 'It was very tiring but because we moved from hut to hut our nights were fairly comfortable. The problem was food. We used up all our rations quickly and became very hungry indeed.'

Three weeks after taking off from Scotland, the W/T operator Haugland cabled London with a short message that offered only a few clues as to their ordeal. 'Happy landing in spite of stones everywhere. Sorry to keep you waiting for message. Snow storm and fog forced us to go down valleys. Four feet snow impossible with heavy equipment to cross mountains.'

Ravenously hungry and starting to show the first signs of malnutrition, the party understood the importance of finding extra provisions to supplement their modest rations. To their delight, Haugland found a stray sheep and two lambs in a gulley. 'We were very, very hungry at this time so we immediately killed one of the lambs and then skinned it on the floor of the hut,' recalled Haugland. 'We cut up the meat and put it into a big kettle with some dried peas . . . It smelled delicious and we all sat down at the table eagerly. But as one of the group (Poulsson) carried the kettle over to us, it dropped onto the floor. We all immediately got down on our hands and knees and even though the floor was very dirty we filled our plates with what we could and ate every last bit. It was delicious.'

Having recovered their strength, the men set out on daily reconnaissance trips to locate a landing place for the Commandos' gliders. They found the ideal location – long, flat and free of rocks and other obstructions – to the south of Møsvatn, roughly ten miles from Vemork.

On 15 November, Haugland cabled London with the news that the snow at the landing place was 30 cm deep and frozen hard. If the weather stayed fine, he estimated that the march to Vemork would take the Commando force about five hours. SOE and Combined Operations held a meeting in London the same day to discuss the first Allied glider-borne operation of the war. They decided Operation FRESHMAN was to be launched in three days' time, during the 'moon period', when the days either side of the full moon would offer good light for the RAF crews to pinpoint the landing zone. SOE put GROUSE on standby to prepare for their arrival. On the 18th, Churchill signed off a memo giving the operation the go-ahead.

The plan, in short, was for the Commandos to be led to the hydroelectric plant by GROUSE, fighting their way if necessary. After overpowering the German garrison there, the demolition teams were to break into the basement and destroy the heavy water canisters, fight their way back out against any reinforcements that had arrived in the meantime, then escape on foot across hundreds of miles of some of the harshest terrain on the planet to the Swedish border – but without skis. The wounded were to be given morphine and left behind. Operation FRESHMAN wasn't officially designated as a 'suicide mission', but that is effectively what it amounted to. It was probably just as well the 34 Royal Engineers of the 1st Airborne Division selected for the task were kept in the dark about their objective until the very last moment.

Even in ideal flying and landing conditions, glider operations were perilous, nerve-shredding affairs, dreaded by the troops – and there were few countries less enticing for a glider pilot than Norway with its rough terrain and challenging, changeable weather. But at 1715 on 19 November, the conditions were as good and settled as could be hoped for and Haugland wired London a message to that effect.

The Royal Engineer paratroopers, heavily laden with weapons and equipment, filed out of the huts at Skitten Airfield near Wick and boarded the two Horsa gliders attached to Halifax bombers. There were seventeen men squeezed into each of the unpowered wooden aircraft, plus two RAF crew sitting at very basic controls. When they took off, just after six o'clock, the weather was fairly mild but the wind steadily picked up as they crossed the North Sea. By the time they reached the Norwegian coast, the gliders were bouncing through strong turbulence. One hundred miles inland, the GROUSE party waited anxiously at the landing zone, listening out for the rumble of the RAF bombers. But they never came.

The details of the Commandos' fate would not become clear until the end of the war, but when only one Halifax bomber returned, the operation planners feared the worst. One of the gliders had crashed into a hillside at a place called Fyljesdal, close to the coast, after the towrope had frozen solid and snapped. Eight of the men had died on impact, one had injured his spine and was paralysed from the waist down, another had broken both his legs, one had shattered his jaw and a fourth had cracked his skull and had difficulty in breathing. Shortly after the crash, two groups of Germans had arrived, one party of regular Wehrmacht soldiers and another of SS troops under the command of a Gestapo officer.

The dead men were dumped in shallow graves and the Germans refused to let the locals give them a proper burial. The five uninjured men were taken to Grini Concentration Camp near Oslo where, after two months' detention, they were taken into woods and executed. A War Crimes trial at the war's end revealed the gruesome fate suffered by the four badly injured British troops at the hands of the Gestapo. Leaving one of them in the cell next door to listen to the torture of his comrades, the Nazi secret policemen battered the other three and strangled them with leather straps. When the Commandos were close to death, their torturers stood on their chests and throats and then injected air into their bloodstreams. All three died a slow death in agony. The fourth man was shot in the back of the head. Two of the torturers were sentenced to death for murder and the third was given life imprisonment.

The fate of the survivors in the second glider was equally disturbing, but the full details of the hours leading to their death have never emerged. An SOE agent reported that the glider crashed near a town called Egersund, killing two or three outright and wounding an unknown number of others. After 'interrogation', all the survivors were shot. The Halifax bomber towing the glider crashed into a mountainside after becoming separated, killing the six-man crew.

The catastrophe of Operation FRESHMAN was also a major setback for Allied efforts to wreck Germany's atomic bomb programme. A map, with Vemork circled in red, had been found at one of the FRESHMAN crash sites. The Germans immediately set about strengthening the defences at the plant and sweeping the area for enemy agents. The GROUSE party was forced to disappear deep into the Hardanger until the danger had passed. SOE cabled them an urgent message, reading: '. . . vitally necessary that you should preserve your safety.' As a further precaution the name of their operation was changed from GROUSE to SWALLOW.

It was now close to a year since the rate of heavy water production at Vemork had been increased by 3,000 per cent. No more time could be lost. Just days after the FRESHMAN disaster, SOE decided to launch a second attempt. This time it would be carried out by a small group of British-trained Norwegian Commandos disguised as British soldiers. The operation would be code-named GUNNERSIDE.

The new plan was as simple as it was daunting. A group of six men from the Linge Company was to be parachuted onto the Hardanger to team up with the SWALLOW/GROUSE party. The ten men would ski to Vemork, break or fight their way into the plant, destroy the heavy water and then escape to Sweden. Unlike their doomed comrades in FRESHMAN, at least this raiding party would have the benefit of skis – equipment that any Norwegian could have told the SOE planners was essential.

Joachim Rønneberg was just twenty-two years old but he was the obvious candidate to lead the raid and would assume command of the combined parties on arrival. 'Rønneberg was one of the most outstanding men we had. He was well-balanced, unflappable, very, very intelligent and tremendously tough,' wrote Colonel Charles Hampton, who ran SOE's Norwegian training school in Scotland. Rønneberg was equally clear as to who he wanted to join him in a venture which would test their courage and physical strength, their will to survive and outdoorsmanship to the limit. 'I wanted strong, physically fit men with a good sense of humour who would smile their way through the most demanding situations,' he said. He chose Knut Haukelid, a formidable operator, as his second-in-command. In his SOE reports, his instructor describes Haukelid as 'exceptionally efficient . . . cool and calculating type who would give a very good account of himself in a tight corner . . . A really sound man and cunning. Has no fear.' He would show all these qualities in abundance by the time the mission had played out. The other four – only marginally less impressive than their leaders – were Birger Strømsheim, Hans Storhaug, Kasper Idland and Fredrik Kayser.

At a meeting with the SOE chiefs in London, Rønneberg and his men were made aware of the enormous risks of the operation. Just in case they were in any doubt about the fate they faced were they to be captured, they were told about Hitler's famous directive ordering the summary execution of all British Commandos. Unknown to the Allies at the time, this had come into force a few days before the FRESHMAN disaster. Rønneberg recalled: 'They told us everything – that those who had survived the crash were shot, or "experimented" on and that some were thrown into the North Sea. They told us that we would be given poison capsules so that we would not have to suffer the same ordeal.'

Using an exact life-size replica of the basement at Vemork, the sabotage party practised laying explosives on the cylinders over and over again until they could do it in the dark. Like SWALLOW, GUNNERSIDE were never told about the deadly capabilities of heavy water, only that its destruction was vital. Their ignorance of the stakes makes the risks they were prepared to take all the more remarkable.

GUNNERSIDE and SWALLOW were to meet at the prearranged landing place, but failing that they would all head to a hut known as Svensbu. After the raid, while the GUNNERSIDE team were to head for the Swedish border, the SWALLOW members were to disappear into the Hardanger and await fresh orders. The parachute drop was scheduled for the 'moon period' around 17 December, with the raid itself pencilled in for the night of Christmas Eve when it was hoped that the German garrisons would be less vigilant than normal. Shortly before they left London for Scotland, they were given a special address by Professor Leif Tronstad, the former chief scientist at Vemork, who had escaped to London and teamed up with SOE. His in-depth knowledge of the Vemork plant was key to the planning of GUNNERSIDE. 'You have no idea how important this mission is,' he told them, 'but what you are doing will live in Norway's history for hundreds of years to come.'

The survival of the SWALLOW party added to the sense of urgency. SOE knew their rations were virtually exhausted and that winter, with its ferocious blizzards and blood-stopping temperatures, was on its way. With German troops scouring the Hardanger area for British-backed agents and W/T operators, the SWALLOW party abandoned the hut at Sandvatn and moved into huts deep in the plateau, where there was even less chance of the Germans finding them. Not long after setting out, a ferocious blizzard blew in with winds so powerful that, according to Poulsson, 'We often had to crawl along on all fours.' It was the onset of one of the worst winters the area had experienced in living memory.

'We had three tasks as we waited for GUNNERSIDE,' said Poulsson. 'The first was to stay alive, the others were to maintain radio contact with England and to establish contact with people who could give us information about what was happening at Vemork and what the Germans were up to.'

All four members of the party were in poor physical condition by this stage. All edible vegetation on the Hardanger had long since disappeared and the migrating reindeer had yet to arrive. To make matters worse, they soon exhausted their store of dry wood. Kjelstrup and Helberg both developed oedema and swelled by about twenty pounds. All four suffered from fevers and nausea. By the time they had reached the Svensbu hut, where they were to team up with GUNNERSIDE, the food situation had become critical. Their rations were all but finished. Only the very smallest amount, which they kept for the direst emergency (i.e. imminent death), remained.

Despite his own wretched state of health, and almost delirious with fatigue and hunger, Poulsson set out day after day, with his Krag hunting rifle slung over his shoulder, and skied for miles across the Hardanger in a desperate search for the reindeer herds. Day after day he staggered back to the hut, empty-handed. Finally, on 23 December, he caught sight of a herd on the distant horizon. The challenge now was to get within effective shooting range without startling them. That was no mean feat, even for a hunter of Poulsson's experience. At the first sign of danger, reindeer flee, and Poulsson knew he lacked the strength to chase them for any great distance over the plateau. Quivering with excitement and nerves, Poulsson stalked the herd for over an hour. He knew the stakes. If they didn't eat soon, he and his men would fall gravely ill and the operation would be placed in serious jeopardy. As he crept closer to the herd, exhausted from the effort and concentration, his foot gave way and he crashed to the ground. The two reindeer closest to him stamped their hooves to raise the alarm and the whole herd disappeared in a stampede over the crest of the hill. 'It was enough to make a man weep,' he said.

The sun was starting to sink behind the mountains as Poulsson dragged his weary body up the next slope. Poking his head over the top of the hill, he was relieved to see the herd had not run far. He lay down and lined up one of the closest animals in his sights. Three cracks split the still frozen air in rapid succession and the herd thundered away into the next valley. It seemed that he had missed. He could see no carcass in the snow and was just about to head back to the hut when, using his binoculars, he noticed what looked like a trail of blood in the snow. He raced forward as fast as his skis would allow him and there, just over the brow, was his injured prey. One further shot from his Krag and the beast slumped to the snow. Laughing wildly with relief, Poulsson took his mug from his rucksack and drank the warm blood spouting from the reindeer's wounds before it froze. After skinning and butchering the animal, he packed the best parts into his rucksack, covered the rest to be collected later, and staggered back towards Svensbu, happy in the knowledge that the long weeks of starvation and malnutrition were over – for the time being at least. When the emaciated SWALLOW leader entered the hut, covered from head to foot in frozen reindeer blood, the other three cheered with joy.

That year's Christmas feast was one that none of them would ever forget and, over the subsequent few weeks, the four of them devoured every last morsel of the reindeer, including nose, lips, brains and eyes. ('The head was the best part,' said Poulsson.) The food that did more than anything to keep them alive was the half-digested reindeer moss they found in the reindeer's stomach. This was rich in vitamin C and carbohydrate, and mixed with blood and heated up came to be considered as a 'delicacy' by the men. Every part of the animal was put to use, including the pelts which were hung up around the hut for extra insulation.

The reindeer had saved their lives and, in doing so, it had rescued one of the most important operations of the Second World War. But bad news soon followed good. London cabled SWALLOW to inform them that the raid had been postponed for a further four weeks. Poor weather had prevented the RAF from dropping the GUNNERSIDE party. The temperature crashed so low on the Hardanger in January that hoar frost lay inches deep on the inside walls and ceiling of the hut. The boredom and frustration of the party was almost as intense as the cold. Helberg filled much of his time making reconnaissance trips to Vemork and his hometown of Rjukan, each time resisting the temptation to visit his family or seek out provisions of fresh food. He often slept in a hut right next to his family home and watched them come and go.

On 23 January the wireless set crackled into life with the news that GUNNERSIDE were on their way again. The four men rushed to lay out the lights at the prearranged landing site. A nearly full moon shone brightly in a star-studded sky. The weather could not have been better but, to the despair of all involved in the operation, the mission was aborted yet again. The Halifax circled over the Hardanger, but the navigator was unable to pick out the dropping zone and, running low on fuel, the pilot was forced to return to Scotland. Fury amongst the planners and the two raiding parties once again gave way to frustration and anxiety for another four weeks. The RAF had lost thousands of men flying behind enemy lines – many of them in Norway – and there was a widespread reluctance to criticise them but, according to the official report of the meeting called to discuss the aborted mission, the plane's navigator was given a severe earbashing. Tensions were high; time was running out.

It was now over three months since the SWALLOW party had parachuted into the Hardanger. It was remarkable that they had survived that long. Could they hold out for another month? The twin pressures of malnutrition and perishing cold were pushing them to the limit. Throughout January and February, the temperature rarely rose above minus 30 degrees Celsius. With little to do but conserve energy and stay warm, they spent most of the time in their sleeping bags. On 11 February, they were put back on standby, but a few hours later a ferocious storm swept over the Hardanger. The winds were so strong it was impossible to move more than a few metres. Five days later, the skies cleared, the wind dropped, and GUNNERSIDE quickly scrambled aboard the Halifax to exploit the break in the weather. They took off at 2000 hours and it was beautifully clear when they approached the Hardanger. Just after midnight, the six men and eleven equipment containers plunged through the dispatching hole into the frozen night from a mere 700 feet. Moments later, they felt the thud of their homeland underfoot and they set about gathering up the containers littered over the landscape. There was no sign of the SWALLOW welcoming party.

They buried the equipment they didn't need for the raid itself under the snow, placed marking stakes and took the bearings so that they could find the location at a later date. The wind was strengthening by the hour. Another storm was gathering. They knew they had to hurry to find Svensbu or some other form of shelter, and they had barely set out when they were engulfed by a violent blizzard. Battered by winds so strong they could move only with the greatest effort, the six men were beginning to fear the worst when they stumbled across a hut called Jansbu. It was a stroke of the greatest luck. Because the visibility was so poor, had the column of skiers been advancing thirty yards either side of it, they would have missed it. As the men warmed themselves by the fire and dried their clothes, the storm shrieked and roared, growing in force hour by hour. 'You felt as if the whole cabin was going to be lifted off the ground,' wrote Rønneberg in his official report.

They set out again when the storm appeared to be subsiding the following morning, but it was only a lull and Rønneberg quickly ordered them to turn back. The combination of powerful winds and deep drifts of snow made progress all but impossible. The storm howled for a week, during which the entire raiding party developed heavy fevers. Without any W/T equipment, they were unable to contact SOE. Sheltering from the same storm a few miles away, SWALLOW were gravely concerned for their comrades.

On 22 February, the storm lifted almost as quickly as it had descended. Clear skies and a dazzling sun revealed the Hardanger in all its snow-blasted glory. Leaving behind more nonessentials to be collected at a later time, they set out on what all knew was going to be a grinding march through tough terrain and extremely deep snow. Taking British uniforms and weapons for SWALLOW plus five days' worth of rations and the demolition equipment, each rucksack weighed twenty-five kilograms. They also had two small toboggans weighing roughly forty kilograms.

As they left the hut, a man claiming to be a hunter appeared. The Commandos were under strict orders to kill anyone who might compromise the successful execution of the operation, but the Norwegians were reluctant to dispatch one of their compatriots unless they knew for sure he was a Quisling. The man gave his name as Kristian Kristiansen; uncertain whether he was a Quisling or 'Jøssing' (a good Norwegian), Rønneberg put him to work pulling one of the toboggans. He turned out to be an excellent guide and first-rate skier, an indispensable extra pair of hands during a gruelling march.

Later that morning, drooping with fatigue, they caught sight of two men skiing hard across the horizon. While the rest of them took cover, clutching their Tommy guns, Haukelid waited to greet them. The two men looked completely wild. Their clothes were caked in filth and reindeer blood, their beards were thick and unkempt, their faces drawn and unhealthy. It took Haukelid some time to register that it was Helberg and Kjelstrup! It was a joyful moment for the two parties. Finally, they had made contact – and all ten men were still alive. After four months of effort and delays, Operation GUNNERSIDE was on. 'We greeted each other with as much emotion as Norwegian men can,' Helberg recorded drily.

After the back-slapping and hand-shaking, they had to decide what to do with the reindeer hunter. Did they kill him or set him free and risk him jeopardising the operation? Rønneberg's instinct told him that Kristiansen could be trusted but, as a precaution, he made him sign a statement that he owned and used a rifle, warning him that it would be handed to the Gestapo if he failed to hold his tongue. (The Germans threatened the death sentence for anyone found carrying a weapon.) They also gave him several days' worth of rations in the hope he would stay up on the Hardanger until the raid was over.

By the time they reached SWALLOW's hut, GUNNERSIDE had covered forty-five kilometres of heavy terrain in sixteen hours. It was an impressive achievement. They were shattered, but their spirits were soon lifted by a feast of reindeer dishes and the chance to exchange news with their comrades. There were just forty-eight hours to go before the ten Commandos launched one of the boldest and most important raids in the history of warfare.

On 25 February, leaving Haugland the W/T operator behind, the raiders set off in driving snow for the hut from which they would launch the raid. Fjosbudalen, as it was known, was the perfect launching point for the attack: close to the plant but difficult to access. Situated 800 metres above the valley, looking to their left was the town of Rjukan, strung out for 2 miles along the main road and the banks of the River Måna. About two miles to the right, hidden from view by a kink in the valley, lay the giant Vemork plant. The slope leading down to the

Vestfjorddalen valley was extremely steep. Descending it would be hard enough; coming back up would be punishing.

Following Operation FRESHMAN, a raft of measures had been taken to beef up security at Vemork and in the surrounding area. A detachment of 30 first-rate German soldiers had arrived to take over the defence of the plant itself, the garrison at Rjukan increased to 200, and at the Møsvatn Dam, troop numbers were quadrupled to 40. Batteries of anti-aircraft guns and searchlights had been installed.

From intelligence from inside the plant and Helberg's recce trips, they knew that every night two guards patrolled the suspension bridge across the gorge connecting the plant to the main road; the guards changed over on the stroke of midnight and floodlights would illuminate the entire plant and immediate area in the event of an emergency.

How to access the plant was an issue that provoked a great deal of debate among the raiders. If they tried to fight their way in over the bridge, the German reinforcements from Rjukan and Møsvatn would quickly be on the scene. If they were to become involved in a prolonged gun battle against a vastly superior, more heavily armed force, there was a risk that they might not be able to lay the explosives. It was unlikely any of them would escape either. If they survived the fight and were captured, they would be summarily executed as Commandos. Still, a minority of the party, including Rønneberg, argued that this approach gave them the best chance of success.

There was one possible alternative. At first light on the day of the attack, Helberg made a final recce to see if it was possible to climb the gorge. The Germans thought it impossible and never patrolled that end of the plant that Helberg had pinpointed. If it was possible to scale the virtually sheer icy wall of rock, it would give the saboteurs a number of advantages. There was a much greater chance they could enter the plant unnoticed, avoid any contact with the enemy and prevent the alarm being raised until the charges were detonated. It also meant they could leave the equipment and provisions for their escape at the hut, allowing them to carry only their weapons and demolition kit, and therefore escape more quickly.

Either way, with giant searchlights lighting up the plant and hundreds of troops scouring the area, the chances of all nine men escaping were very slim. This was partly because the Germans would work out that there was only one exit route open to the saboteurs – up the steep slope opposite the plant. Behind the plant was a towering cliff almost one kilometre high, and taking the only road through the valley was not an option. To get out of Vemork, they must either cross the bridge or climb back down the gorge, negotiate the river, cross the main road and then make the energy-sapping climb up the same, near-sheer valley wall they had descended earlier. The party was as good as resigned to not making it to safety. 'Our chances of being trapped in the valley were very great indeed,' recorded Rønneberg. 'We knew that we might not come through it.'

When Helberg returned from his mission, he revealed that though the ice on the river was starting to thaw, there was a narrow point where they might be able to cross. On the other side, he pointed out, there was a band of small trees linking the bottom of the gorge to the plant. If trees could climb the gorge, so could they, Helberg argued. A vote was taken and the climbing option carried the day. The group were split into two: a covering party led by Haukelid and consisting of the SWALLOW members Helberg, Kjelstrup and Poulsson, and the demolition party led by Rønneberg and including Strømsheim, Kayser, Idland and Storhaug. Their operational orders covered every possible eventuality. 'If fighting starts before the High Concentration (heavy water) plant is reached the covering men shall, if necessary, take over the placing of the explosives. If anything should happen to the leader, or anything to upset the plans, all are to act on their own initiative in order to carry out the operation. If any man is about to be taken to prisoner, he undertakes to end his own life.' The raiders weren't aware of the stakes that rested on the raid. Were they to fail, the Allies had just two courses of action left open to them: a saturation bombing raid that would most likely claim the lives of scores of their compatriots, or blowing the dam and flooding the valley, killing hundreds of innocent Norwegians, including dozens of their own family members.

The conditions were perfect when the nine saboteurs, dressed as British soldiers and carrying British papers, left the hut at 2000 hours and began the long descent. It was cloudy and windy. What they didn't want was a still night with a bright moon. They were travelling light, which was just as well, given the intense physical exertions ahead of them. Between them they carried five Tommy guns, three Colt .32 pistols, seven Colt .45s, ten Mills bomb hand grenades, two sets of explosive charges and fuses and a small quantity of food. The wet snow was three feet deep in places and made it impossible to proceed on skis. Advancing on foot, with their skis and poles slung over their shoulders, the men regularly sank up to their chests in the drifts. On reaching the powerline, they buried their skis, dashed across the main road and disappeared into the darkness at the bottom of the gorge as fast as the snow and rock allowed them.

The river ice was thawing rapidly in the mild air and the one stretch that Helberg had singled out as passable now had three inches of water running over it. The ice cracked as, one by one, they shuffled across to the foot of the cliff. Looking up at the virtually vertical rockface, there was some doubt cast on Helberg's optimism, but one after the other, they yanked themselves upwards, grasping roots and branches and icy outcrops for support. One slip or loose stone and they would tumble to their death. All nine men were first-rate outdoorsmen and there were no mishaps, although by the time they scrambled onto the railway tracks at the top they were sodden with sweat from the strain.

A few hundred metres along the tracks, they could just make out the dark outline of the Vemork plant's two enormous main buildings. The faint rumbling of the machinery inside was carried along on the wind. Like clockwork, on the stroke of midnight, the two sentries pacing up and down the suspension bridge were relieved by a new pair. In planning the fine details of the advance, the raiders had decided to wait for thirty minutes, figuring the vigilance of the guards would start to fade. The nine men sat patiently in the shadows of the towering cliff at the eastern end of the plant before making their move. They crept towards the plant's fenced perimeter and crouched. Haukelid sprinted up to a set of high wire-mesh gates and snapped the thick chainlock with a pair of shears. The covering party were the first into the compound, bursting through the gate to take up their positions. The demolition team followed and quickly broke open a second gate leading to the basement where the heavy water was stored. So far so good. The only setback was that the moon had appeared and some of the lights inside the factory had been left on.

Leaving one man on guard, the other four members of the demolition party split into pairs. A cellar door and a second entrance that were meant to have been left unlocked by a contact inside Vemork hadn't been. (The contact, it transpired, had been taken ill and failed to come to work.) Thanks to Tronstad's meticulous planning of the operation, one option remained: Rønneberg and Kayser climbed a ladder and crawled into a narrow cable shaft. Pushing their demolition equipment ahead of them, it took several minutes to wriggle their way to the far end of the shaft. They slid down a ladder and burst into the room housing the cells of high-concentration heavy water, overwhelming the terrified Norwegian guard. After locking the doors, Kayser held the guard while Rønneberg set about laying the sausage-shaped explosive charges on each of the eighteen cylinders. Both men were at pains to show the guard the insignia and stripes on their British uniforms. Fearing reprisals against the local population, they left further evidence, in the form of their English-made tools, that this was a British operation, and not one carried out by the Resistance.

The original plan was to lay two-minute fuses but, fearing that would give the plant engineers time to dismantle them, the raiders opted for shorter versions – a courageous decision that increased the risk of the party getting caught before they had cleared the compound. Rønneberg was poised to light the fuses when a Norwegian civilian walked into the room. Visibly taken aback by the sight of the Commandos, at the point of Kayser's gun he was made to join the guard with their hands above their heads. Outside, the covering party were getting worried. It had been almost half an hour since they had seen the demolition team.

When Rønneberg lit the last of the fuses, Kayser ordered the two captives to sprint upstairs as they all made for the cellar door. The door had barely shut when they heard the first of eighteen muffled explosions from behind the thick stone walls. Within seconds, one and a half tons of concentrated heavy water – the essence of Germany's atomic bomb programme – was gushing across the floor into the drains. The strong wind had helped soften the thump of the charges. Loud noises were not uncommon in the valley at this time of year in any case. Ice cracked and large quantities of snow often fell down steep slopes, especially during the thaw. But expecting some reaction from the garrison all the same, the nine raiders took cover and waited. Sure enough, the door of the barracks house swung open and the silhouette of a soldier appeared in the light from within. Swinging a torch from side to side, he moved slowly towards some tin drums. Haukelid was crouched behind them. There were three Tommy guns and five pistols pointing at the soldier's back as he pulled up just short of the drums, a few feet from Haukelid. The beam of his hand torch brushed the Norwegian's head; his comrades flicked off their safety catches. The guard stood for a few moments, then turned slowly and made his way back to the barracks. As the door shut, Rønneberg gave the hand signal for the team to pull out.

The next few minutes were to be critical. It was imperative they put as much distance between them and the plant as possible before the alarm was raised. Clambering to the foot of the gorge as quickly as they could without risking a fall, they found the Måna was flowing much faster than it had been just a couple of hours earlier and the ice was that much more unstable as they dashed across. Hauling themselves up the icy bank towards the main road, the party froze on the spot when the eerie wail of the plant's alarms broke the night's silence. Grabbing their skis and poles, the nine men melted into the darkness of the woods at the foot of the slope before them.

Walking switchback rather than straight up the steep slope, several kilometres and hours of draining marching lay ahead of them, but with every German soldier in the region pouring into Vemork, they had all the motivation they needed to press on without delay. Their route followed the open area beneath the cable car used by sun-starved locals in the winter to get onto the plateau above the town. It was the only plausible route, but there was a danger that the plant's searchlights might reveal them, and the Commandos were surprised that the lights had not been turned on immediately. An even greater worry was that the Germans would turn on the cable car and dispatch troops to the top, but that fear was never realised either. At 0500, after three hours' backbreaking marching, they dragged their weary bodies the final few steps onto the plateau above.

'It was a beautiful morning as we watched the sun rise,' recalled Rønneberg. 'The sky was lit up in a lovely red colour and we sat there in silence eating chocolate and raisins . . . We were all very, very happy. Although we said nothing as we sat there I think we all felt great pride. But we also spared a thought for our British friends who died in the gliders disaster . . . From now on our struggle was with Norwegian nature.'

The next stage of the escape was to head for a hut owned by a Rjukan shopkeeper at a remote location called Langsja where they would rest up before heading back to the Svensbu hut. The wind howled over the Hardanger as they set off and, having not slept for the better part of two days, it was a major effort to drag their aching limbs against the force of ever-strengthening gusts. They made it to the hut with no more than an hour to spare before another violent blizzard burst over the plateau. Although they were unable to press on, the fresh snow did at least cover their tracks from the cable car and force the Germans to spread their troops over Telemark's vast wilderness.

In the valley below, the Germans were struggling to understand how the 'impregnable fortress' of Vemork had been breached and its precious contents destroyed without so much as a shot being fired. General Wilhelm Rediess, the head of the Gestapo in Norway, urged reprisals against the local population after inspecting the damage, despite conceding that the raid had, in all probability, been a British operation. General von Falkenhorst, commander of German forces in Norway, overruled him on the grounds that it had been a military act. Von Falkenhorst, an old-fashioned Wehrmacht officer with a distaste for the practices of the Gestapo, was in open admiration of the raiders, describing the attack as 'the most splendid coup I have seen in this war'. He was later dismissed from his post for refusing to implement the policies of the Nazi Reichskommissar Josef Terboven who, amongst other brutal acts, had ordered savage reprisals against the villagers of Televåg for sheltering two Norwegian officers.

After a good night's rest and revitalised by some hot food and drink, the GUNNERSIDE party set out the following morning into the snowstorm for Svensbu. It was tough going and it wasn't until 2130 that they finally arrived. At the start of what would turn out to be a heart-stopping personal adventure, Helberg peeled off to return to the Fjosbudalen hut to collect the civilian clothes and faked Norwegian identity documents he would need over the coming months. The plan was to meet the rest of the team at Svensbu, but there was no sign of him over the next two days and his comrades feared for his safety.

At this point, the eleven men of the operation (including

Operation Gunnerside:
Jens Anton Poulsson, leader of the advance party that became
severely weak and malnourished as they waited for the assault team.

Operation Gunnerside: The Vemork Power station today.
The raiders scaled the cliffs out of picture, to the left.

Operation Gunnerside:
The winter conditions on Norway's Hardangervidda mountain plateau are amongst the harshest on the planet. The advance raiding party, all expert outdoorsmen and skiers, were pushed to the limit of endurance for four months leading up to the assault.

Operation Gunnerside:
Joachim Rønneberg led the attack on the night.
The escape on skis to Sweden proved to be
an even greater challenge.

Operation Chariot: HMS *Campbeltown* wedged into the outer lock gate.
The German troops on deck were unaware of the giant explosive charge below their feet.

Operation Chariot: A German soldier passes the body of a dead Commando in the morning after the remarkably bold raid on St. Nazaire dockyard.

Operation Deadstick: Royal Marine Commandos move through Colleville-sur-Orne on their way to relieve forces at Pegasus Bridge.

Operation Deadstick: Three of the six Horsa gliders that brought Howard's force in the first hours of D-Day to capture the bridge over the Caen Canal at Bénouville, subsequently known as 'Pegasus Bridge'.

Operation Deadstick: Pegasus Bridge, safely under British control, thanks to the efforts of Howard and his small force. The gliders can be seen in the distance.

Skinnarland, the local SOE agent) were to split into three separate groups. Five of the GUNNERSIDE party – Rønneberg, Idland, Kayser, Strømsheim and Storhaug – were to make a 400-kilometre journey to the Swedish border. Haukelid and Kjelstrup were to stay in the Hardanger, wait for the German searches to pass and then team up with the Resistance. Poulsson and Helberg were to head to Oslo before deciding on further action. Haugland and Skinnarland, the W/T operators, were to lie low until it was safe and await further orders from London. Convinced that Helberg had either been captured or killed, Rønneberg and his team strapped on their skis and pushed off for the long cross-country trek towards neutral Sweden.

For eleven days following the raid, the British authorities, including the Prime Minister, waited anxiously for news of the outcome. Haugland and Skinnarland had been unable to find a message left for them by the sabotage team at one of the huts they had been using. It was only when Haukelid and Kjelstrup arrived that they learnt the good news. Shortly before midnight on 10 March, the wires back in the UK came to life and the coded message began to arrive. Deciphered, it read: 'Operation carried out with 100 per cent success. High Concentration plant completely destroyed. Shots not exchanged since the Germans did not realise anything. The Germans do not appear to know whence they came or whither the party disappeared.' SWALLOW's momentous message was greeted with relief and delight in Downing Street, Whitehall and the SOE

HQ in Baker Street. Hitler's hopes of beating the Allies to an atomic bomb had suffered a major setback – but, as events were soon to show, Operation GUNNERSIDE had not killed off his hopes once and for all.

Such was the urgency attached to capturing the Vemork saboteurs that General von Falkenhorst and the dreaded Terboven, the two most senior Germans in Norway, personally supervised the search over the weeks that followed. The senior officer at the Vemork plant was dispatched to the Eastern Front as punishment. At the height of the searches, over 2,000 German troops were deployed, as well as several hundred Norwegian Nazis from Quisling's NS party.

When the sabotage party had set out to Vemork, Haugland and Skinnarland packed up their W/T apparatus and set up camp high in the mountains above Lake Møsvatn where they knew the Germans never ventured. From the safety of their snowhole, through the binoculars they watched the German troops combing the valley. A state of martial law was declared in the Telemark region with no one allowed to leave without official permission. The Norwegians, however, laughed at the incompetence of the Germans' hunt for the perpetrators. Looking for suspicious ski tracks was an obvious place to start, but with so many soldiers involved they ended up creating an enormous confusion of tracks that killed off any leads.

Eager to avoid the more populated areas of eastern Norway, Rønneberg had decided to take the long route to Sweden, heading north at the outset before turning back to the southeast. SOE had made up three sets of escape maps, each of which contained twenty-six smaller, more detailed ones of the areas they would pass through. The weather and skiing conditions had been first rate when they had set out, but it wasn't long before they hit trouble. Their rucksacks were heavy with equipment and poorly designed: the straps bit hard into their shoulders and put extra strain on their backs. They also had to heave a heavily loaded sledge, which was a gruelling effort through the wet snow and over rocky scrubland. Even Rønneberg, not a man to complain easily, recorded in his notes for the operational report that their escape was 'an awful labour'.

Making sure they weren't spotted added to the effort, forcing them to take detours around open spaces, main roads, towns and villages. Before each short stretch of the journey, two of them went ahead to reconnoitre the area before the others followed. The landscape, often shrouded in fog or snow, was a bewildering confusion of hills, valleys, forests and lakes, criss-crossed with tracks and paths. Unable to establish their location from the maps, they often had to rely on the compass to guide them. On several nights they were forced to sleep in their sleeping bags in the open, wet through with freezing sweat and melted snow.

On the fifth day, their spirits now at a very low ebb, the temperature plunged again but, in a rare stroke of good fortune, they came across an unoccupied farmhouse where they helped themselves to the stores of flour and bannock bread (hard, unleavened biscuit-style bread). In the remote regions of Norway, where many people kept huts or second homes, it is a custom to let strangers use them on the understanding that they replace, or leave some payment in kind for any provisions they use. Needless to say, the saboteurs weren't in a position to repay the generosity.

On the evening of the sixth day, they crawled on all fours over a lake that was starting to thaw in darkness, climbed almost 1,000 metres of steep hill before breaking into a hut. The following day, the temperature rose sharply, which was a mixed blessing because it made the snow wet. By the afternoon, it was raining, and progress became even slower and exhausting; by nightfall, the sodden conditions forced the exhausted party to stop. Over the days that followed the party made good progress, but there were fresh problems: as winter continued its jostle with spring, the temperature dropped again, and their supplies were rapidly running out.

Unable to find a hut to break into, for two nights they were forced to sleep in the snow in their sleeping bags. With their rations almost exhausted, they had to veer from the route to seek out provisions, raiding huts for flour and bannock bread. The nearer they got to the Swedish border, the more alert they had to be, as there was a greater concentration of German and Norwegian Nazi units there. Navigating was more straightforward when they were high up because they could see the land and consult their maps, but down in the valleys it was far harder to work out where they were. The raiders were tantalisingly close to freedom when they got lost in the mesmerisingly uniform landscape.

They were heading for the Glåma, the longest river in the country, which runs roughly parallel with the border. When they found it, they were dismayed to discover it was entirely free of ice. They were forced to steal a boat to cross it. The following two nights were spent out in the open again in wet clothes and sleeping bags. No one slept. They were too cold and too hungry. The final leg was especially hard-going. 'It was dreadful broken and stony country, through scrub and thick woods, with no visibility,' Rønneberg noted.

Finally, just after eight in the evening on 18 March, 400 km and two weeks after they had set out, bedraggled, worn out and famished, the five men crossed into neutral Sweden. They shook hands, slapped each other on the back and, best of all, lit their first fire in the outdoors since leaving Britain. The following morning, after burying all their incriminating equipment, they changed into civilian clothes and walked along a main road until they were picked up by a police patrol and taken to the local sheriff and then to hospital where they washed and had their clothes disinfected and dried. The following day, the Swedish police happily accepted their cover story that they had escaped from a German work camp. Issued with the relevant identification papers, they continued to Stockholm and reported to the British legation, who arranged for their return to the United Kingdom.

SOE were quick to understand the trials the men had overcome during their arduous escape. 'The difficulties of this march in winter conditions with the added strain of short rations and hard lying make it a most noteworthy achievement,' an SOE memo states. Back in Britain at the end of March, Rønneberg noted movingly about his adopted country: 'On our arrival we were handed a cup of tea. It was a strange feeling because here I was back in Britain, but I felt like I was at home. We often used to refer to it as home when we were in Norway and when I look back on the war I will never forget the welcome that the British showed us.'

Rønneberg, meanwhile, had compiled a comprehensive report of the raid (which can be read in the National Archives at Kew), attached to which is a handwritten message from a senior government figure (only a very few knew of the heavy water threat). It reads: 'A magnificent report of a great effort. Well planned and beautifully executed. If you return the report to me I will have a condensed edition made for the P.M.'

The destruction of the heavy water and the safe return to the UK of the men who carried it out was by no means the end of the story. There was a great deal of drama to be played out yet. In early April, SWALLOW reported to England that Helberg had been shot trying to escape the Germans. Tributes were duly paid by SOE and his Norwegian comrades. This was wrong. Helberg was very much alive and enjoying a remarkable adventure. The story of his escape, which he wrote up on his return to the UK, amazed even his SOE commanders, who witnessed plenty of high adventure in their roles. His boss Colonel Wilson scrawled a note on Helberg's report: 'The attached is an epic of cool headedness, bravery and resource.'

After the raid, Helberg and Poulsson both headed east for Oslo and met, as arranged, in a café the following week. Poulsson left for Sweden a few days later in order to return to Britain. Helberg's long-term plan was to make contact with the resistance movement Milorg back in Telemark after lying low for a few weeks while the Germans hunted for the raiders. In the short term, his main priority was to move to a safer place the cache of incriminating equipment that GUNNERSIDE had left near the Jansbu hut where they had sought refuge from the snowstorm after their parachute drop. Were the Germans to find it, there was a strong risk of reprisals against the locals, dozens of whom had already been arrested and taken in for interrogation. After a couple of weeks in Oslo, Milorg said it was safe for him to return to the Hardanger. He left Oslo on 22 March, unaware that the Telemark region was in fact still crawling with Germans.

Helberg spent his first night back on the Hardanger in a hut that was burnt to the ground the following day. The Germans – furious at being unable to track down the 'British' saboteurs – were venting their fury on the locals. Still oblivious to the large concentration of German troops in the area, Helberg skied off to the Jansbu hut. Pushing open the door, he found the entire contents of the hut strewn all over the floor. He immediately turned round and saw three German soldiers skiing towards him at speed. Quickly strapping his skis back on, Helberg took his Colt .32 from his rucksack and put it in his pocket. As he pushed off, the Germans opened fire on him, the bullets kicking up puffs of snow around him. 'I increased my pace so they had to stop shooting and then a first-class long-distance ski race began,' recalled Helberg in his official report. 'I had a half year's training to my credit and was in splendid form.'

Two of the Germans turned back after an hour or so but the third, a very strong and accomplished skier, kept up the chase. Helberg was a strong uphill skier so he headed for the mountains in the hope of shaking him off. He also skied straight into the low, brilliant bright sun in order to dazzle the German if he attempted a potshot. Helberg was weighed down by a heavy rucksack and his skis were in a poor state because he had not had a chance to wax them. Slowly the German gained on him. After about two hours Helberg reached the lip of a steep hill and, fearing his pursuer would catch him on the descent, he decided to stop and settle the matter in a shootout. The German pointed his Luger at him and bellowed '*Hande hoche!*' ('Hands up!), but was taken aback when Helberg pulled out his Colt .32. Helberg stood stock still and let the German empty the whole magazine of his pistol. He knew the Luger was not effective beyond a range of about fifty yards and the German was further away than that. When he had fired his last bullet, the hunter became the hunted. Helberg quickly closed on him, took aim and fired. The German slumped to the ground.

Darkness was fast enveloping the Hardanger as Helberg headed back down to the floor of the valley. Halfway down, he felt the earth disappear from under him – he was falling over a very high precipice, as high as forty metres, Helberg estimated. His landing was cushioned by deep snow but he knew instantly that he had broken his left shoulder. To his relief, his skis remained intact and he pressed on, in excruciating pain and exhausted after a day and a half on his skis. Heading towards a town called Rauland where there was a house he knew, he was stopped by a German patrol. Unruffled as ever, Helberg calmly produced his identity card and told the Germans that he had been helping in the search for the British saboteurs. When he arrived at the house, he was disappointed to find it occupied by a group of German soldiers, but once again he passed himself off as a pro-German and settled down for a night of cards and drinking games. So well did he get along with the men who had been tasked with hunting him down, that one even bandaged up his arm in a sling and arranged for him to see a German doctor.

The following day a German Red Cross car was laid on to transport the smiling British-trained Commando to the town of Dalen. There he was to spend the night in a hotel before continuing to Oslo by boat and train for hospital treatment. It was typical of Helberg's run of luck that Terboven, the country's ruthless Reichskommissar, arrived at the hotel that night to use it as a base from which he could conduct the searches. Terboven moved into the room next door and SS guards were posted along the corridor. Helberg was caught in the centre of the spider's web.

Early the next morning, hours before sunrise, a Gestapo officer ordered Helberg to join the other Norwegian guests in the lobby where they were made to wait for six hours. This was a nerve-racking time for Helberg. Not only was he the only single person among the guests, he also had a suspiciously sunburnt, weather-beaten face that could only have been acquired from spending a very long period out in the open. Finally, an officer arrived to explain why they had been rounded up. At dinner the previous evening, an attractive young girl had spurned Terboven's public overtures and insulted him. Enraged by this display of Norwegian defiance, the Reichskommissar had ordered that all the guests were to be sent to the notorious concentration camp at Grini. Women over fifty and very elderly men were allowed to stay, but the seventeen others were shepherded onto a bus and told that they would be shot on the spot if they attempted to escape. An SS guard sat at the front of the bus by the only door and three more SS men were on motorbikes with sidecars in the escort.

Sitting next to the pretty girl whose boldness had so enraged Terboven, Helberg deliberately struck up a loud, boisterous conversation with her in order to draw the attentions of the SS guard. Sure enough, the German, like a bee to a honeypot, made his way to the back of the bus and indicated that he and Helberg were to swap seats. As the bus slowly negotiated the winding, climbing road, Helberg saw his chance, pulled open the door and leapt out. He hit the frozen ground hard, aggravating his shoulder and smacking his head. He ran into the woods, chased by the shouting Germans. Reaching a high fence that he could not scale, a stick grenade exploded a few yards away, hurling him to the ground. He hauled himself up, sprinted back past the bus and into the dense woods on the other side. A grenade exploded behind him and another hit him in the back, but it didn't go off until he had scampered clear of its blast range. The Germans fired intermittently into the dark, but after a few minutes they returned to their vehicles and continued their journey. It was these shots that led to the report given to SWALLOW by the Resistance that Helberg had been killed as he tried to escape. To avoid punishment for allowing him to get away, the German guards probably reported that they had killed him.

That night Helberg sought sanctuary in a lunatic asylum in a town called Lier where he had heard that the staff were Jøssings. It was past midnight when he arrived, exhausted, soaked to the skin from the cold rain, and his shoulder and head throbbing with pain. He was immediately taken in, fed, washed, clothed and treated by a doctor. In the morning he was taken five miles down the valley to a hospital in the larger town of Drammen, where he was treated for eighteen days before being released. At the end of May, after three months as a fugitive in his country, Helberg escaped into Sweden and boarded a plane for Britain.

Estimates that it would take a year before the Vemork heavy water plant would return to its preraid operational levels proved wide of the mark. The Germans went to great lengths to repair the damage quickly, replace the destroyed apparatus and resume full-scale production. In July, Skinnarland cabled London with the depressing news that production would be back to full capacity within a month. Once again, the top brass in Whitehall convened to consider their options. Nothing was ruled out.

A 'coup de main' attack, similar to the GUNNERSIDE raid, was out of the question. Germans had made major improvements to their defences at Vemork, surrounding the plant with rows of thick barbed-wire barriers and minefields. All doors bar the main entrance to the building were bricked up and the windows had wire meshes fitted to stop bombs being thrown or fired through them. More troops had been drafted in to beef up the garrisons.

The only plausible option was a saturation bombing raid. The major drawback of such a plan of action was that innocent Norwegians were likely to die and the entire plant, upon which the local economy depended, would probably be razed to the ground. (Fertilisers for agriculture made up roughly 95 per cent of Vemork's production.) 'Precision' bombing was little more than an expression in World War Two. The reality was that bombers dropped their payloads over the area of the target from a great height and hoped enough of them scored a direct hit. With the heavy water stored in the basement of a solidly built concrete and stone structure, hundreds of heavy, high-explosive bombs would have to be used.

The Norwegian authorities in London were sure to protest vehemently and an SOE memorandum of 20 August 1943 suggested that their High Command and government-in-exile should be kept in the dark about the plans. For the Allied authorities the deaths of innocent civilians and damage to a small local economy was a price worth paying to halt a programme that might wreak far greater destruction in times to come.

One man who didn't indulge in too much soul-searching over

the air raid was Major Leslie Groves, the head of the US atomic bomb project known as 'Manhattan'. He insisted that the destruction of the Vemork plant was an urgent priority for the Allies and it was partly down to his powers of persuasion that the US government overcame its misgivings and rubber-stamped the plan. The job of carrying out the raid was handed to the US 8th Air Force. The first the Norwegian authorities in London were to hear of the attack was after it had taken place.

On 16 November, a massive fleet of 300 Flying Fortresses and Liberators roared off from the US bases in East Anglia and turned for Norway. Almost half of them split away from the main force to draw off the Luftwaffe fighters. The remaining 162 made a straight line for Vemork. The first wave of aircraft were 20 minutes early and, knowing that the Norwegian workers would not yet have left the plant for their lunch break, they made a circuit to kill time. This humane gesture was to prove costly. When the bombers returned the German gunners were waiting for them. Almost immediately the air was thick with smoke from the bombs, the steam in the cold air, the aircraft exhaust fumes and puffs of flak. From the outset, the plant was almost completely obscured and from 12,000 feet, it was more in hope than expectation that the Flying Fortresses and Liberators dropped 711 thousand-pound bombs and 201 five-hundred-pound bombs in just 45 minutes.

Almost all of the bombs missed the target and caused widespread devastation in the usually quiet and peaceful valley. The RAF photographs and the intelligence sources on the ground confirmed the planners' worst fears. Far from destroying the plant and its heavy water stocks, Vemork had barely been scratched. Out of the 1,000 or so bombs dropped, only 18 landed on the site. Some of the power had been knocked out – but that was easily fixed – and several inconsequential outbuildings destroyed, but the operational capacity remained entirely unaffected. To add to the despair, an air-raid shelter full of women and children was hit. Twenty-two locals were killed in all. The Norwegian authorities back in London were enraged and a furious argument ensued that jeopardised future cooperation on vital missions – not least on how they might now proceed with a new plan to destroy Germany's atomic capability.

In a further unwelcome consequence of the raid, the Germans decided that the heavy water was too vulnerable to be stored in Norway and they began making plans to move the operation to Germany. The intelligence caused panic in London and Washington and a blizzard of top secret memos blew down the corridors of power in both cities. The Germans planned to transport the heavy water to Hamburg, by train, ferry and then ship; the Allies planned to intercept and destroy it en route. Such was the urgency, the memos make clear, that likely reprisals on the local population were accepted as a price that would have to be paid for the destruction of the deadly cargo. On 7 February SWALLOW (Skinnarland) cabled London to report that the heavy water was going to be moved out of Vemork in the near future. The situation was now so critical that the news was immediately passed on to Churchill's War Cabinet. Within an hour of sending his message, Skinnarland received an urgent message ordering him to organise an attack.

There was only one realistic candidate for the job: Knut Haukelid, the one member of the GUNNERSIDE party to remain in the area. Skinnarland tracked him down at his hideaway thirty miles away on the Hardanger. Under normal circumstances, Haukelid would have wanted several weeks to plan his attack down to the last detail, but time was not a luxury he enjoyed. To compound the challenges, the Germans had recently stepped up their sweeps of the area, hunting out the Resistance, and his journey back to the Rjukan area on 13 February was fraught with danger.

Skinnarland received hard information from his contacts that the heavy water was to be loaded onto a ferry, called *Hydro*, on the night of 20 February at the heavily guarded dock area at Mael, ten miles along the valley from Vemork. Haukelid's plan was to blow up the ferry when it was over the deepest point of Lake Tinn. To do so, he would have to somehow find a way past the guards, get onto the ferry, lay the charges and escape before it set sail. The ferry was the principal link to the railway network and was frequently used by the locals. Many of them were certain to die if Haukelid was able to pull off his bold plan.

In the days leading up to the heavy water's removal, dozens of Gestapo agents arrived in Rjukan to reinforce the army detachments and local police. Skinnarland's agents, working inside Vemork, arranged the programme for loading the heavy water in such a way that it would leave on the Sunday ferry. On Sunday there was only one scheduled trip from Mael, which meant there was little chance of the Germans postponing its departure. What's more, with most locals resting at home, it was likely there would be fewer casualties.

Haukelid built two rudimentary time-bombs using alarm clocks with traditional bells on top. The hope was that at the exact time he predicted that the ferry would be in the middle of the lake, the hammer would strike the alarm bell and detonate the charges. The risks were obvious – any heavy movement of the boat could set off the homemade devices at any time – but, given the haste and the urgency, there was no obvious alternative. On 18 February, Haukelid made a recce to Mael, bluffed his way onto the ferry and disappeared into the holds to work out where best to lay the explosives. He found his answer in a watertight compartment in the bow of the boat where crew members were highly unlikely to venture.

Haukelid couldn't carry out the raid on his own. He needed help to carry the explosives, he needed a driver and he needed lookouts. The three men chosen to help were confirmed patriots: Rolf Sørlie, a member of the Resistance, plus Alf Larsen and Knut Leir Hansen, who were both engineers at Vemork. Only Sørlie, of the four, would remain in the area. The rest would flee to Sweden.

While Haukelid was carrying out his recce, the Germans began to load the heavy water stocks onto the freight wagons amid the tightest security at Vemork. Under the bright glare of giant floodlights, one by one the thirty-nine drums were carefully stored and secured. Twenty-four hours later, the train pulled slowly into the Mael ferry port. At 0100 Haukelid and his three accomplices set out from Rjukan. Leaving Larsen at the car, the others completed the last stage by foot. Bravado and composure under pressure were the order of the day from here in. Striding into the port as if they were dockyard workers, they passed the guards standing by the freight wagons lit up by floodlights. Incredibly, there appeared to be no German on the boat or guarding the entry to it, and most of the crew were playing cards at the far end of the boat. They darted below deck where they were confronted by a crew member. Haukelid had no choice but to take a gamble. He told the man they were Jøssings on the run and needed somewhere to hide their belongings. Happily, the man nodded and let them through. Haukelid also now had the perfect excuse if he was discovered in the depths of the boat.

Haukelid and Sørlie descended to the third-class deck where they wriggled through a hole in the floor into the bottom of the vessel. It was pitch black and there was freezing cold water a foot deep, through which they were forced to crawl with no more than eighteen inches between the water and the deck above. Working by torchlight in the very confined space, Haukelid fastened the charges to the wall and set the alarm for 1045. A few millimetres separated the bell hammer from the detonator.

The three men slipped out of the dockyard and melted away into the night. Haukelid was sitting on a train to Oslo the following morning, nervously inspecting his watch as it ticked down to 1045. The following morning's newspapers carried the news: the ferry had sunk at the deepest point of the lake, just as Haukelid had hoped. Skinnarland sent the following telegram to London: 'The Ferry was sunk on Sunday. Unfortunately some people drowned. Our people are OK.' A further telegram from SOE in Stockholm confirmed the news, stating that the 500-ton ferry had gone down in three minutes with the loss of eighteen lives, fourteen Norwegian and four German. Nineteen people were rescued from the icy waters.

News of Haukelid's brilliant coup was greeted with joy in London and Washington. Hitler's hopes of beating the Allies in the race to build an atomic bomb now lay 1,000 feet below the surface of Lake Tinn. With the Allies now in the ascendancy on the battlefield, the Führer's last chance of victory had been sunk.

Buried in the bundle of SOE documents relating to the raid at the National Archives in Kew is a small, frayed memo dated 14 April 1943, which reads: 'What rewards are to be given to these heroic men?' The identity of the man asking the question is given away in the address: 10, Downing Street, Whitehall. It is signed off with the initials 'W.S.C.' No one had followed the drama of the heavy water mission more closely than the Prime Minister, and no one was more eager to recognise the courage and skill of the young men who brought about such a happy ending to the saga. Rønneberg and Poulsson were duly rewarded with the Distinguished Service Order, the Military Cross was granted to Haugland, Idland and Haukelid, and the Military Medal to Helberg, Kjelstrup, Kayser, Storhaug and Strømsheim.

Skinnarland was awarded the Distinguished Conduct Medal later in the war. When the full story of the Telemark raid emerged after the war, there were many who felt the eleven men deserved a great deal more.

Operation Chariot

27/28 March 1942

It was shortly before midnight when Lieutenant Nigel Tibbits left the bridge of HMS *Campbeltown* and went below to activate the fuses connected to the huge charge inside the watertight, cement casing built into the forward compartments of the old destroyer. Using long-delay pencil fuses, it was impossible to set an exact time, but the young naval demolition expert had no doubt that within six to ten hours, the four-and-a-half tons of explosive in the form of twenty-four depth charges would tear the ship to shreds – as well as anything else within the vicinity of its huge blast range. Whether her captain up on the bridge,

Lieutenant Commander Stephen 'Sam' Beattie, would succeed in guiding the ship onto the target was another matter. To do that, over the coming hour, the naval force would have to negotiate six miles of the Loire's myriad of treacherous shoals and mudflats and survive the pounding barrage of one of the most heavily defended stretches of coast anywhere on the planet.

HMS *Campbeltown* sat at the centre of the naval force, now in battle formation, steaming at fifteen knots towards the yawning mouth of the Loire estuary, twenty-five miles south of the Brittany peninsula. The gun crews were closed down in their positions, the eighty Commandos of Group Three, who had been kept out of sight below deck throughout the long crossing, put on their steel helmets and collected their weapons and equipment. On *Campbeltown*'s port and starboard sides, two columns of high-speed motor launches, carrying the Commando assault and demolition troops of Groups One and Two, bounced over the flat surface of the Atlantic. There were twelve of them in total and, though fast, their wooden hulls and the extra fuel they carried on deck made them vulnerable. The convoy was spearheaded by Motor Gun Boat 314, the HQ vessel, containing the two commanders of the raid, Commander Robert Ryder, who was in charge of the naval force, and Lieutenant Colonel Charles Newman, leading the Commandos. Tucked in behind them, on either side, were two torpedo motor launches. Two other torpedo boats provided protection at the rear of the convoy. Twenty miles to the southwest, the crews of destroyers HMS *Atherstone* and HMS *Tynedale* who had escorted them from Falmouth waited in the darkness, on high alert for enemy patrols and U-boats.

They were still twelve miles off and no land could be sighted through the misty gloom when Ryder and Newman spotted gun flashes dead ahead to the northeast. A glance at the time told both men that the RAF had arrived over St Nazaire, according to plan. Soon the horizon was ablaze with tracer and searchlights. On all 18 vessels, the nerves of 611 men began to tighten and the banter faded to tense silence as they went to action stations.

As the convoy slid towards the estuary opening, they passed the eerie sight of the wreck of the troopship *Lancastria* lying on its side, sunk by German bombers two weeks after Dunkirk, with the loss of over 4,000 lives, in Britain's worst ever maritime disaster. The time was 0025 and, moments later, they arrived at the buoy that marked the final positioning from which they would head into the Loire through the maze of natural obstacles hidden below the dark surface of the water. The operation had been timed to take place inside a tight window when an unusually high spring tide would allow the destroyer *Campbeltown* to make an alternative approach to St Nazaire, up the centre of the great river out of sight, if not out of range, of the many coastal gun installations.

The closer they moved to St Nazaire, the shallower the water became, increasing the risk of beaching on one of the many of the sandbanks lurking below. As they passed over the notorious Banc de Châtelier, all aboard the *Campbeltown* froze as they felt the destroyer scrape the seabed and wedge to a halt – not once but twice. The alarm of the men was matched by the relief they felt as each time she pulled clear and continued on her way, undetected by the crews of the many medium and heavy coastal guns pointing in their direction. The convoy was still over seven miles away – or forty minutes – and to the troops waiting below and the crews manning the vessels, it was surely only a matter of time before the German defences sprang into life and the battle erupted. But onwards they crept, inching ever closer to the giant dockyard and further away from the mighty coastal guns guarding the entrance to the estuary.

A light breeze carried the stench of the mudflats and seaweed through the cold air as the gunners stared down the barrels of an array of light armaments, including Bren, Lewis and Vickers guns, Oerlikons and other anti-aircraft cannon, each man waiting for the German onslaught. It was around 0100 when the first of the sixty-five Wellingtons and Whitleys of the diversionary bombing raid turned for home, thwarted by thick cloud and Churchill's express orders not to endanger French civilians. They had dropped no more than half a dozen bombs, causing virtually no damage, and had succeeded only in arousing the suspicions of the German commander Kapitan zur See Karl-Conrad Mecke in charge of the port's air defences. He ordered the AA gunners to hold fire, the searchlights to be switched off and all troops to be on high alert for a 'landing'. The force was under two miles from the target when a German lookout on the coast reported the sighting of an inward-bound convoy, but his warnings were dismissed by all the commanders – except Mecke, who was convinced that there was 'some devilry afoot'. By the time the drone of the last RAF bomber had faded away, the Germans were fully prepared for a seaborne attack. Every gunner was at his station with his armament depressed and angled to meet the potential threat heading up the estuary. All infantry units had been roused from their barracks and were heading towards the dockyard.

At 0122, the blinding beams of two large searchlights, one from either bank, were turned on, lighting up the entire British flotilla in a flash. Sporadic fire opened up from the shore, but there was confusion amongst the German defenders. Surely 'Fortress St Nazaire' could not be under attack? And the destroyer at the heart of the convoy not only looked distinctly German, it was flying the German Ensign.

As the Germans dallied, Commander Ryder's German-speaking signalman bought the raiders a few more precious minutes. Answering the naval light signal to identify themselves, the signalman sent a long reply by Morse code: 'Have Urgent signal. Two damaged ships in company. Request permission to proceed without delay.' A second request to identify themselves from a separate signalling station delayed the inevitable a few more seconds. To the disbelief of the British commanders, by the time the German defences realised they had been duped, the raiders were under a mile from their target.

At 0128, Beattie ordered the red, white and black Ensign of the Third Reich to be hauled down and the White Ensign to be broken out. Battle was officially commenced. The German response was one of uncontained fury. A devastating barrage from every gun in the harbour opened up on the British flotilla. *Campbeltown*, her guns blazing, surged at full speed through the maelstrom. 'All hell was let loose' is the phrase that crops up over and over in the eyewitness testimonies of those fortunate enough to survive it. Operation CHARIOT, by far the most hazardous raid undertaken by Combined Operations, had reached its critical moment. They had two hours to achieve their strategically vital objective. It would come to be known as 'the greatest raid of all', but a great many of those who took part in it would not live to tell the story. Of the 611 sailors and Commandos who had set sail from the Cornish coast 36 hours earlier, only 242 of them would make the return journey.

St Nazaire was one of five major ports on the Atlantic coast of Vichy France which the Axis powers converted into U-boat bases to wage a deadly underwater war against the Royal Navy and the Allied merchant convoys. By the end of 1941, Brest, Bordeaux, Lorient, La Rochelle and St Nazaire had been so heavily fortified that they were almost invulnerable to attack from sea or air. The U-boat pens were encased in concrete so thick that, in the very unlikely event that the RAF were able to land a dozen 500-lb bombs right on top of them, the high explosive would cause only minor damage. The success of Germany's U-boats against the Allied convoys in the Atlantic threatened to starve Britain out of the war and deny her armed forces the raw materials and resources necessary to defend the last free corner of western Europe. But, in the late summer of

1941, when the strategists from all three services first sat down to discuss a proposed assault on St Nazaire, the U-boat pens were not the main subject of discussion. This was partly because the planners knew that German subs could use the other bases on the coast, and partly because the solidly built pens, deep inside the harbour, would be very difficult to destroy. But, principally, the pens were treated as a target of secondary importance for the simple reason that St Nazaire raised the spectre of a much greater threat to the British war effort – the *Tirpitz*.

The largest and most powerful battleship in Europe and the pride of Germany's Kriegsmarine, *Tirpitz* had recently completed her sea trials, and was ready to enter the Atlantic and Arctic to wreak havoc amongst Allied convoys already struggling under sustained attacks by the U-boats. Churchill referred to *Tirpitz* as 'the beast' with good reason. The bare statistics of her specifications were enough to send a shudder down the spine of even the saltiest Royal Navy captain. With an overall length of just under 800 feet and displacing over 50,000 tons when fully laden, she had a maximum speed of 30 knots and could outrun the fastest destroyers, the whippets of the high seas. With a range of 9,000 miles, she could remain out at sea for long periods of time. The thickness of her armour, especially around her belt and turrets, made her virtually unsinkable by conventional shelling. Armed with eight 15-inch guns and twelve 5.9-inch guns, plus dozens of AA guns and eight 21-inch torpedo tubes and four reconnaissance flying boats, her armament was so powerful that the Admiralty determined that two battleships and an aircraft carrier would be needed to defeat her. These capital ships needed a significant fleet of cruisers and destroyers to protect them, meaning that the mere threat of *Tirpitz* venturing out of port was sufficient to tie up a huge amount of naval assets. 'The destruction, or even the crippling, of this ship is the greatest event at sea at the present time,' said Churchill. 'No other target is comparable to it. The entire naval situation throughout the world would be altered.'

In all, the Allies would launch more than thirty-six major operations to sink the *Tirpitz* while keeping her confined in waters where she could inflict no damage on her enemies. So long as there was a war to be won at sea, it was vital that *Tirpitz* did not enter it. St Nazaire featured in the planning from the outset because it possessed the only dry dock in Europe with sufficient capacity to accommodate the giant battleship for refuge and repairs. The theory was that if the British could somehow deny the *Tirpitz* a safe haven in the Atlantic, she would never dare venture out of the Baltic or the fjords of Norway and risk the fate of her sister ship a few months earlier. The *Bismarck*, having sunk HMS *Hood* in the Denmark Strait, was immediately hunted down and sunk by the Royal Navy as she ran for St Nazaire for repairs to damage caused by torpedoes from Swordfish biplanes.

Aerial bombing was a long way from being a precise science at that time and the lock gates of the 'Normandie' dry dock were far too small a target for the RAF bombers operating from several thousand feet. An amphibious assault on the port was the only plausible option, though it was one fraught with grave peril and major logistical challenges. When such an attack was first proposed, all senior officers connected with its planning understood the great hazards it would entail for those they tasked to execute it. Admiralty files reveal the minutes of an inter-services meeting on 19 September in which it was suggested that protection forces should be landed in the harbour to hold positions while demolition groups went about their tasks. There was agreement around the table that an extremely high casualty rate was a price worth paying. 'If this operation is to be carried out I think we must accept the very possible if not probable loss of the landing parties,' the minutes note. 'If they achieved the destruction of the 5 lock gates it may be considered that the operation should be carried out in spite of the regrettable loss of life.'

Admiralty, Air Ministry and Combined Operations files from the autumn of 1941 reveal the heated disputes between the services and other government officials over the details of the proposed attack. Eager to hit targets of their own choosing, and with resources increasingly limited by heavy losses, the RAF were reluctant partners from the outset. The number of aircraft they offered for a diversionary bombing raid fell far short of the figure sought by their colleagues in the Navy and Army. Churchill, worried about casualties to French civilians, narrowed the scope of their usefulness still further by insisting the RAF could only drop their bombs if the dockyard targets were clearly visible. The Navy, meanwhile, despite standing to gain the most from neutering the

Tirpitz, were averse to the idea of sacrificing any of their precious warships in an enterprise that would end in the certain destruction of at least one of them. The Army, as ever overstretched and under-resourced, saw little point in committing several hundred of its best men to an operation that, in all likelihood, would end in their death or capture. Such was the wrangling that, in a memo dated 18 October, Charles Lambe, the Director of Plans at Combined Operations, called for the operation to be scrapped.

But the squabbling stopped in early January with intelligence reports that *Tirpitz* had been declared ready for combat operations and was preparing to leave Kiel in the Baltic and sail north to Trondheim on the Norwegian coast. The Admiralty took this as evidence that the most powerful battleship afloat in western waters was preparing to break out into the North Atlantic. Tackling the *Tirpitz* was given urgent priority. Lord Louis Mountbatten, who had been appointed Director of Combined Operations in October, now had the full attention of the three services.

Combined Operations HQ worked closely with several intelligence organisations to plan the raid, which was code-named Operation CHARIOT and given the approval of the Chiefs of Staff Committee on 3 March. The main objective of the operation was to put the Normandie dry dock out of action. The planners had established that the only feasible way to do this was to convert an obsolete destroyer into a floating ammunition dump and ram her into the outer gate of the dock, having negotiated an estuary made highly treacherous by the sandbanks below her surface and the network of heavy gun batteries strung out along her banks. Long-delay fuses would detonate several tons of high explosive several hours after the raiders had withdrawn. As soon as the destroyer made impact, Commando demolition groups were to storm ashore and cause as much damage as possible to the port installations while protection parties kept the enemy at bay. Their tasks completed, the survivors were to re-embark in a flotilla of smaller ships known as Fairmile Motor Launches and, protected by destroyers waiting out at sea, run the gauntlet of German retaliatory strikes on the return voyage to home waters.

There was no part of the operation that didn't carry the highest risks to those taking part in it. Surprise was the key. The further the force could sail up the Loire estuary without being detected, the greater their chance of pulling off the most daring amphibious raid ever undertaken. The odds against the raiders could barely have been longer, nor the stakes higher but, were they to succeed in their mission, they would have accomplished two great feats. Not only would they have forced the enemy to strengthen his defences all along the western coast of Europe by allocating men and materials urgently required elsewhere, they would have effectively eliminated *Tirpitz* from the war at sea.

Lieutenant Colonel Charles Newman, commander of No. 2 Commando, was chosen to lead the assault forces on the ground. A civil engineering contractor by trade, he had served sixteen years as a territorial officer with the Essex Regiment before the war. At thirty-eight, he was relatively old, and his friendly, avuncular manner only reinforced the impression and endeared him to his men. There are few pictures of him without a pipe stuck in his mouth and a smile on his distinctive face. He had a large, very hooked nose (broken several times), a small moustache and a large pair of ears that, according to one of his junior officers, gave him the appearance of a kindly elephant. Behind the cheerful, relaxed manner, however, lay the soul of a warrior, who demanded the highest standards from those in his command.

No. 2 Commando were to provide 173 men, roughly half the unit, to form the assault and protection groups in the raid. The five assault groups, each comprising two officers and a dozen other ranks men, were to assist the Navy in attacking targets during the approach. Once the landing parties were ashore, they were to attack enemy positions, blockade possible lines of enemy approach and cover the withdrawal of all troops during re-embarkation. Each of the seven protection parties was made up of one officer and four men and armed with three Thompson submachine guns and one Bren gun between them. They were to defend the target positions while the demolition teams, armed only with Colt pistols, went about their tasks. Anticipating combat at extremely close quarters, 2 Commando's second-in-command, Major Bill Copland, was ordered to oversee the training of 100 men in the dark arts of nocturnal street fighting. The demolition teams were to be made up from groups of officers and men from 1, 3, 4, 5, 6, 9 and 12 Commando. Newman's HQ group, two demolition control parties, Copland's 2iC group, a reserve of fourteen men and a twenty-eight-strong special task party completed the complement of landing forces. The special task party was ordered to attack the defences at the southern entrance of the dry dock if HMS *Campbeltown* were to get into difficulties and failed to ram the gate.

The demolition parties, working in groups of five to thirteen men, underwent an intensive three-week training course in dockyard demolition, beginning in the shipyard of Burntisland on the Firth of Forth under the expert supervision of two Royal Engineer captains, Bill Pritchard and Bob Montgomery. Pritchard, who had been awarded a Military Cross for blowing a bridge under enemy fire during the Dunkirk evacuation, was the son of the dock master in Cardiff and, having trained as an engineering apprentice in the dockyards of the Great Western Railway, there was probably no one better qualified in Britain to offer advice on how best to destroy the installations of St Nazaire. At the heart of his training methods was the belief that the total destruction of an installation as large as the Normandie dry dock could only be achieved by the placing of explosives in the structure's weakest spots. The positioning of the charges, he argued, was far more important than the amount of explosive used. By coincidence, Pritchard and his friend Montgomery had drawn up plans on how best to destroy St Nazaire dock as part of a Royal Engineering theoretical training exercise.

After Burntisland, the demolition group was split into two and transferred either to Cardiff's Barry docks or Southampton's King George V dry dock, whose design had been based on the one in St Nazaire. Each of the ten demolition parties concentrated on the destruction of specific targets, including lock gates, bridges, pumping stations, winding machinery and power houses. By the time the sappers assembled at Falmouth with the rest of the raiding force, they had been put through their paces so intensively that – it was said without exaggeration – they would able to carry out their tasks in pitch darkness or wearing blindfolds.

The Commandos were split into three groups, each with its own subparties of assault, protection and demolition teams. Group Three, the largest, would travel and disembark from the *Campbeltown* after she had rammed the outer gate of the dock. Groups One and Two were dispersed among the motor launches, and were to land at two separate points, from where their demolition and protection parties would fan out. Group One was to land and secure the Old Mole, about 600 yards south of the Normandie dock, and destroy the enemy gun positions protecting the southern quays. This was one of the key tasks of the raid, for it was from the Mole, a 100-yard-long stone jetty, that all the troops were to re-embark. The demolition parties were then to advance into the nearby Old Town and destroy targets including the power station, swing bridges and lock gates of the smaller, new entrance into the main basin of the docks. Group Two, under the command of Captain Micky Burn, were to rush ashore at the Old Entrance to the St Nazaire basin, halfway between the Old Mole and the Normandie dock, eliminate various gun installations, destroy the locks and bridges at the Old Entrance into the basin and then form a defensive block to prevent an enemy counterattack. Group Three, under the 2iC Major Bill Copland, were to knock out the gun emplacements and hold the area around the *Campbeltown*, before the demolition teams set about destroying all the operating machinery associated with the Normandie dock.

Commander Robert Ryder was serving an unofficial punishment, languishing in a dull desk job as naval liaison officer to the Army's Southern Command in Wilton, when on 26 February 1942 he was summoned to London to a meeting at Combined Operations HQ. He was more surprised than anyone to find himself sitting around the same table as Lord Mountbatten and Admiral of the Fleet Sir Charles Forbes, the Commander-in-Chief, Plymouth. His surprise turned to astonishment when he was informed that he had been selected as the naval commander for a major inter-service assault on an enemy-held port. Only a few months earlier, the thirty-four-year-old adventurer, who had taken part in several global expeditions, had received a letter from the Admiralty informing him that he had 'incurred their Lordships' displeasure'. The Admirals' discontent related to an incident twelve months earlier when the Commando ship he captained, *Prince Philippe*, was sunk following a collision in thick fog. British Admirals never like to see one of their ships slip beneath the waves and, although he was not held responsible for the loss, Ryder was sent for a 'rest cure with the Army' in Wiltshire. It was a job wholly unsuited to Ryder's adventurous temperament.

Until his mishap off the West Coast of Scotland, Ryder had

distinguished himself as a sailor of great courage and daring. He had served in submarines, sailed from Hong Kong to the UK in a boat he helped build himself, and he had commanded a three-masted topsail schooner during an expedition to the Antarctic. Shortly after the outbreak of war, the Q-ship he commanded (a heavily armed, disguised merchant vessel) was torpedoed in the Atlantic and he spent four days adrift clinging to a wooden plank before being rescued. Sitting around a Whitehall table with the Royal Navy's top brass, Ryder might have been excused for believing that he had been forgiven for the collision incident. After the war, he wrote that, to his great amusement, he was to discover that he had been chosen for the St Nazaire job because there was no other officer of suitable experience available.

Ryder had shown he was a highly resourceful man, but even he was going to be hard-pressed to pull together the many elements of a complex plan in just over three weeks. He was not helped by the fact he had no support staff, no office and, crucially, no old destroyer with which to ram the outer lock gate of the dry dock. The inability of the Admiralty to produce a suitable ship to be sacrificed in the raid was threatening once again to scupper the entire operation. On the last day of February, while all other elements of the force were being hastily assembled, Mountbatten vented his fury on his brother officers in the Senior Service. The Navy had offered a large submarine destined for the scrapyard instead, but this was considered by both Ryder and Newman to be wholly unsuited to the nature of the operation. In a terse, handwritten MOST SECRET memo from Combined Operations, an official scrawled that Mountbatten 'urgently requires a decision by Monday as to the destroyer'. Having considered and dismissed all other options, Mountbatten dangled the warning that the operation would have to be cancelled if the Navy was unable to deliver an expendable vessel by the meeting of the raid's planners three days later. The threat of being held responsible for the raid's abandonment appears to have had a remarkably galvanising effect on the Admirals. Within days, the HMS *Campbeltown* was on her way from Portsmouth to Devonport for a very rapid refit.

The UK's shipyards were building new warships as fast as it was humanly possible but at this stage of the war, Navy resources were stretched to the limit. The reluctance to commit any vessel to certain destruction – no matter how outdated and decrepit – was understandable, but if there was one ship that the Royal Navy could probably survive the war without, it was the *Campbeltown*. She was launched in 1919 as the USS *Buchanan*, one of fifty antiquated warships given to the Royal Navy by the United States in exchange for the lease of some of Britain's naval bases around the world. On her last legs, she would have been no match in a fight with the Kriegsmarine. Converting her for the raid involved two main challenges: 1) allowing for the addition of almost five tons of explosives she had to be made light enough to pass over the Loire estuary's many shoals; 2) she had to be modified to resemble a German destroyer.

That both these engineering feats were completed within ten

days was a testament to the hard work and skill of the men of the Devonport dockyard. All her compartments below deck were stripped out, her three 4-inch guns, torpedoes, depth charges and forward gun were removed and replaced with a light, quick-firing 12-pounder and eight 20-mm Oerlikon AA guns. Anticipating heavy fire from the German coastal guns, the bridge and wheelhouse were plated with extra armour. Two further rows of armour were installed along the sides of the ship to protect the Commandos lying on the open deck during the final approach. Her rear two funnels were removed and the forward two were reduced and repositioned at an angle to resemble those of a German destroyer. The huge explosive charge, secured in a concrete block, was placed in a hidden compartment between the bridge and the bow, where it was likely to cause the greatest amount of damage to the dock. Ryder was delighted when the elderly captain of the *Campbeltown* was replaced by Lt Cdr Sam Beattie, an old friend who had joined the Navy in the same year. Beattie had plenty of experience on destroyers and Ryder wrote later: 'I could wish for no one better.'

Combined Operations' original plan of attack envisaged the use of two lightened destroyers, one to ram the Normandie dock and the other to act as an escort and troop carrier. But if securing one old destroyer had proved hard enough, acquiring two was impossible. Faced with the problem of transporting over 100 Commandos laden with weapons and demolition equipment to and from the target, the planners found there was only one plausible alternative and that was to deploy a flotilla of 'little ships'. This was to be made up of sixteen Fairmile 'B' motor launches (MLs), a gun boat and a motor torpedo boat. Twelve of the MLs were to transport small squads of Commandos and the four others were each mounted with two torpedo tubes to boost the force's firepower. It promised to be a cramped voyage for those on board. In normal circumstances, the MLs had a crew of sixteen, but that number was increased for the raid.

The sixty-five-ton vessels, designed for escort, patrol and anti-submarine roles, could reach a maximum speed of twenty knots, but their speed would be of little help when they came within range of St Nazaire's coastal defences. Made from plywood, they were completely ill-suited to the task of assaulting one of the most heavily defended ports in the world. The thin sheet of armour around the small bridge was small comfort for the crew within. The Commandos on the deck outside were even more vulnerable – even a rifle bullet could breach the ship's timber sides. In order to extend their range for the 850-mile return voyage, each of the vessels was fitted with an additional fuel tank, on the deck, carrying 500 gallons of highly combustible petrol. It would take just one accurate or lucky shot from the shore to turn one of the mini-troop carriers into a floating inferno. Given the extreme frailty of the motor launches, the element of surprise during the approach to the target was imperative. The closer they advanced to the target, the greater their chances of success.

The guns under which it was necessary for the flotilla to pass were truly formidable, even for far more heavily armed and armoured ships than the little wooden motor launches. At the entrance to the estuary, the Germans had made major improvements to the existing French installations. In all, St Nazaire was protected by over 70 guns, ranging in calibre from 75 mm (of which there were 28 pieces) to 150 mm and 170 mm, and to the massive 240-mm railway guns a few miles to the north at La Baule, positioned to engage enemy ships long before they reached the estuary. In addition to the heavier artillery, there were over forty 20-mm to 40-mm calibre guns that doubled as anti-aircraft and coastal defence weapons. If an attacking force succeeded in negotiating these forbidding layers of defence, a further bulwark awaited them in and around the town itself where over 5,000 German troops, military and naval, were stationed.

In mid-March, all the elements of the raiding force began to assemble at Falmouth on Cornwall's south coast. The motor launches that would carry most of them were already in harbour when the troops of 2 Commando arrived from their training base on the west coast of Scotland aboard the troopship *Princess Josephine Charlotte*. The demolition groups, having completed their intensive rehearsals on the docks of Southampton and Cardiff, slipped into the town at the same time. In order to maintain a veil of secrecy over the operation, all the Commandos were ordered to remain out of sight below deck. Spies were known to operate in every naval port in the world during the war. Loose talk and slack security could compromise the operation. A cover story was invented to mislead the gossipers and safeguard CHARIOT from intelligence breaches. Word was put about that the flotilla was being organised into 'Tenth Anti-Submarine Striking Force' for a sweep of U-boats out in the Bay of Biscay.

In order to familiarise the troops with conditions at sea, the Commandos were embarked in the motor launches and other small ships and taken around the Scilly Isles, forty miles off Land's End. They set off in rough weather that soon developed into a strong gale. By the time their Navy hosts decided to seek shelter in the bays of the Scillies, virtually every one of the 250 soldiers had been sick. Back in Falmouth, two further weeks of training exercises focused on approaching the target, and on disembarking and reboarding in the dark. On 18 March, Newman summoned his thirty-nine officers and divulged the nature of the mission. The following day, one by one, the officers revealed the plan to the men they would be commanding on the night. Only the name of the port was withheld, but several immediately guessed its identity. Throughout the army contingent, the reaction was one of excited astonishment mixed with trepidation. Most of the young men had never seen combat, but they were savvy enough to understand the scale of the challenge and the grave risks it involved. The Commandos were a volunteer organisation and it was in that spirit that Newman offered the opportunity for his men to pull out and, without recrimination or dishonour, return to their regular units. No one took him up on his offer.

A detailed model of the dockyard was displayed in the briefing room aboard the troopship and, one after another, each of the

Commando subgroups filed in to have their specific tasks spelt out. Once the raid was underway, Newman's military HQ was to be set up at the Old Entrance to the harbour where Group Two was to have disembarked. Communications on the night were to be carried out by radio and by runners. The original plan to take six bicycles was considered impractical and was dropped. All tasks were to be completed within two hours. The signal to withdraw was to be made first with green and then red flares. In an emergency, if the operation had to be aborted, all flares would be fired at once and the crews of every ML would sound their klaxons. The operational orders issued to Newman and Ryder stipulated a number of security precautions. All badges and distinguishing signs were to be removed (except badges of rank) and no papers or letters disclosing the identity of the unit or formation were to be taken ashore. Recognition between the men on the ground was to be made by the use of surnames plus a password and countersign.

Useful French and German phrases were learned by all ranks. In French, the expressions were to be forceful and helpful: *'Obey and you'll be OK . . . Disobey and you'll be killed . . . Where are the Germans? . . . Get out! . . . Shut up!'* In German, the phrases were designed to intimidate and mislead. They included: *'Scum . . . Quickly for God's sake . . . You're surrounded . . . We're two battalions . . . It's a whole army . . . Hands up!'*

The Commandos' uniform included special-issue boots fitted with rubber soles for silent movement (which soon came to be known as 'commando boots'). The orders regarding uniform and appearance continue: 'oldest battle dress, roll-neck sweaters, first field dressing, knives (fighting), Mae Wests, 2 identity discs around neck, gaiters, steel helmets, no respirators, faces and hands clean, scrubbed skeleton order [= *clean faces & hands, bare minimum kit*], full water bottle slung, no entrenching tool.' Special carrying equipment was also issued to those armed with grenades, Tommy guns and mortars. The conclusion of the Operational Order, signed off by Admiral of the Fleet Forbes, reads: 'In an operation of this nature, difficulties may arise which have not been foreseen. I rely on all officers and men to overcome these by the display of initiative and the aggressive spirit.'

On the night of 21/22 March a full-scale dress rehearsal was carried out at Plymouth and Devonport under the ruse of testing the dockyards' defences. It quickly turned into a fiasco that depressed the planners and participants in equal measure (although it brought some cheer to those tasked with the defence of one of Britain's most important naval bases). The approaching raiders were immediately picked up by the port's defences after the crews of the ships had been blinded by the searchlights. Had the exercise been for real, the entire party would have been blown out of the water long before they reached the target.

On 25 March, seventy-two hours before the force was sched-uled to depart, a distinctly Germanic-looking *Campbeltown* caused a stir when she slid into Falmouth Harbour. Just 22 days after the Chiefs of Staff had given the operation the go-ahead, 21 ships, one submarine, and 611 sailors and highly trained soldiers were ready for action. The operation was scheduled for the night of 28/29 March when the tides in the Loire were at their highest, but eager to make the most of the favourable weather, Commander Ryder brought the timetable forward by twenty-four hours. On the afternoon of 26 March, escorted by the destroyers HMS *Atherstone* and HMS *Tynedale* and a lone Hurricane fighter, the flotilla slipped out of the Cornish harbour at 1400 and headed towards the Bay of Biscay. A gentle swell rolled beneath the ships and a mellow, hazy sunshine filled the skies above, but the calmness of the scene did not fool anyone aboard. The Operation Order insisted on military personnel staying out of sight. If anyone was to come above they had to do so in a naval duffle coat or oilskins. 'It is essential that reconnaissance enemy aircraft should NOT learn the presence of Military on board,' the order reads. For most of the passage, the Commandos remained below deck in fairly cramped conditions, relieving the tension with nervous banter and jokes.

The 420-mile voyage to St Nazaire had been plotted so as to maintain the impression that the flotilla was on a U-boat sweep. The course that had been set took them well past the Brittany peninsula into the Bay of Biscay before they turned sharply and steamed for the French coast under the cover of darkness. As soon as it had left the relative safety of home waters, the flotilla went into anti-submarine formation. If an enemy ship or reconnaissance aircraft did spot them, it would have appeared that the British convoy was on a routine passage to Gibraltar. In this way, it was only in the final few hours that the raiding force's true intentions might be suspected.

As darkness began to fall, the last of the escorting Hurricanes swept low over the ships and headed back to England. The Ensign of the Third Reich was hoisted aboard so as to try and fool any Vichy fishing vessels they might encounter. The night passed without incident and, to the dismay of Ryder and his crews, daybreak ushered in a beautifully clear day with brilliant visibility. It was shortly after 0700 and the force had just turned east for France when the alarm was raised. *Tynedale* spotted a U-boat, its periscope up, seven miles to the northeast. Ryder understood the critical importance of the moment: he must either destroy the enemy boat or force her to dive before she radioed in the sighting of the flotilla.

Tynedale was immediately ordered to go after her. Casting off the HQ motor gun boat (MGB) she was towing, the destroyer, flying the German Ensign, sped towards the sub at a maximum speed of twenty-seven knots. The U-boat fired off a pyrotechnic rocket that burst into five stars as a recognition signal. The *Tynedale* replied with five long flashes of her Aldis lamp. At 4,000 yards, *Tynedale* ran up her White Ensign and opened fire. If she had closed any further, it would not have been possible to depress her guns low enough to hit the target. Giant plumes of water burst around the U-boat but the near-misses were not near enough to cause any damage. The U-boat (U-593), damaged from an earlier confrontation with the British, had tried but failed to launch a torpedo at the *Tynedale*. She had no option but to crashdive and wait for the inevitable pounding beneath the surface. Minutes later, the German crew felt the mighty percussion of depth charges. Such was the force of the explosions that U-593 was forced to the surface, but she quickly dived again, strafed by *Tynedale*'s short-range guns from close range. HMS *Atherstone* was now at the scene and the two destroyers swept the area using ASDIC underwater detection device. But dropping to about 500 feet below the surface and reducing her speed to a barely perceptible one knot, the U-boat evaded her hunters. After two hours the destroyers broke off the search and rejoined the flotilla. Ryder's main fear was that the U-boat had succeeded in reporting the British presence before diving. There was nothing for it but to continue as planned. All would be revealed in the coming hours. If the Germans ashore had been alerted, Operation CHARIOT was badly compromised.

For two hours, no enemy reconnaissance aircraft was spotted as the flotilla continued its course towards the French coast. But shortly before midday, the raiding force came across two French fishing vessels. Enemy radio operators were known to operate from these boats and Ryder was under orders to sink any that he encountered. *Atherstone* and *Tynedale* went alongside them and, having taken off the crews, sank both vessels. The captains of both boats gave their word that there were no wireless sets on board either of the craft. By that time, Ryder was reassured that the U-boat they had engaged had been unable to dispatch a sighting report to her Coastal Command. (After the war, it was discovered that U-593 had surfaced in mid-afternoon and the captain made a report that contained one highly significant mistake. He said the British flotilla was heading west, away from their intended target. They were in fact heading southeast. The German coastal commanders assumed the ships were en route to Gibraltar and decided not to send out the five destroyers that patrolled that area. It was a very poor error of judgement by the U-boat crew, and it would not be long before they were made to understand its magnitude.)

Darkness had fallen when one of the motor launches, ML 341, reported that she had lost the use of one of her engines and was unable to keep up with the flotilla's fifteen-knot pace. Coming at such a critical time, just a few hours before Z-hour, this was a blow on a number of counts. The Commandos on board were an assault group tasked with capturing and holding the Old Mole, the re-embarkation for the raiding force. One of the two back-up launches, ML 446, that had been brought for just such an eventuality, took the troops and a medical team on board, but they were two hours behind the others by the time the handover was completed. Pushing twenty knots, ML 446 succeeded in rejoining the flotilla, but she was forced to line up at the rear of the formation. There was now no chance of the assault party spearheading the attack on the Old Mole and that was a major cause for concern, as the demolition groups that would now go in before them had little more than a few pistols between them.

It was shortly after 2000, five and a half hours from Z-hour, when the force reached 'point E' off the French coast and came to a stop. Ryder and Newman transferred from *Atherstone* to MGB 314, which hauled out to the front of the force as the rest of the ships fell into battle formation. Two torpedo boats,

ML 160 and ML 270, were positioned behind them at the head of two columns of motor launches, twelve of them in total, to the port and starboard of HMS *Campbeltown*. Two further torpedo boats, ML 446 and ML 298, brought up the rear. Ryder was astounded that the flotilla had steamed so close to the heavily patrolled French coast without being detected. So far, the good fortune had been all British.

Navigation was now the key challenge. The submarine HMS *Sturgeon*, which had sailed from Plymouth twenty-four hours before the flotilla, was to act as a navigational mark for the raiders. From that position, the force would be able to follow the precise course charted for them through the treacherous shallows of the Loire estuary. The rendezvous point was known as Position Z and the responsibility of leading them there fell to Lt Bill Green in the lead gun boat. In the pitch-black night and with no landmarks to assist him, it was some feat that Green not only brought them to the very spot but he did so almost to the second. It was exactly 2200 when *Sturgeon's* beacon flashed out of the darkness. Passing within hailing distance of the sub, the crews exchanged greetings before it slipped beneath the surface, leaving no more than a ripple. At the same time, the destroyers *Atherstone* and *Tynedale* broke off from the force and steamed away from the coast to await the return of any ships that survived the most ambitious, large-scale amphibious raid ever undertaken by British forces.

By coincidence, six hours earlier, Admiral Karl Donitz, supreme commander of Germany's U-boat fleet, had made an inspection of St Nazaire and asked Kapitänleutnant Herbert Sohler, commander 7th Submarine Flotilla, what the chances were of the British attacking the port from the sea. He was reassured that an amphibious assault was out of the question. Both men were preparing for another good night's sleep when 611 British souls steamed through Position Z and into the mouth of the Loire. In three-and-a-half hours' time, the German commanders would discover whether Sohler's conviction held true.

When the White Ensigns on the ships were hoisted, the raiders were still six minutes short of their target. The 360 seconds had felt like six days to those who survived the gunfire of one of the most heavily defended military bases in the world. 'It is difficult to describe the full fury of the attack that was let loose on each side,' Ryder wrote after the war. 'Owing to the air attack, the enemy had every gun, large and small, fully manned, and the night became one mass of red and green tracer.'

When MGB 314 – the command boat spearheading the approach – reached the east jetty, close to the entrance of the harbour, she was greeted with a burst of fire from the guard ship moored there. Passing no further than 200 yards away, the British gun boat responded with a heavy fusillade from her pair of two-pounders and heavy-machine guns, knocking out one of the German gun positions. The *Campbeltown* and the other ships followed 314's example and, in the confusion, German guns also pounded the hapless ship, which was unable to depress its AA guns low enough to attack the flotilla.

The *Campbeltown*, the largest of the vessels, began to attract fire like iron filings to a magnet. Scores of shells of all sizes punched holes in her hull and waves of machine gunfire swept over her decks. There was not a part of the old destroyer that didn't feel the full force of German gunnery skills. The Commandos, lying on the decks behind the reinforced armour plates, could do nothing but pray that the flying shrapnel and ricocheting bullets failed to come their way. Casualties were sustained from the opening seconds of the battle and they mounted rapidly. The bridge of the *Campbeltown* drew such a weight of fire that Commander Beattie ordered his men to the wheelhouse below, where thin armour plates at least offered some protection from the efforts of the gunners of the smaller armaments. The range of vision from there, however, was reduced to a small slit, no more than a foot wide, and it was through that gap that Beattie had to direct the destroyer onto a relatively small target that he hadn't yet managed to identify.

With a shower of bullets and shells crashing into the hull, the thickly bearded Commander squinted through the slit, desperately trying to pick out the outer lock. *Campbeltown* was close to its full speed of twenty knots when a giant searchlight fixed the wheelhouse and left Beattie blinded by its powerful beam. Almost instantaneously, his helmsman slumped to the floor, mortally wounded. The telegraphist immediately leapt forward to take the wheel, but he too was cut down on the spot as fire raked the wheelhouse. Tibbits, the demolitions expert, calmly stepped into the breach to steer the ship. There were just seconds now before impact.

Beattie knew that if he failed to ram the outer lock gate head-on, Operation CHARIOT would be remembered as a very costly catastrophe, a waste of a great many talented, brave young men. He kept his eyes on the gun boat in front, waiting for it to bank to starboard and allow him an open run at the dock. At that moment, a huge shell from one of the larger gun emplacements crashed into the twelve-pounder gun forward of the bridge, instantly killing the gun crew and many of the Commandos lying around it, and leaving many others stunned or writhing in agony. The massive explosion left Beattie dazed and dazzled, but through the smoke he recognised the landmarks of the harbour from the planners' scale model back in Falmouth. Passing the Old Mole on his port side, he realised he was off course and ordered a sharp wheel to the starboard. As Tibbits swung the destroyer back on course, Beattie could now see the lock gate of the giant dock dead ahead of the point of his bow.

Battering her way through a maelstrom of tracer and incendiaries, punctured by a hundred shell holes, the dead and wounded lying on her decks, but her guns still blazing, the *Campbeltown* surged towards the entrance at full steam. The motor gun boat swung away to starboard. 'Stand by to ram,' ordered Beattie calmly. Those still alive inside the wheelhouse clung for dear life to whatever support they could find and braced themselves for the impact. The dark outline of the dock's structure appeared to rise out of the water before the impact. A split second later, over 1,000 tons of warship travelling at 20 knots smashed into the thick metal wall of the gate. The violence of the collision shook the ship from bow to stern, sparks and debris flew in all directions and the harsh sound of metallic grinding filled the air. What was left of the bow of the old destroyer hung over the lock gate, pointing skywards at an angle. The impact was so powerful that the front of the ship was crushed back by twelve metres. Through a barrage of artillery fire, with his men falling dead around him, Beattie had guided her straight into the centre of the target. The four and a half tons of explosive below deck were sitting right on top of the gate. He could not have been more precise in his positioning of the charge had he placed it there with a crane. It was 0134 hours. Beattie, a stickler for precise timing, looked at his watch and was heard to mutter: 'Hmm, four minutes late.'

Leaving their dead and wounded comrades behind for the medics and the crew to attend to, the Commandos of Group Three leapt over the sides of the wrecked destroyer and, splitting into small parties, sprinted for their assigned targets. Behind them in the harbour bloody carnage was being played out as the two columns of motor launches, carrying Commando Groups One and Two, were shredded by withering enemy fire. Proving to be every bit of a problem as they had been in the rehearsal exercise, the searchlights lit up the little ships in a brilliant light that allowed the shore gunners to pick them off almost at will. The small, lightly armed wooden craft were no match for the big-calibre shells or the sheer volume of fire from the smaller guns. Very soon after the battle had begun, many of the launches were ablaze and cries of agony rang out across the water, mingling with the burst of shells and the rattle of machine-gun fire in a hellish chorus.

The starboard column, carrying Group Two, was to land her Commandos at the Old Entrance to the harbour's main basin, 100 yards from where the *Campbeltown* had come to rest. The first motor launch, ML 192, had been hit by a shell during the approach and was burning furiously alongside the east jetty. Her captain gave the order to abandon ship and the wounded were lifted into the Carley float life rafts. Nine soldiers were killed or too seriously wounded to continue and four crewmen were also lost. But Captain Michael Burn, the party's leader, and four others managed to jump into the water and scramble ashore, swimming past the dead body of one of the section commanders as they did so.

The second and third launches in the column overshot the disembarkation point after the crew were caught in the glare of a powerful searchlight. As they turned round to head back, ML 268, which had been fourth in the column and was carrying a large contingent of eighteen Commandos, was hit by relentless, close-range fire as she made her approach. She burst into flames and then blew up as the auxiliary fuel tank on deck and the demolition party's explosives caught light. Half the crew jumped overboard in time but sixteen soldiers were killed in a huge explosion.

ML 156, the fifth of Group Two's six launches, had already taken heavy fire when a direct hit on the bridge severely wounded its captain Lieutenant Fenton, the leader of the Commando assault group, and a number of his men. The ship's second-in-command took over and pressed on towards the Old Entrance but, when heavy fire claimed him and the third officer, as well as one engine and the steering gear, there was no option but to withdraw.

Witnessing the bloody mayhem on the northern side of the Old Entrance, Lieutenant Rodier in ML 177, the final boat in the column, diverted at the last moment and went alongside the steep stone steps on the other side of the small quay where the enemy fire was lighter. His quick thinking almost certainly saved many lives and ML 177 thus became the only one of the six ships in Group Two to succeed in putting its troops ashore. It was, however, a hollow success, as there were no demolition parties to support. They were on their own. At this point, Commander Ryder's gun boat appeared and disembarked Lieutenant Colonel Newman and his HQ party at the northern steps of the entrance. Some of the German guns had been silenced by now and CHARIOT's military commander was able to get ashore without the loss of any of his seven men.

Using his loud-hailer, Ryder ordered Rodier to go to the *Campbeltown* and take off as many of the wounded Commandos and crew as he could. At the same time, ML 262 under Lieutenant Burt, one of the launches that had overshot the Old Entrance, arrived on the scene. The Commandos she carried were jumping onto the quay when the southern winding shed, a stone's throw across the water, exploded with an ear-shattering blast. It was heartening for the others to know that at least some demolition parties had managed to get off the water and reach their target. Moments later, the five-man party responsible for laying the charge – Lieutenant Smalley's from the *Campbeltown* group – ran down the quay. ML 262, which had just re-embarked a separate party, took them aboard. As they headed out, they came under heavy fire again and suffered a number of casualties, including Smalley who was killed outright. The launch was damaged too but Burt managed to escape downstream.

ML 267 under Lieutenant Beart, carrying a reserve of fourteen Commandos, had turned back to make a second attempt at the Old Entrance but, under heavy fire, burst into flames as she tried to land her men. Jumping overboard to escape the flames, nineteen crew and Commandos died in the water, most of them machine-gunned in the burning oil. The lucky ones were drowned. Ryder witnessed the horrific fate suffered by so many from his starboard column as his gun boat raced down to the Old Mole to assess Group One's progress there. In his report, he wrote: 'On leaving the Old Entrance, however, I could see that matters had fared badly there. The approaches were floodlit by searchlights from all directions and a deadly fire was being poured on the M.L.s still gallantly attempting to go alongside.'

While the Commandos in the motor launches battled the devastating enemy fire to try and get ashore, their colleagues on the *Campbeltown*, many of them already carrying wounds, were pouring over the sides of the stricken destroyer. They too were feeling the full force of the enemy guns that continued to spray the ship from both sides of the river. As they did so, Commander

Beattie immediately set about arranging the withdrawal of his crew and the wounded before scuttling his ship. The plan was to send the destroyer to the bottom so that if the charge failed to detonate, the entrance to the dock would remain blocked to the *Tirpitz* for up to a year.

The two assault groups were the first into the fray but their exit was impeded by the number of wounded men lying in the blood-spattered gangways and well-deck. There was no option but to drag some of them out of the way in order to get the attack under way. Urged on by Newman's 2iC, Major Copland, the men of 2 Commando hurried through the smoke, flames and raking fire to clamber down the hanging ladders to the dock. Lieutenant Roderick's party descended by the starboard side of the bow and quickly silenced a gun emplacement, strafing the gunners with their Tommy guns and disabling the gun with a small explosive. Working in small groups, covering each other in fire-and-move advances, Roderick's men used a shower of grenades to destroy their second target, a 3.7-cm flak gun that had been hammering the *Campbeltown* from its position on a nearby roof.

A third gun they were to target had already been silenced by the Navy's guns and, their tasks complete, Roderick's men set up a blocking position to thwart a German counterattack. In the space of those few, frenetic minutes, four of his men had fallen. The other assault party, led by Captain Roy, destroyed a gun position that had been hastily abandoned at the sight of the Commandos streaming along the dockside, firing Brens and

Tommy guns from their hips. The emplacement was put out of action and Roy took up position, as per their orders, at the Old Entrance bridge, which they were to hold until all the demolition squads had withdrawn to the evacuation point on the Old Mole.

The first demolition team from the *Campbeltown* into action, led by Lieutenant Chant, had reached their target before the immediate area had been cleared of enemy guns. Chant and one of his sergeants, Chamberlain, were carrying severe wounds sustained in the run up the river. Struggling to walk, Chant had taken injuries to his leg, arm and hands, while Chamberlain had been hit in the shoulder and had to ask one of his 'buddies' to carry his heavy haversack laden with explosives. Their task was to destroy the pumping house, next to the *Campbeltown*, which would render the dock tidal and prevent the *Tirpitz* and all other large warships from using it for a great many months. It was considered the most important of all the demolition assignments.

Having blown the door to the pump house, Chamberlain, who was weakening by the minute, was left to guard the entrance while Chant and three sergeants disappeared below. Each carrying 60 pounds of explosives on their backs, they descended the labyrinth of stairs into the bowels of the echoing chamber as quickly as the darkness and Chant's wounds allowed them. Working in the gloom by the light of their torches, it was now that their intensive training back at Southampton's King George V dock paid off. The layout of the machinery was just as they had been led to expect and, one by one, each of the four peeled off to their assigned positions and quickly set about laying their charges. As they finished, Chant was starting to fade and one of his men had to help him climb back to the top as the slow fuses burnt down behind them. Shortly after they had taken cover, the pump house exploded in an enormous roar that reverberated across the dockyard. Adding the finishing touch to their demolition work, the group lit the oil pouring out of the structure and withdrew over Roy's bridge, hurrying to the Old Mole ready to re-embark.

The final group of Commandos off the *Campbeltown*, and the largest, had been handed the most hazardous of the demolition tasks. They were to destroy the northern lock gate and its winding shed. To reach their target, however, they had to run the gauntlet of heavy German fire for 300 yards along the eastern, or left-hand side of the Normandie dock. The group was split into two parties: the first, four NCOs under Lieutenant Purdon, was to blow the winding machinery. The second, eight NCOs under Lieutenant Brett, was to attack the lock gate. Their numbers were boosted by the addition of a reserve demolition group under Lieutenant Burtinshaw. Lieutenant Etches, who was in overall charge of the group, was forced to stay behind having suffered serious shrapnel wounds to both legs and an arm shortly before the *Campbeltown* made impact with the southern gate. Two men of five in a heavily armed protection squad had also been incapacitated and remained on board.

Stepping over the dead, the dying and the wounded to get to the ladders at the forward end of the besieged destroyer, Purdon, Brett and Burtinshaw led their men down the sides and into the thick of the battle. They advanced to their target in short bounds, taking cover from the beams of the searchlights and the raking crossfire as and when they could. The heaviest fire was emanating from a German position midway along the dock and it was clear there could be no further progress until it was neutralised. Drilled to perfection by months of training, the three-man protection squad went into action. While one drew the fire, the other two crept forward and lobbed in grenades, killing all inside.

The two demolition squads had infiltrated deeper into the heart of enemy territory than any other and they soon found themselves under intense fire from a number of positions, including the heavier-calibre guns of the ships moored inside the giant basin to their left. Brett was injured early on and Burtinshaw and six others were killed as the casualty toll mounted rapidly. But, undaunted, the others continued with their tasks. With no officers left standing in the group, Sergeant Carr took control and, having abandoned plans to lay explosives inside the structure, he set about detonating the underwater explosives that had been lowered over the side. Moments later, a muffled boom was followed by the sight of giant fountains of water shooting into the air and pouring through the holed structure into the dry dock. Leaving their dead comrades where they lay, the survivors, each one suffering at least one wound, staggered back through the tumult of gunfire towards the bridge held by Roy's small, heavily reduced assault party. As they disappeared into the night, Purdon and his men lit the fuses on their charges on the machinery inside the winding shed, echoing those set off by

Lieutenant Smalley a short time earlier at the southern end.

With battle raging in all parts of the dockyard, Lieutenant Colonel Newman and his seven men waited anxiously at the HQ they had established in a building at the Old Entrance close to the bridge held by Roy. His protection party had perished on the water but he was soon joined by the only full Commando party to have made it ashore – from Rodier's ML 177. He deployed the group, commanded by Troop Sergeant Major Haines, as the HQ's makeshift protection party, doing his forlorn best to exercise some sort of control over the chaotic scenes around him.

Five hundred yards to the south of Newman's HQ, the six launches of the port column of the raiding force were attempting to land the Commandos of Group One on the Old Mole. The fate they suffered under the German guns was every bit as horrifying as that of their comrades from Group Two at the Old Entrance; the courage of their efforts to get ashore was as awe-inspiring as it was hopeless.

As the first of the six, ML 447, under Lieutenant Platt, had already absorbed significant punishment as it closed on the heavily defended stone jetty. Two machine-gun positions on the Mole raked the vessel, and casualties lay strewn upon her deck as Platt tried to bring her alongside the steps. Captain Birney's fifteen-strong assault party had already been reduced to roughly half its strength when an artillery shell scored a direct hit and flames engulfed the ship. Platt gave the order to abandon ship, but though a few managed to scramble ashore and some were picked up by one of the torpedo boats, most were drowned or gunned to death in the water.

As at the Old Entrance a few hundred yards to the north, only one of the six launches managed to get their men ashore. Once Birney's assault party had been wiped out, there was no chance of the rest overcoming the German defenders behind the walls of the jetty, who outnumbered and outgunned them. ML 457, under Lieutenant Collier, the second in the column, somehow survived the relentless German enfilade from above and managed to disembark one demolition team under Lieutenant Walton, the protection party under Second Lieutenant Watson and a small demolition control party under Captain Pritchard. The fifteen men who made it into the dockyard amounted to 18 per cent of the total number of Commandos scheduled to land at the Old Mole.

With next to no support, their fate was sealed the moment they began to scramble up the greasy stone slipway towards the German gunfire that was intensifying by the minute. But they pressed on nevertheless, trying to ignore the harrowing screams of their friends and comrades from ML 447 in the water below. As the small groups of men made a dash for their targets, more Germans arrived to strengthen the defences at the Old Mole, extinguishing, once and for all, any hope that the troops ashore could be evacuated from there as planned. As the Germans tossed grenades over the walls onto the landing points below, the weight of fire raining down was so great and the scene so chaotic that the remaining four motor launches were forced to withdraw back into the middle of the river. So it was that of the twelve troop-carrying vessels, only one from each column had succeeded in putting their men ashore.

Moments after the last of his Commandos had clambered ashore, Collier's motor launch (ML 457) burst into flames. Lieutenant Burt in ML 262 rushed in to help but both were shattered by enemy fire. There were few survivors. Within minutes, the parties that had managed to land at the Old Mole were also in disarray as they battled in vain to carry out their orders. Lieutenant Walton lost his life trying to blow up the bridge connecting the Old Town to the centre of St Nazaire in an attempt to block German reinforcements. Captain Pritchard died of a deep wound to the stomach, almost certainly at the point of a German bayonet as he rounded the corner of a building. Lieutenant Watson's team were beaten back by ferocious German defence and fought their way through the dock installations to Newman's HQ at the Old Entrance.

To his mounting frustration, Lieutenant Wynn, commanding the motor torpedo boat MTB 74, had been forced to watch the battle unfolding on the dockside, unable to contribute anything more telling than some covering fire for the rest of the force. Commander Ryder had held him back to torpedo the *Campbeltown* if her scuttling charges had failed to detonate, but once the old destroyer was lying safely on the bottom and stuck fast on the lock gate, Wynn was handed his chance to play his part in the action. Speeding towards the Old Entrance, Wynn unleashed two torpedoes at the lock gates leading to the U-boat basin.

Both hit the target and, with their time-delay fuses activated, sank to the river bed. He returned to the *Campbeltown* and embarked as many wounded men as he could accommodate before making his escape towards the mouth of the estuary.

It was now that his good nature got the better of him and disaster struck. Orders stipulated that none of the withdrawing vessels were to stop under the German guns to pick up survivors but, spotting two men on a life raft, Wynn didn't have the heart to roar past them. The speed of the torpedo boat was its only protection against the mighty coastal guns and, as soon as he slowed, one of them traversed its giant barrel. Moments later, two 170-mm shells crashed into the boat causing devastation. Wynn, severely injured, was rescued by his Chief Petty Officer. Together with the others who survived the massive blasts, they abandoned ship. As many as two dozen men clung to the one Carley float life raft as it was pulled out to sea by the power of the retreating tide. When it was later intercepted by a German patrol boat, Wynn was one of only three men still alive.

The three other motor torpedo boats had provided covering fire during the attempted landings and, using their speed to dodge incoming shells, survived the early exchanges of the action. ML 270 and ML 160 were later hit by shells but managed to patch up the worst of the damage and limp out to sea. ML 298 under Lieutenant Nock was less fortunate. Braving the heavy fire of the German defences, Nock took the boat into the Old Mole and the Old Entrance searching for Commandos to evacuate; finding none, he headed back out into the river. The boat had been hit several times during the night and a fire on board soon drew the attention of the coastal gun batteries as she sped for the relative sanctuary of the open sea. When a volley of large-calibre shells crashed on her wooden decks, the result was carnage and destruction. The few that survived had no choice but to abandon ship and put their lives at the mercy of the tides.

Commander Beattie and Lieutenant Tibbits, the two men who had guided the *Campbeltown* onto the target, were among fifty or so naval personnel and Commandos who had been taken aboard Lieutenant Rodier's ML 177, many of them carrying severe wounds. They had almost reached the mouth of the river when they were hit by a shell that killed most on board, including Rodier and Tibbits. Those who weren't killed outright died of their wounds in the freezing water. Beattie and the few other survivors were later rescued by the Germans after several hours in the water.

Commander Ryder, aboard his HQ gun boat MGB 314, was horrified by the grisly spectacle in the harbour. Bodies of men floated in water, the badly wounded cried out in agony, motor launches exploded and smouldered, oil burned on the surface of the river and fountains of water burst skywards from the shower of shells raining down from the coastal batteries.

'All this time MGB314 was lying stopped about 100 yards off the Old Entrance,' wrote Ryder in the Dispatch submitted to the Admiralty two weeks later, 'and although fired on continually by flak positions and hit many times she was by the Grace of God not set ablaze. On looking round the harbour, however,

I counted about seven or eight blazing M.L.s and was forced to realise that MGB314 was the only craft left in sight . . . It was clearly impossible for MGB314 to return. With some thirty to forty men on board and her decks piled with seriously wounded I decided at 0250 that she was in no position to take off the soldiers we had landed. It was unlikely that MGB314 would survive another five minutes with the fire that was being concentrated in her direction so I left at high speed.'

As she withdrew downriver, the gun boat was caught in the glare of the searchlights and immediately subjected to heavy crossfire from both banks. In spite of being badly wounded, Able Seaman Bill Savage, the gunlayer manning the forward gun, a quick-firing three-pounder, kept up a vigorous stream of return fire. Savage, who was completely exposed without an armoured gunshield to protect him, must have known it was only a matter of time before the sheer weight and accuracy of the enemy's many guns got the better of him. The citation for his posthumous Victoria Cross stated that it had been awarded 'in recognition not only of the gallantry and devotion to duty of Able Seaman Savage but also of the valour shown by many others, unnamed, in motor launches, motor gun boats and motor torpedo boats, who gallantly carried out their duty in entirely exposed positions against enemy fire at very close range.'

It was as obvious to Newman as it had been to Ryder that there was going to be no evacuation as planned. He too could see the blackened hulls of the smouldering motor launches out on the oil-choked river. Roughly 100 Commandos, many of them wounded, had slowly congregated, group by group, around the HQ building by the Old Entrance. With every minute that passed, more German reinforcements poured into the town, pinning the British down with their backs to the river. The question facing Newman was simple: surrender, or try and fight their way out and head for neutral Spain? There was only going to be one answer. Surrender was not covered in the Commando training manual.

The only possible escape route was through the dockyard and the outskirts of the Old Town, over a narrow bridge spanning the southern entrance to the U-boat basin, into the labyrinth of backstreets and alleys and out into the countryside. The Commandos were running out of ammunition, they were heavily outnumbered and many of them were carrying wounds, but their one advantage was their street-fighting skill.

The men spilt up into five groups of about twenty and moved out in the darkness through the network of warehouses. Almost immediately, a series of skirmishes broke out and the crack of grenades and rattle of machine-gun fire echoed across the giant submarine basin. Several men fell in quick succession with wounds too severe for them to continue. All their comrades could do was inject them with morphia, wish them luck and press on.

The Commandos regrouped at the end of the warehouse complex and paused in the shadows of a building, pondering their next move. To their right, they could see the bridge, but to reach it they had to dash across over 100 yards of open ground. Heavy fire was pouring in their direction from buildings and a machine-gun pillbox on the town side. But there was no talk of giving up. As one, eighty men rose from the shadows and burst towards the bridge, firing their weapons. Writing about the event after the war, Lieutenant Purdon recalled: 'A hail of enemy fire erupted as we crossed the bridge, projectiles slamming into its girders, bullets whining and ricocheting off them and from the cobbles. There was a roar of gunfire and the percussion of "potato masher" grenades as we neared the far end.'

The defenders fled at the sight of the stampeding British troops, who immediately split and disappeared into the back-streets of the town centre. The charge was a heroic gesture of defiance by the Commandos but, for the great majority of them, it was to be their last. The Germans had surrounded the town and cordoned it off with heavily armed checkpoints while hundreds of other troops carried out an intensive sweep, street by street, house by house. Some Commandos holed up in homes, cellars and alleyways, while others chose to break out while there was still darkness to cover them. The close-quarter fighting continued for several hours but, as the sun cast its watery light over the French port, it became obvious that, with ammunition almost expended, any further attempt to flee would end in certain death.

Newman and the other survivors were gradually rounded up and taken up the road to the de-luxe hotel L'Hermitage in La Baule, which had been converted into a temporary hospital and prisoner camp. Here they were reunited with other 'Charioteers' – soldiers and sailors – who had been plucked from the river or found wounded around the dockyard. Over three-quarters of the 200 raiders who were captured were carrying at least one wound, some so severe that several men did not survive to make the transfer to the permanent POW camp a few days later. Only five men succeeded in evading capture. Helped by French civilians along the route, all of them made it safely into Spain and back to England, rejoined their units and saw further action before the war was out.

Daylight revealed an apocalyptic vision in St Nazaire. Dead bodies, British and German, were strewn around the dockyard and streets of the town. Some were floating in the harbour; others lay washed up on the banks of the Loire. Buildings had been turned to rubble, fires burned and sunken ships and boats sat low in the water, billowing smoke. On realising the hopelessness of their situation, the Commandos slowly emerged from hiding and gave themselves up throughout the morning and afternoon, but the town remained tense for many days afterwards. Sporadic bursts of machine-gun fire crackled through the streets as nervous Germans, expecting to find a 'Tommy' in every nook and cranny, leapt between doorways and alleys firing at shadows.

The raid had come as a huge shock and it quickly reverberated through the chain of command back to Berlin. There was open fury among Hitler's High Command that a small raiding party had managed to infiltrate such a heavily defended and strategically vital centre of German military operations – and wreak so much devastation. Some of the locals, meanwhile, thought the long fight through the night heralded the start of their country's liberation and attacked German soldiers, triggering a brutal crackdown by the authorities.

In general, the Germans treated their British captives with decency, and over the coming days they would bury their enemies with full military honours. But there were a few instances of cruelty and inhumanity. Some of the severely wounded were dumped unceremoniously into transports and others were treated harshly by some medical orderlies at L'Hermitage.

As the Commandos were continuing the fight in St Nazaire, the eight of the seventeen 'little ships' that had survived the pounding of the coastal gunners were racing to make their rendezvous with *Tynedale* and *Atherstone*. The destroyers, however, were running late, having encountered a group of enemy torpedo boats, which they saw off after a brief but fierce engagement. Ryder's gun boat (MGB 314), which was taking on water having been holed on the starboard, came across the torpedo boat ML 270 as they left the Loire and they both went alongside the destroyers shortly after daybreak to transfer their wounded into the care of the medical teams. Two other launches (ML 156 and ML 446) had already done the same, having arrived an hour earlier. Once the rest of the men and the crews were taken aboard the warships, the four smaller vessels were scuttled and the destroyers made smoke to get away from the heavily patrolled coastline as quickly as possible. Three other launches – ML 160, ML 307 and ML

443 – were several hours ahead of them, having decided to make the most of the darkness and head straight back to England. They were the only ones of the original eighteen to make it from Falmouth to St Nazaire and back.

The crew and Commandos aboard ML 306, under Lieutenant Henderson, had good reason to believe that they had slipped the German net too. By 0530, they were some fifty to sixty miles from the mouth of the estuary and making good speed towards the safety of home waters. The fourteen Commandos aboard, who had not managed to get ashore, were feeling aggrieved at having missed out on the main action when they felt the engine cut and heard the call from the bridge to go to action stations. Henderson had spotted the phosphorescence from the bow waves of an enemy destroyer squadron.

One of the five, the *Jaguar*, broke away from the others to investigate and, quickly identifying the suspicious vessel as a small British motor launch, Kapitänleutnant Friedrich Paul approached her, expecting her to surrender. Henderson and the Commandos aboard had no intention whatsoever of capitulating, in spite of the fact their vessel was over ten times lighter, made from wood not steel and one of her two Oerlikon 20-mm guns was jammed. The only other armaments were two .303-inch Lewis machine guns mounted on the bridge and the assorted small arms of the Commandos, which didn't amount to a great deal as nine of the men were part of a demolition team and carried nothing more powerful than a Colt pistol.

Jaguar turned on her searchlight and opened up with all her light weapons. A murderous enfilade tore through the British ship from close range, shredding wood and flesh. The German captain could have sunk the launch at any point with his main armament but he wanted to have it as a prize and, once he had overcome his shock that he had a fight on his hands, he seemed to be enjoying the sport being offered by the spirited Tommies. A game of cat-and-mouse followed as Henderson tried to out-manoeuvre the destroyer, which was attempting to ram him. When *Jaguar*, which was faster, managed to make impact, the launch was turning away, but the shunt was powerful enough to catapult several men overboard. German guns poured fire into the British vessel, knocking out the Oerlikon and inflicting very heavy casualties. When the crewman manning the Lewis guns was cut down, Sergeant Tom Durrant leapt up to take over the position.

Fed up with the resistance, Paul finally brought his main 4.1-inch guns to bear and a single shell into the flimsy craft caused death and devastation. Paul's call to surrender was met by a heavy burst from Durrant's Lewis guns. Durrant sustained wounds from the German guns to both arms, both legs, chest, head and stomach but he continued to battle his superior oppo-nent as if they were meeting on equal terms. A repeated call to give up drew an even longer burst from Durrant before he was finally silenced, slumping to the deck mortally wounded.

With the naval officers and senior crewmen all dead, dying or wounded, Lieutenant Swayne, the demolition group leader, finally offered their surrender. Of the twenty-eight men on board, twenty lay dead or wounded. The survivors were taken back to

France where they were reunited with their comrades at L'Hermitage. The following week Kapitänleutnant Paul, a chivalrous commander of the old school, sought out Lieutenant Colonel Newman at the POW camp in Rennes, and reported the brave fight put up by the men aboard. He singled out Durrant in particular for his gallantry, recommending the Sergeant receive the highest award for his heroic, bloody stand.

As the morning wore on, back in St Nazaire, the Commandos still fighting, in hiding or in captivity were dismayed not to have heard the *Campbeltown* go up. It seemed that either the fuses must have failed or the Germans had discovered the huge charge and made it safe. After so much blood had been shed, it was a bitter blow that the main objective had not been achieved. The scuttled ship on the lock gates represented a serious inconvenience rather than a major catastrophe.

Once the fighting was over in the dockyard area, the Germans began the task of taking away the dead bodies that lay in great numbers around the quays, jetties and warehouses. (The Germans removed their own dead first and left the British till later, so that the locals were led to believe their occupiers had scored an overwhelming victory.) Hundreds of people, mostly German servicemen, crowded down to the Normandie dock to witness the extraordinary spectacle of the British destroyer lying over the southern lock gate, its crumpled bow angled towards the sky over the empty dock and its stern sitting heavily on the river bottom on the other side.

The German naval authorities who went aboard to examine her were at a loss to understand why the British would go to such lengths and sacrifice the lives of so many frontline troops. The lightened destroyer was never going to have the weight or force to destroy the gate, so why bother? As an act of defiance to show that the British were not a spent force, it was an impressive performance, but in practical strategic terms, it had achieved very little. The destroyer could be dismantled and the lock gate patched up.

The clock had just struck twenty-five minutes to eleven and Lieutenant Commander Beattie was in the office of one of the port buildings, wrapped in a blanket, wondering why the charge had failed to blow. At the very moment his interrogator was mocking the costly stupidity of the raid, the *Campbeltown* offered a retort far more potent than any words the exhausted Beattie could have done. An almighty explosion, as loud as anyone in the vicinity would ever hear, shattered the relative calm that had been restored to the Atlantic port.

The roar of the blast was heard across town and many miles beyond. Around the town, buildings shook, windows shattered, and people standing hundreds of yards away were blown off their feet. Between 350 and 400 people, mostly enemy servicemen aboard the destroyer or alongside the dock, were killed instantly. Their number included several senior officers accompanied by their collaborating mistresses. Body parts rained down on the dockyard. The front of the ship ceased to exist, the lock gate was blown to pieces and collapsed, and what was left of the

Campbeltown was swept into the dry dock by several million gallons of water from the estuary.

In the short term, the eruption caused panic and fury among the Germans and did little to speed up or improve the quality of the medical attention being received by the wounded at La Baule. Many suffered at the hands of vindictive orderlies, enraged by the news of the explosion. Around St Nazaire, startled troops, fearing a fresh attack and a civilian uprising, rushed through the streets, firing their guns at any figure they suspected of being unfriendly. Homes were turned upside down and the locals manhandled as the search for the 'Tommies' intensified. Two days later the town had once again settled down into some form of normal life when the delayed-action torpedoes fired by Lieutenant Wynn's boat blew up the lock gate to the U-boat basin and sparked more pandemonium and paranoia.

On that first morning, to the hundred or so British soldiers and sailors still within the area, all facing a long spell in captivity, the deafening boom of the *Campbeltown* explosion was a sound as satisfying as it was shocking. In one ear-splitting second, a gallant defeat had been transformed into a glorious victory. The Normandie dry dock had been put out of action for years to come. *Tirpitz* would find no refuge or respite from Royal Navy guns in St Nazaire now. Not one of the 169 deaths had been in vain.

Of those 169 men to give their lives, 105 of them sailors and 64 Commandos, most perished during the attempted landings in the ferocious start to the action. Medals were showered on the raiders, many of them posthumously, but it took many years to piece together the whole story. Newman and Beattie, two central figures in the drama, and 200 other participants languished in German POW camps until the end of the war in Europe three years later. Savage, Durrant, Newman, Ryder and Beattie were all awarded the Victoria Cross. Four Distinguished Service Orders, seventeen Distinguished Service Crosses, eleven Military Crosses, fifteen Military Medals, four Conspicuous Gallantry Medals, five Distinguished Conduct Medals, twenty-four Distinguished Service Medals, four Croix de Guerre were also awarded and fifty-one men were Mentioned in Dispatches. *Tirpitz* never dared venture out into the Atlantic and spent the rest of her life trying to thwart relentless Allied attacks. She finally met her end up a Norwegian fjord in November 1944 when she was sunk by RAF Tallboy bombs.

Operation Deadstick

6 June 1944

When planning for the Allied invasion of Europe began in earnest at the start of 1943, teams of military strategists scoured highly detailed maps of Normandy looking for weak spots and strongpoints in the terrain. Once the beaches for the amphibious landings on D-Day had been chosen, attention focused on thwarting a German counterattack that risked driving the British, US and Canadian forces back into the sea. Their eyes were inevitably drawn to a small pinprick of a village, deep behind enemy lines, lying midway between the coastal town of Ouistreham and the city of Caen, roughly four miles from the centre of each. The sleepy hamlet of Bénouville comprised no more than a few houses, a church, some smallholdings, a maternity hospital and a café. Hardly could the locals have guessed that, back in England, some of the sharpest military minds in the world had identified their tiny community as the key to D-Day's success.

The reason for Bénouville's importance lay right beneath the feet of its inhabitants in the form of two small bridges running consecutively over the Caen Ship Canal and the River Orne. The waterways are almost exactly parallel to one another, separated by 400 yards of flat farmland. Whoever controlled the bridges on 6 June 1944 controlled the course of the battle on the left-hand – eastern flank – of the invasion. If the Allies could somehow capture the bridges before the dawn landings began, and hold them until major reinforcements arrived, they would close off the only feasible route for a German counterattack against the British Army landings at Sword Beach. It was from this direction that German 711th Infantry Division and the tanks of the formidable 21st Panzer Division would race to engage the British as they waded ashore and attempted to break out. In short, whoever held the bridges held the key to D-Day.

It was decided that the most effective way of seizing the bridges was by a glider-borne *coup de main* operation, under the cover of darkness, a few hours before the main assault forces came ashore. The task would not just represent a mighty responsibility but also a mighty challenge. The 6th Airborne Division, commanded by Major General Richard 'Windy' Gale, was tasked with securing the left or eastern flank of the Allied invasion. Gale asked Brigadier Hugh Kindersley, the CO of the division's glider infantry brigade, to recommend the best group of men to carry out the assignment. Without a second thought, Kindersley put forward 'D' Company, 2nd (Airborne) Battalion, Oxfordshire and Buckinghamshire Light Infantry, known to all as the 'Ox and Bucks'.

It would have come as a major surprise to his first commanding officer in the King's Shropshire Light Infantry that the gap-toothed private by the name of John Howard would one day play a leading role in the largest invasion in the history of warfare. Howard was plagued by homesickness as a young recruit, but he persevered. He had served for six years when, in 1938, he applied for an officer's commission only to be turned down in spite of having all the necessary qualities and qualifications. Snobbery may well have been a factor. Howard was from a working-class background. His father was a barrel-maker at Courage Brewery in London and barely brought home enough money to feed and clothe his nine children.

After joining the police, Howard rejoined his regiment when war broke out and rose rapidly through the ranks. This time, there was to be no social prejudice to hold him back. Within five months he was Regimental Sergeant Major and was offered a commission and joined the Ox and Bucks. By mid-1942, he had been promoted to Major and took command of a Company that he soon turned into one of the finest in the British Army.

After impressing the staff officers during a three-day exercise to find the best unit for the D-Day assignment, Howard's D Company (D Coy) was chosen to spearhead the British assault. The planners considered that two platoons were needed to seize each bridge but, in case of heavy casualties or the loss of a glider, D Coy's four platoons were reinforced with two extra ones. Howard chose two from B Company, commanded by Lieutenants Dennis Fox and 'Sandy' Smith. Most of the 170 men that made up the *coup de main* party were from London or its suburbs. Howard was invited to play a significant role in planning the specifics of the assault. The two landing zones he chose for the six troop-carrying Horsa gliders were situated in fields between the Caen Canal and the River Orne, so that if the Germans blew one of the bridges, the force would not be stranded on the far bank.

The final three-week training course, which began in late April at Ilfracombe in Devon, was extremely tough even by Howard's exacting standards. Howard was a great sports enthusiast and he set out to create a culture of fierce competition among his men. His training methods were imaginative and resourceful. He switched between day and night exercises in order to simulate the reality his men would experience on the battlefield. He took the company to bombed-out areas of Southampton to accustom them to a street-fighting environment in a war zone. Only Howard knew why the men were being pushed to the very limits of their endurance, but slowly they began to suspect that they had been assigned some form of special mission. Others might have been pushed to the brink of mutiny by Howard's punishing regime, but his men not only respected him, they genuinely liked him. For a start, he would never ask them to perform an assignment he wouldn't carry out himself. He was strict but down-to-earth, 'one of the boys' at heart who had risen through the ranks and never forgot his humble background. Far from being aloof and removed, Howard would often sit down with the other ranks and polish his boots with them.

When the training was over, the entire battalion was told to march the 130 miles back to their camp at Bulford on Salisbury Plain, carrying eighty pounds of weapons and equipment. D Coy completed it in just four days, two of them in torrential rain and two under a scorching sun. It was this Herculean effort that convinced the higher authorities once and for all that Howard's men were the right ones to carry out one of the most momentous tasks in the history of the British armed forces. Under Howard's training regime, D Coy of the Ox and Bucks, a harmless-sounding unit, had become elite Special Forces in everything but name. Howard was nothing if not meticulously thorough. He thought deeply about every scenario that might unfold on the night and trained all his men in each of the tasks they were assigned so that they were interchangeable.

At the end of May, the extended group of D Coy was split up from the rest of the battalion and driven from Bulford to a camp in the village of Tarrant Rushton in north Dorset, five miles from the picturesque market town of Blandford Forum. As the men climbed down from the trucks and saw the canvas community, the barbed-wire fencing and the guards patrolling the perimeter, they realised that this was no ordinary transit camp. When they were informed that they were not to leave the camp under any circumstances, speculation was rife as to the nature of the special mission they had been assigned. Training was light so as to minimise the risk of injuries. The weather was hot for the first few days and the men spent much of the time sunbathing or playing football and other sports. In the evening, they played cards, gambled, watched films in the tented cinema or went to the NAAFI to supplement their meals. The food, by all accounts, was dreadful, even by the low standards of army catering.

On the morning of 27 May, Howard summoned six platoon commanders to his Nissen hut, the only solid structure in camp, which served as the briefing room. Maps, aerial photographs and Top Secret files lay in neat piles and a twelve-by-twelve-foot scale model of Bénouville, exact in its detail down to the last bush and ditch, sat on a table in the centre of the room. It was now that Howard revealed D Coy's mission and objective. Slowly and methodically, Howard talked his junior officers through every phase of what had been code-named Operation DEADSTICK. The room soon became thick with cigarette smoke as the men, poring over the model and the RAF's recce photographs, ran through every step and possible eventuality. It was almost midnight when the meeting broke up.

Straight after breakfast the following day, the group filed back in and another entire day was spent going over the procedure.

That evening, Howard addressed the entire extended company and finally put an end to the mounting speculation. He told them everything except the name of the place where they were going. Over the following week, platoon by platoon, the men were summoned to the hut and talked through the operation, until every last detail was drummed into them. 'They stood round the model, at first struck dumb by its complexity, fascinated and impressed by its detail, and before long they all seemed to know every inch of the area on which they would be working,' Howard wrote in the private papers that were published almost sixty years after the event.

The following day, the twelve pilots of the six Horsa gliders were brought over and introduced to D Coy. 'A damn good crowd,' Howard called them and, helped by some inter-service banter, they quickly struck a close bond with the men who would carry them into battle. Only one jarring note was struck: the pilots were horrified by the combined weight of men and equipment that their unpowered, plywood aircraft were expected to carry. There would be thirty fully laden men in each Horsa, plus extra equipment and ammunition, which made them about three-quarters of a ton overweight. There was no choice but to jettison valuable provisions and equipment. For Howard, the hardest part of all was telling two men from each glider that they'd have to stay behind.

The invasion of Normandy was scheduled to take place on Monday 5 June. Each day in the week leading up to it, fresh aerial reconnaissance photographs and intelligence were fed into the planning of the operation. On 29 May, Howard was alarmed to learn that poles designed to stop aircraft landing were being constructed in the very fields that he had designated as their landing zones. Known as 'Rommel's asparagus', after the German General who had ordered their construction along the Normandy coast, the poles were laid out at intervals and would tear off the wings of all but the smallest aircraft. Howard was told that the white dots in the photographs were just the holes that had been dug, not the poles themselves. But he was only partly reassured. He harboured two fears that would nag him until the moment the gliders were scheduled to land. Firstly, with the holes now dug, it was obvious that the poles could be installed at any time. Secondly, did their appearance suggest that the Germans had got wind of the operational plans and were busy reinforcing their defences in anticipation of their arrival?

Four days before they were scheduled to be flown in, the men were reminded of the dangers that awaited them in France when they were each issued with a small survival kit to help them escape through enemy territory. They were given a small amount of French francs and a number of items to sew into their battledress, including silk maps of France, a file, a hacksaw blade, fishing hooks, a trouser button with a compass embedded in it and Benzedrine tablets or 'Bennies', a stimulant to help the exhausted stay alert, which were especially popular with bomber pilots.

Major General 'Windy' Gale, commander of the 6th Airborne Division, came down to Tarrant Rushton to address the troops, delivering the memorable lines: 'The German today is like the

June bride. He knows he is going to get it, but he doesn't know how big it is going to be.' By Friday night, with forty-eight hours to go, the weather turned for the worst as the hot spell gave way to strong winds and a heavy grey sky. On Sunday morning, a dispatch rider roared up to the camp on his motorcycle and handed Howard a brown envelope. Inside, there was just one word: 'Cromwell' – the code-name confirming that D-Day was on the following morning.

Howard's first course of action was to get the entire company to sit down and write a letter to their loved ones. Most of the men found this task far harder than anything they were asked to do out in the field. Writing the letter put the challenge that lay ahead into sharp focus. Each man asked himself the same question: *Is this the last contact I will have with home?* Even Howard admitted, years later, that he could barely write to his wife Joy for all the tears welling up. Most of the older soldiers had children and it was especially hard for the eight men in the company whose wives were pregnant.

The weather deteriorated as the day went on and by late afternoon gales were lashing the Channel. Howard was not surprised to be informed that the invasion had been postponed – but he was worried. The longer they waited, the more time the Germans had to strengthen their defences at the landing sites. As wind and rain lashed against the canvas, making sleep almost impossible, Howard prayed all night for a rapid improvement in the weather.

* * *

The planners for Operation DEADSTICK were lucky to have a first-class source of intelligence in Bénouville. The Gondrées owned a café situated right next to the canal bridge; every day for four years, the proud French family had served the troops of the local German garrison. When they picked up significant news of German activities, the information was quickly passed along the Resistance's chain of communication and transmitted to England. Their German customers never suspected for a moment that Thérèse and Georges Gondrée, a friendly and apparently guileless couple, were in fact members of the Resistance. Thérèse came from the Alsace region on the border with Germany and spoke the language of the occupying forces almost fluently. Georges had worked for over a decade as a clerk in Lloyds Bank in Paris and spoke perfect English. Thérèse listened to the troops in the café and passed on any noteworthy news to Georges to translate. He then forwarded the information to the leader of the local Resistance – a Madame Vion, who ran the local maternity hospital a few hundred yards along the canal. Madame Vion then passed it on to the radio operator in Caen, who tapped out the coded message for the intelligence people back in England. Thérèse and Georges often plied their German customers with the local hooch Calvados, an apple brandy, in order to loosen their tongues. The speed with which information was relayed back to the UK was illustrated in the final days leading up to D-Day. On the Friday, Thérèse discovered that the detonator for the demolition charges on the canal bridge had been placed in the machine-gun bunker at the eastern end.

By Sunday, Howard was reading the memo in his briefing hut in north Dorset.

The wider intelligence network had provided a comprehensive breakdown of German defences and troop numbers in the area. The bridges were defended by men from a fifty-strong garrison made up of conscripts from occupied countries, mostly from Eastern Europe, but commanded by German NCOs and officers. They were armed with light machine guns, four light anti-aircraft guns and one anti-aircraft machine gun. The bulk of the defences were centred on the left or eastern end of the canal bridge where there was an anti-tank gun in a reinforced concrete bunker surrounded by a series of sandbagged trenches. Gun pits sat at the other corners of the bridge. The river bridge, a quarter of a mile away to the west, was guarded by gun pits, but was nothing like as heavily defended as the canal crossing.

Major Hans Schmidt, the commander of the local garrison, was under orders to place explosive charges on the bridges ready to be blown in the event of an attack. But, fearing that the French Resistance would either defuse them, or detonate them as part of their strategy of sabotaging transport links to disrupt German movements, he decided to keep the charges in a nearby bunker and put them in place when they received news of the invasion.

Howard's orders from Brigadier Nigel Poett, commander 5th Parachute Brigade, included the lines: 'The capture of the bridges will be a *coup de main* operation depending largely on surprise, speed and dash for success. Provided the bulk of your force lands safely, you should have little difficulty in overcoming the known opposition on the bridges. Your difficulties will arise in holding off an enemy counterattack on the bridges, until you are relieved.'

Thanks to the intelligence from the Resistance and the photographs from the RAF's aerial reconnaissance unit, Howard knew every detail of the local defences – except for one. So as not to undermine the morale of his men, a key piece of information was deliberately withheld from him by his masters at the Planning HQ on Salisbury Plain. Stationed in Caen, five miles down the road, was the 125th Panzer Regiment of the 21st Panzer Division, commanded by Colonel Hans von Luck. The regiment was a very well-equipped, elite unit, trained in the art of counter-attacking. Von Luck was one of the most experienced and capable tank commanders in the German Army, hardened by years of heavy fighting in Poland, France, North Africa and the Eastern front. He was an old-school Prussian who enjoyed a clean fight and had developed an admiration and liking for his British foes in the North Africa campaign. Von Luck and the 2,000 men of 125th Panzer Regiment were the 'difficulties' to which Brigadier Poett was referring in his orders. The 'relief' would be provided by the men of 7th Battalion, 5th Parachute Brigade, 6th Airborne Division. Whether there would be any forces left for them to relieve was another matter.

The first challenge was to get the assault party safely onto French soil. The men were to be flown over the Channel in Horsa gliders towed by Halifax bombers that would release them close to the Normandy coast. From that moment on, the lives of the twenty-eight men crammed into each of the wooden aircraft lay in the hands of the pilots, who had been specially handpicked and trained for the assignment. All twelve were highly skilled airmen who had been put through intense training programmes for the D-Day landings. Glider pilots were a precious asset in the Normandy landings and orders stated that, in a break with normal practice, they were not to be risked in the battle on the ground and that they were to be returned to England at the earliest practicable time for the next mission.

Glider operations had many advantages over parachuting. They could deliver a large body of men to a single spot ready to go straight into action. They were able to carry heavy items of equipment. They approached the landing zone in silence and, with a high descent rate, the pilots could put them down in a very tight landing area. Unlike paratroopers, glider infantry needed virtually no additional training. But there were also many shortcomings and hazards to glider-borne operations. Gliders need flat terrain on which to land and, at 80 mph, even the smoothest landings were violent, painful experiences that often ended in death and injury. The Sicily landings of 1943 high-lighted a number of problems. More than 250 men had been drowned after the gliders were released too early by their towing aircraft.

Gliders were also very vulnerable to interception by enemy fighters while being towed, as well as to anti-aircraft and small-arms fire during the final approach. Several gliders were shot down in Sicily by Allied gunners who mistook them for the

Luftwaffe. As a result of those blue-on-blue incidents, to aid identification all Allied aircraft involved in the Normandy invasion were painted with black and white stripes on their wings and fuselage.

The assault party was split into two groups of three platoons, one to assault the canal bridge, the other to seize the river bridge. The six Horsas would carry a platoon each. The first group, which was scheduled to land shortly after midnight, was to capture the canal bridge. To do that, a handful of troops in the lead glider had to sprint from the aircraft to take out the machine-gun bunker that stood on the eastern bank of the canal, no more than 100 yards from where they had landed. The rest of the platoon, meanwhile, were to storm over the bridge and secure its western end, which led into Bénouville village. The two other platoons in the group would clear the other enemy positions.

The three platoons of the second group, landing a short distance away, would carry out a carbon-copy manoeuvre at the river bridge. D Coy would then settle into defensive positions and wait to be relieved by paratroopers landing a few miles to the east. Codewords and recognition signals were issued: if the canal bridge was successfully captured, it was 'Ham'; for the river bridge 'Jam'. On being told this, the men could be heard wandering through camp shouting 'Ham and Jam!' If all went to plan, Howard's lightly armed men would have to wait no more than an hour for airborne reinforcements to arrive. In turn, the paratroopers would be relieved in the late morning by a large force of Commandos arriving by sea. How the Germans reacted in the hours immediately following D Coy's assault would be the key factor. 'Surprise, speed and dash' were the words used by Poett to describe how Howard's men were to take their objectives. They might equally have been included in the orders issued to the German units tasked with the counterattack.

The morning after the scheduled day of departure, Howard's prayers for fine weather were answered – at least in part. It was still blustery and the Channel was still running heavy, but the gales had subsided and clearer weather was forecast overnight. Howard waited anxiously for news. That afternoon, the dispatch rider returned and Howard was handed another brown envelope, once again containing the codeword Cromwell. The camp was filled with a nervous excitement that mounted as the day wore on. The most momentous challenge in the lives of the 180 soldiers and pilots of Operation DEADSTICK drew ever closer – a challenge deeply connected to the lives and fortunes of hundreds of thousands of Allied servicemen who would follow them into the action in the days and weeks that followed. And it was upon the skill and courage of those servicemen that the fate of the Free World and Occupied Europe depended.

After a well-attended church service, a meal with all fat removed was served to the men that evening to reduce the risk of airsickness. (Howard and many of his men had vomited on every training flight in the Horsas. The motion of the glider was different to a powered flight and it induced nausea in most passengers.) The rest of the evening was spent checking equipment, weapons and provisions. The men put on their battledress, blackened their faces and, as the light began to fade, they lined up on parade for the final time at the camp. 'Everyone was grossly overloaded – and some of the smaller chaps were visibly sagging at the knees under their heavy loads,' Howard recalled in his diaries. He addressed his men for the last time and was almost overcome by the emotion of the occasion. In his own words: 'I am an emotional man beneath the surface, a fact that would have surprised many who knew me then, and I found addressing the men as they went into battle very moving. I found my voice breaking several times as I wished them all the best.'

When the men boarded the trucks for the short journey up the hill to RAF Tarrant Rushton airfield, some of them were so heavy with kit they had to be lifted and shoved into the back. RAF personnel from the admin buildings came out to wave them off, instinctively aware that a special mission was about to be launched. The gliders had their numbers, from 91 to 95, chalked onto the fuselage and white 'D-Day stripes' painted on their sides and wings. The first three, containing Howard's group, were destined for the canal bridge; the second, led by his 2iC Brian Priday, for the river bridge. A little further in front were the six Halifax bombers, the paint of their new stripes adding some freshness to their war-weary frames.

Pilots and soldiers greeted each other warmly, bantering amongst themselves over mugs of hot tea and cigarettes. Ever the perfectionist, Howard walked amongst his men, checking that they had blacked out properly. Those who hadn't were dispatched to supplement their battle paint with the grime from the exhaust of the trucks.

At 2240 the men synchronised their watches. The men squeezed aboard the gliders through the side door, took their places on the floor of the wooden aircraft and snapped on their harnesses. Howard, the last to board, and with a 'terrible lump' in his throat, went to each glider and shouted some final words of encouragement. From each one he was met with shouts of 'Ham and Jam!' One by one, a minute apart, the six Halifaxes roared down the runway, their gliders on tow, and climbed into a dark sky of broken cloud to 6,000 feet. The largest invasion in history was underway.

The six gliders rolled and bounced in the wind as the Halifaxes pulled them over the Sussex seaside town of Worthing and out to the Channel. All along the coast below them, the largest invading force ever assembled lay waiting to go into action. The twenty-eight men in the back of each glider sat on the floor leaning against the wooden sides of the fuselage, the whites of their eyes gleaming in their blacked-out faces. The atmosphere was thick with smoke and song as the young troopers pulled nervously on cigarettes and belted out a medley of music hall favourites.

The lead glider was piloted by Staff Sergeants Jim Wallwork and John Ainsworth and carried Howard and Number 25 platoon led by Lieutenant Den Brotheridge. They were to be the first troops into the fray, tasked with the vital role of seizing the canal bridge. As soon as the Normandy coast appeared on the distant horizon, Wallwork shouted his order to prepare for cast-off. The men fell silent and waited for the lurch as the two aircraft decoupled and the glider dived below the clouds before levelling out. It had just gone midnight. They had reached the point of no return. Dead or alive, wounded or intact, the men of D Coy, Ox and Bucks were three minutes from their long-awaited encounter with destiny.

When Brotheridge dragged open the side door a few minutes later, the chill night air swept through the cramped compartment. Fields and hedgerows rushed beneath. The only sound was the stream of the air as the unpowered glider floated towards earth. There was a reason why the troops who flew in them called the gliders 'silent coffins'. The pilots took their bearings from the glistening waterways of the canal and the river, to their right, which cut through the landscape from the coast. Straight ahead of them, six or seven miles distant, balls of orange flame and towers of smoke rose up through the searchlight beams and tracer around Caen as Allied bombers laid aerial siege to the medieval city. Wallwork turned the glider sharp right on Ainsworth's order and then once again to set up the final approach.

The two bridges were now clearly visible through the Perspex windscreen, but this was not the time to celebrate the navigational skills that had brought them to their target so skilfully. Everyone on board knew what was coming next and they braced themselves. The men linked arms and raised their feet over their heads ready for impact. There was no such thing as a smooth landing in a glider and many legs had been broken in the past. Wallwork battled the controls and adjusted the wing flaps as the glider, wobbling from side to side, went into a steep descent towards the little triangular field by the canal. Wallwork pulled up the nose and the world outside raced by at 100 mph when the seven-ton, sixty-seven-foot-long aircraft made impact with the uneven ground. The glider bounced twice before sliding along the field in an ear-splitting, wood-splintering crash. The nose of the aircraft was sticking into the barbed-wire fence, fifty yards from the bridge, exactly where Howard had jokingly asked Wallwork to place it back at Tarrant Rushton.

The force of the crash-landing had thrown the two pilots through the windscreen and left the men in the back momentarily stunned. Howard's harness had snapped and he smashed his head on the roof. When he came round, he thought he had been blinded until he realised that his helmet had been pressed down over his eyes. Glider One had broken up on impact, dust and debris filled the air, and the only sound was that of groaning men injured in the crash.

Moments later, as Howard and 25 Platoon staggered out of the wooden wreckage, Glider Two, piloted by Staff Sergeants Boland and Hobbs, made a near-perfect landing close by. Glider Three, with Staff Sergeants Barkway and Boyle in the cockpit, came in between the first two, but theirs was not a happy landing. The Horsa broke up as it slid into the marshy end of the field and into a pond, which had gone undetected during the planning. Barkway and Boyle were catapulted out of the disintegrating cockpit and into the water. Semi-concussed, they hauled them-selves out past the heavily laden body of Lance Corporal Greenhalgh who lay dead in the water. (It is thought that he may have drowned while unconscious.) Such was the force of the impact that Lieutenant Sandy Smith, the leader of 14 Platoon, was also hurled through what remained of the cockpit. The German sentries on the other side of the bridge heard the crash of the gliders but they had grown so accustomed to the Allied bombing raids over the years that they assumed the noise was falling debris or a stricken bomber.

Meanwhile Lieutenant Brotheridge, hobbling from the heavy landing, took off towards the bridge with his men in close attendance. Gunfire erupted as they charged down the bridge firing Sten and Bren guns from the hip. Brotheridge was the first to reach the far end and had just thrown a grenade into a gun pit when he was cut down by a burst of Spandau machine-gun fire that sliced through his neck. He slumped backwards to the ground, the first combat casualty of the Normandy invasion. Tracer streaked back and forth and the air was filled with the rattle of machine-gun fire, the thud of grenades and the cries of men. Brotheridge's platoon wasted no time in dispatching the gun crew as their leader lay slowly bleeding to death. On hearing the news, Howard's first thoughts were for the young Lieutenant's wife who was eight months pregnant.

As the three platoons of Group One cleared trenches and gun positions, Howard set up his command post at the end of the bridge near the landing zone along with his wireless operator

Lance Corporal Ted Tappenden. The glider pilots, meanwhile, staggered through the dark, stunned into semi-consciousness during the landings. Staff Sergeant Barkway, one of the pilots in Glider Three, which had crashed heavily, was almost immediately felled by machine-gun fire that almost ripped off his arm. (It was later amputated.) But Boyle, and the other glider pilots who had escaped serious injury, braved the enemy fire to lug weapons, ammunition and equipment from the aircraft to Howard's command post next to the bridge. Wallwork, covered in blood from a gash to the head, freed his copilot Ainsworth who was trapped under the nose of their Horsa and, ignoring his orders to keep clear of the fighting, worked tirelessly to bring up supplies for the troops.

The three gliders of the second group, a few minutes behind the others, were also experiencing mixed fortunes as they attempted to land in the field alongside the River Orne. Only Glider Six, carrying Lieutenant Fox's 17 Platoon, managed to come down in the designated landing zone. Glider Five, with Lieutenant 'Tod' Sweeney's 23 Platoon, came down three fields away, almost half a mile short of the bridge. What had happened to Glider Four, carrying 2iC Priday and Lieutenant Hooper's 22 Platoon, no one knew. They were nowhere to be seen and Tappenden was unable to raise them over the wireless. Howard began to fear the worst.

Sweeney's men set off as fast as the terrain and their loads allowed, crashing through hedges and sprinting across the fields towards the bridge, all the time fearing they might have arrived too late to take the German defenders by surprise. They could hear the crack and boom of battle in the distance and saw the tracer licking through the darkness. When they arrived at the river bridge, panting and sweating under their heavy loads, they were surprised to find Lieutenant Fox's men already in position. There was mild disappointment among all the men that they had taken the bridge without a fight. Two mortar bombs had been sufficient to send the crew of the machine-gun post sprinting for safety. The W/T set at Howard's command post soon crackled into life. The word 'Jam' confirmed the capture of the river bridge.

Back at the canal, Lieutenant Wood and his men had cleared out the trenches and positions assigned to them on the 'home bank' and were on their way back to report to Howard when they were raked by machine-gun fire. Three bullets tore into Wood's left leg, shattering his thigh bone. His Sergeant and one other also collapsed under the heavy fire. Wood tried to stand up but couldn't. It would be many hours before he could be evacuated to a divisional aid post, and in the meantime all his men could do was splint his leg with a rifle and give him and the two others an injection of morphine.

Within fewer than five minutes of landing, Howard had only one infantry officer left standing, Lieutenant Smith whose platoon had been badly mauled during Glider Three's violent landing. In addition to Greenhalgh's death, two others had been badly injured, including his Sergeant. Smith had twisted his knee in the crash and he was limping as he led his men across the bridge to reinforce Brotheridge's platoon. On reaching the other side, a German soldier stood up from behind a wall by the Café Gondrée and threw a stick grenade at him. Smith cut the German down with his Sten, but the grenade exploded and tore the flesh on his wrist down to the bone. Not until he and his men had cleared out all the German positions did he allow himself to be treated.

Captain John Vaughan of the Royal Army Medical Corps, the one qualified doctor in the assault party, had been knocked out when Glider Three had broken up on landing, and he was wandering around in a stupor when Howard spotted him. An unmistakable sight with his large drooping moustache, Vaughan was plastered in foul-smelling mud, having been thrown into the pond on impact. After giving him a swig of whisky from his hip-flask, Howard pointed him in the direction of the casualty command post that had been set up near the river bridge. The first casualty he attended to was Lieutenant Wood, whose thigh had been shattered by machine-gun fire – the first injury in what was to prove a very busy night for the dazed doctor.

The five-man Royal Engineer parties attached to each platoon leapt beneath both bridges to cut wires and remove explosives. They were astounded to discover that no charges had been fixed to the structures. So long as Howard's assault force could hold their positions for an hour or so, there was no chance now of the Germans blowing the bridges. Cries of 'Ham' and 'Jam' echoed back and forth across the waterways as the three platoons finished mopping up the slit trenches and machine-gun nests. Within ten minutes of the lead glider careering into the landing zone, Howard had achieved his primary objective of seizing both bridges intact. The months of hard training had paid off. It was a brilliantly executed *coup de main* operation but, as the men took up position in the slit trenches and gun pits, every one of them knew that the real battle was about to begin.

It was ten minutes to one, a little over half an hour after the Ox and Bucks assault party had gone into action, when the men craned their heads skywards. What started as a distant humming soon turned into a loud drone as scores of aircraft filled the darkened skies. The moon cast its light through the broken cloud, revealing a sight, described by all who saw it, as one of the most magical and uplifting of their lives. Hundreds and hundreds of paratroopers were floating towards earth, the silk canopies of their chutes billowing above their heads. They were falling into landing zones lit up by ground flares in farmland a mile or two beyond Bénouville. To their disgust, they could also see streaks of German tracer rising up to greet the men of the 5th Parachute Brigade in blatant violation of the Geneva Convention.

Howard immediately reached for his pea whistle and blew the 'Victory-V' signal – the letter V in Morse code – and continued to repeat it at regular intervals through the night. The shrill blasts carried for miles through the night air over the flat land-scape. Some of his men grumbled that Howard was only rousing the Germans and giving away their position, but after the battle many of the paratroopers who had fallen far and wide of the landing zone commented that it was the sound of the whistle that had guided them to the bridges. Howard ordered Tappenden to send the message to Brigadier Poett, commanding the 5th Parachute Brigade, that the bridges had been captured. 'Ham!' and 'Jam!' . . . 'Ham!' and 'Jam!' . . . 'Ham!' and 'Jam!', the Corporal repeated over and over. But no matter how often he said it or how loudly, there was no reply.

The drop of the main body of the 5th Brigade was nothing like as accurate as had been hoped. Poor visibility and strong winds were partly to blame, and some of the ground flares, guiding the men down, were laid too far to the east. The net result was that a great number of the men landed in difficult country far from their forming-up points. There was a good deal of confusion as different units became tangled up with each other. Much of the equipment, including the heavy weapons, could not be recovered until daylight. Without mortars and medium machine guns, the already mighty task of keeping the counterattacking Germans at bay was going to be even more of a challenge.

Minutes after the gliders had landed, Brigadier Poett and his HQ unit were dropped a mile to the east of Bénouville, amongst a group of pathfinders from the 22nd Independent Parachute Company, whose job it was to set up the ground flares at the drop zones. Disorientated at first, the sound of gunfire helped guide him through the crop fields to the canal bridge around which Howard had established the bulk of his defences. With no prior warning of his arrival, Howard was a little taken aback when he saw the tall figure of his Brigadier striding over the bridge towards his command post shortly before one o'clock. Tappenden was still monotonously repeating 'Ham and Jam!' into the wireless when he arrived, and Poett explained that their own sets had been lost during the drop.

Howard's delight at the sight of the paratroopers' floating to earth gave way to an anxiety that mounted with every minute that they failed to arrive. The original schedule envisaged the Brigade's 7th Parachute Battalion reaching the bridges roughly one hour after Howard, but as they were now scattered all over the countryside, that seemed highly unlikely.

Shortly after Poett's arrival, the ominous, grating sounds of heavy armour could be heard along the coastal road from Ouistreham, entering the northern end of Bénouville in the area around the church known as Le Port. At the same time, firing broke out behind them near the river bridge, where a section from Tod Sweeney's platoon was carrying out a fighting patrol. Four soldiers, advancing along the towpath towards the bridge, were met with raking Bren gun fire and died where they fell. Sweeney's men were horrified to learn the following day that one of the dead was a British paratrooper who had been captured.

A few minutes later, Sweeney's platoon braced themselves for a major engagement. 'We heard the grinding of gears and the noise of what sounded like a very heavy vehicle coming round the corner,' Sweeney wrote years later. 'I thought, *Well, here we go. This is the first tank attack.*' The only defence they had against heavy armour was the hand-held PIAT antitank gun, an unreliable, wayward weapon at the best of times that had to be fired from extremely close range to be effective. Headlights appeared around the corner and the men could make out the distinct sound of vehicle tracks grinding over the tarmac. Sweeney sent a message over the W/T to Howard but, as the vehicles swept around the corner, Sweeney's worst fears were allayed. It was a motorcycle and an open-topped half-track officer's vehicle.

The whole platoon opened up as one, blasting the rider off his motorbike, which veered off the road into the river. The tyres of the half-track were blown out in the hail of fire and three men leapt out as a grenade was hurled in their direction. The driver and one other were gunned down as they tried to flee. The third was captured – and he was not at all happy about it. With good reason. He was Major Hans Schmidt, the garrison commander of the bridges who, on seeing hundreds of paratroopers drifting down, was racing to take up his position when he ran into Sweeney's men. Severely wounded in the leg, he ranted at his captors in perfect English, and continued to do so as he was led to Captain Vaughan's casualty clearing station between the two bridges. Still shouting, Schmidt proceeded to inform the magnificently moustached doctor that Hitler was going to hurl the British straight back into the sea. He then demanded to be shot for having lost his honour in allowing the bridges to be captured. The doctor soon shut him up by jabbing him in the buttock with a syringe full of morphia.

In Caen, five miles to the south, Colonel Hans von Luck of the 125th Panzer Regiment was growing increasingly agitated.

Hearing the news that thousands of British paratroopers were landing up towards the coast, he had roused his men and readied his tanks. Had he advanced immediately to meet the threat, events on D-Day might have taken an altogether different course. But, because of the Führer himself, he was unable to do anything but sit in his HQ and await orders from Berlin. Increasingly suspicious and dismissive of his generals, Hitler had demanded complete control of his armoured divisions; at one o'clock on the morning of 6 June 1944, no one in his staff dared disturb the dictator while he slept. In a further stroke of ill-fortune for the Germans, Field Marshal Erwin Rommel, the man in charge of repelling an Allied invasion in France, had flown back to Germany the day before to celebrate his wife's fiftieth birthday, having been told by his naval authorities that the sea was too rough for amphibious landings. "It is my firm opinion . . ." wrote Von Luck in his memoirs, "that by exploiting the initial confusion among the enemy after their descent we would have succeeded in pushing through to the coast and probably also in regaining possession of the two bridges over the Orne at Bénouville."

While Sweeney and his men apprehended Major Schmidt at the river bridge, the rest of Howard's men back at the canal crossing prepared themselves for the scenario they had all been dreading: a German counterattack with tanks. They could hear the heavy armoured vehicle crunch and clank its way slowly towards them in the darkness. With the paratroopers of the 7th Battalion still nowhere to be seen, their only means of defence was the misfiring PIAT. Lieutenant Fox's platoon was patrolling around Bénouville with the other four platoons dug in around the bridge. His Sergeant, 'Wagger' Thornton, who was in charge of the PIAT, understood that the three-pound high-explosive bomb needed to be fired from a range of no further than fifty yards to be sure of penetrating the armour. Thornton showed extraordinary composure as he held the thirty-two-pound gun steady and waited for his moment. For his comrades waiting in the trenches and gun pits to the rear, the tension was unbearable as the tank rumbled towards the T-junction at the end of the bridge. When the tank was virtually on top of him, Thornton fired. Private Eric Woods, who was lying alongside the Sergeant, recalled many years later: 'It must have been a direct hit on the tank's magazine, for there was an almighty explosion and ammunition continued to explode for more than an hour afterwards. The two remaining tanks quickly retreated from whence they came.'

In hindsight, Thornton's cool act of courage was a key moment in the Normandy invasion. The continuing explosions from the tank's magazines gave the impression to all in the vicinity that the British force at the bridge was very heavily armed and involved in a ferocious action. There was the added advantage that the British troops scattered over the countryside used it as a homing beacon. 'The Paras who were beginning to muster in the surrounding countryside thought we were having a hell of a fight at the bridges . . .' wrote Howard. 'The continuing firework display of the exploding tank helped to guide many of the members of 7 Para who were lost in the Normandy countryside down towards the bridges.'

The 600 men of the 7th Parachute Battalion – 7 Para – began landing shortly after D Coy had captured the bridges, but an hour later there was still no sign of them and no contact over the wireless. By about 0100 only fifty of them had reached the rendezvous. A bugler repeatedly blew the rallying signal but only a small number of the force staggered out of the darkness over the next hour or so. 7 Para's CO, Lieutenant Colonel Geoffrey Pine-Coffin (known as 'Wooden Box' to his men), decided he could wait no longer and gave the order to move off to the bridges, even though they numbered just 150 men, and had no mortars, no machine guns and no wireless. Pine-Coffin claimed his men arrived at Bénouville at 0140. Howard said it was 0300. Brigadier Poett said it was shortly after 0230. Whenever it was, there was plenty of chat from D Coy when the Paras finally trooped over the bridges. 'Howard's men were naturally in very high spirits and much friendly banter and chaff took place as the Battalion had hurried past them,' Pine-Coffin wrote in his account of the invasion. 'They had done a most splendid job which rendered the task of the Battalion immeasurably easier.'

Pine-Coffin automatically took over command from Howard, whose men became the battalion reserve responsible for the defence of the river bridge. Pine-Coffin's much-reduced force took over the defence of the canal bridge and pushed out a bridgehead towards the west. 'The distance between the two bridges was only about four hundred yards, but it contained plenty of evidence of the thoroughness with which Howard's men had done their job,' Pine-Coffin added. 'Many of the Battalion got their first sight of a dead German on that bit of road and few will forget it in a hurry, particularly the one who had been hit with a tank-busting bomb whilst riding a bicycle. He was not a pretty sight.'

At first light, the Germans began to target the small force of lightly armed Paras around the bridge. Snipers were operating from the church tower to the right and from the windows of the maternity hospital, an old chateau, to the left. It was to be nightfall before the sniper threat was finally extinguished, but not before the German marksmen, firing high-velocity rifles with unerring accuracy, had taken a heavy toll on the British forces. Lieutenant 'Sandy' Smith recalled that he had just had his wrist bandaged when a sniper shot the medical orderly treating him straight through the chest. There was no point in the British wasting the precious little ammunition they had left by firing back wildly in the vague direction of the threat. They had no choice but to put up with the punishment.

The situation became so hazardous that Doctor Vaughan was forced to relocate his aid post from his position in between the bridges to the Café Gondrée, at the T-junction by the canal bridge where the bulk of the Paras were now dug in. The Gondrées, who had provided so much intelligence about the area, greeted their liberators with tremendous warmth and generosity. Thérèse kissed the blackened faces of every British soldier she met. When it was safe to do so, Georges went into the garden and dug up the crates of champagne he had buried to avoid serving it to the Germans. All day, he dished out the champagne for casualties, medics and soldiers, while a fierce battle raged outside as the Germans launched a series of powerful counter-attacks to retake the bridges.

Relentless, accurate sniper fire was not the only danger that dawn brought. Lieutenant Richard Todd, who was to become a film star after the war, described, in a newspaper article, the scene he witnessed from his slit trench near the church. 'Minutes before first light, a shattering cacophony erupted, with a glare that made full daylight seem pale as the softening-up bombardment of the German coastal defences began,' wrote Todd, who was to play Howard in the film *The Longest Day*. 'For about half-an-hour the din, the vibration of air and ground, the magnitude of that assault, was far beyond anything I could have imagined. Hundreds of aircraft, American and British, rained thousands of bombs along that strip of gun-positions, trenches and pill-boxes that menaced the landing of our seaborne invasion force. Artillery and batteries of rocket-launchers firing from special craft at sea poured a continuous hail of shells across the water, while naval guns, including the big ones of HMS *Warspite*, helped pulverise the defences. From our grandstand position at Le Port, I felt sorry for the poor sods cowering in those German bunkers. How could they possibly emerge and fight back? But they did, and with impressive vigour.'

At around 0600 or 0700 or 0800, two or three Spitfires – depending on which account you read – were spotted circling directly over the bridges. Seeing the Allied recognition signals that had been laid out, the fighters dived steeply and then came in low over the bridges, waggling their wings in the 'victory roll'.

They were greeted with loud cheers from the positions around the bridges. One of the Spitfires dropped a parcel in the field as it sped past. When one of Howard's men brought it in, they were delighted to discover it contained the morning newspapers from England.

Champagne, 'Spits' and newspapers might have provided a morale-boosting distraction, but the situation in which the British airborne troops at the bridges found themselves was an increasingly ugly and desperate one. Fighting intensified as the morning wore on and the casualty count grew steadily. Another hundred or so paratroopers trickled into the bridges, but the bulk of the heavier weapons never arrived and small pockets of Paras battled heroically to hold the position as they waited for the main relief to arrive. These were the seaborne Commandos of the 1st Special Service Brigade under Lord Lovat who were fighting their way inland from the beaches.

The Germans attacked the bridgehead from all directions and from land, water and air. Patrols probed the British defences and, from time to time, a full counterattack led by tanks was launched. At one point, the Paras' regimental aid post was overrun and all the wounded killed, including the Padre trying to defend them. The weakened Paras hung on grimly, urged on by shouts of encouragement from their CO Major Nigel Taylor, even as he lay on the ground with a shattered leg. There was no battle front as such. The action was as fluid as it was intense, but every counterattack and every infiltration of the area by the enemy was beaten off.

The Germans attacked from all angles. At one point a gun boat crept up the canal from the direction of the coast, with its crew hidden below deck but its powerful 20-mm gun clearly visible. Lieutenant Wood's 24 Platoon, now commanded by a Corporal, waited until it was in range and then opened up, first with a hail of small-arms fire and then with a blast from the PIAT gun. Its steering disabled, the boat swerved into the canal bank and the crew were captured. A second boat appeared from the opposite direction shortly afterwards, but two rounds from a PIAT prompted its skipper to make a hasty U-turn and retreat towards Caen.

Shortly after 0900, lying in their slit trenches and gun nests, exhausted by a night of fighting, the troops at the crossings witnessed a peculiar but awe-inspiring sight. Marching in step down the middle of the road between the bridges were three lofty figures in red berets and immaculate battledress. As the sniper rounds whistled through the air, not one of them flinched or broke stride. Closer inspection revealed the new arrivals to be none other than General 'Windy' Gale, Commander of 6th Airborne Division, flanked by Brigadier Hugh Kindersley, commander of 6th Air Landing Brigade, and Brigadier Nigel Poett, Commander of 5 Para Brigade. 'For sheer bravado it was one of the most memorable sights I've ever seen,' wrote Todd.

Taking a chance among the flying rounds, Howard strode out to meet the three senior officers and saluted them. Half hoping for a verbal slap on the back for his men's efforts, the Major was disheartened when General Gale scowled at him, pointed to an antitank gun lying in the grass and told him to have it stowed away. The men strode on to visit Pine-Coffin in 7th Battalion's HQ at the end of the canal bridge. 'The General found Pine-Coffin and his men in fine form, in spite of the hammering they were getting,' Poett recalled. 'He was left in no doubt that Pine-Coffin would hold his position.'

In the middle of the morning, a German bomber was spotted diving steeply towards the canal bridge. The troops scrambled for cover, pressing down their 'battle-bowlers', braced for the explosion. A 1,000-lb bomb, dropped with perfect precision, hurtled towards the bridge, crashed into the side with a metallic clatter and then splashed harmlessly into the water. Had it detonated, the bridge would have been torn to shreds and dozens of men killed and wounded.

In spite of mounting casualties and no sign of reinforcements, or of their heavy weapons and wireless sets, 7 Para continued to hold the Germans at bay throughout the morning in the wooded Le Port area around the church and in the lanes and fields in Bénouville. It was twelve hours after the Ox and Bucks troops had seized the bridges that Colonel von Luck at last received his orders from Berlin to launch a concerted counterattack. But when the tanks of his 125th Panzer Regiment rolled northwards out of Caen, their location was reported almost immediately by Allied aircraft. Von Luck, a veteran of all Germany's major campaigns, knew what was coming. Minutes later the bombs began to rain down from aircraft and naval guns offshore, inflicting significant damage on men and machines.

But Colonel von Luck's regiment was one of a dozen units within the 21st Panzer Division operating in the area, some of which continued to press the bridge positions backed up by artillery. Howard was not the only commander wondering how much longer the overstretched, outnumbered, outgunned and exhausted force could hold out. General Gale had been certain that Pine-Coffin's men would hold firm, but that had been three or four hours earlier. The Paras' casualties had risen to almost sixty, roughly a third of the depleted force that had managed to reach the bridges. Howard had lost two killed and fourteen wounded from his assault party and he was short of a whole twenty-eight-strong platoon and his 2iC. (It transpired later that their glider had come down eight miles away alongside the wrong river.) The Germans, growing ever more organised, were tightening their grip on the defensive perimeter. Howard was looking at his watch for the umpteenth time that day – it was one o'clock – when a curious sound, cutting through the rattle and boom of the guns, made him look up. One by one his men and the Paras did the same.

'After all the earlier din of battle it suddenly became very quiet,' Private Denis Edwards of 25 Platoon, whose section had been sent up to reinforce the Paras around the church, recalled in his postwar account. 'Even the Germans had stopped shouting to each other, when suddenly, in the uncanny stillness of that spring day, I heard a sound that will live with me for the rest of my days . . . One of the lads shouted *"It's them – it's the Commando!"* and we all let out a cheer as the noise grew louder and we recognised it as the high-pitched and uneven wailing of bagpipes! Shouting and cheering . . . and abandoning all caution, we were up on our feet and leapt over the wall into the church-yard again, yelling things like *"Now you Jerry bastards, you've got a real fight on your hands.'"*

A long line of green berets, stretching as far as the eye could see, ran along the canal towpath back towards the coast. The relief, in the impressive form of the 1st Special Service Brigade, had indeed arrived – and they were bringing with them some desperately needed heavy weapons, including a tank. Accompanied by his piper Bill Millin hammering out 'Blue Bonnets over the Border', the lanky figure of Lord Lovat was at the head of his men, cutting a somewhat eccentric figure in his heavy Aran wool white jersey. If the British were delighted by the arrival of the powerful Commando force, the Germans were less pleased. As Lovat's men turned onto the bridge, every sniper in the area lined up one of the hundreds of new targets. The men of D Coy, dug into trenches and foxholes at either end, watched appalled as every few seconds a heavily laden Commando, exhausted from his fighting march from Sword Beach, slumped to the ground, felled by a high-velocity bullet. But still Lovat and his men kept marching. No one flinched, no one dived for cover. Onward they strode, cheered by Howard's men and the Paras. Lovat wrote later that he had run across the bridge but Howard remembered him walking calmly, unfazed by the bullets whistling and ricocheting around him.

Howard and his men would stay in position until midnight,

but for them the hard fighting that day was over. Almost exactly twenty-four hours after the first glider slammed into the turf and battle commenced, D Coy Ox and Bucks handed over to the Royal Warwickshire Regiment, packed up their equipment and prepared to rejoin the remainder of their battalion in the town of Ranville. With the snipers now silenced, Howard's men marched away into the darkness in silence. Most of the men couldn't resist turning round for one last look at the crossing, which from that day onwards has been known as 'Pegasus Bridge', after the winged-horse emblem of the British airborne forces: named in their honour, and in that of the other brave young men who came from the sky to liberate it.

Author Acknowledgements

Firstly I would like to thank Niall Edworthy, whose passion and enthusiasm has driven this book forward from the start. There are several people I must also thank for helping me transform *Raiders* from a mere idea to the book you are holding in your hands now. A great deal of research has been done, mainly at The National Archives in Kew and for that I am very grateful to Roger E Nixon (Military & Historical Search) and Daniel Starza Smith for digging out the relevant files and sifting through reams of documents to locate the relevant material. On their behalf, I should also thank the ever-helpful staff at Kew as well as the archivists at the Fleet Air Arm Museum at Yeovilton.

Also to Ben Dunn at Random House. And of course, as ever, Lord Waheed Ali, for all his support.

Picture Acknowledgements

© Imperial War Museums (H 17365); © Imperial War Museums (D 12870); © Imperial War Museums (B 5288); © Imperial War Museums (B 5067); © Imperial War Museums (B 7033); © WoodyStock/Alamy; © Norimages/Alamy; © Trinity Mirror/Mirrorpix/Alamy; © Bettmann/ CORBIS; © Hulton-Deutsch Collection/CORBIS; © Norway's Resistance Museum; © Poperfoto/Getty Images; © Poperfoto/Getty Images; © Poperfoto/Getty Images; © Poperfoto/Getty Images; © Hulton Archive/Getty Images; © Underwood archives/Getty Images

Sources & Further Reading

Operation ARCHERY

The National Archives, Kew
Supplement to the *London Gazette*, 2 July 1948 (Dispatch to
  Admiralty by Admiral Sir John Tovey)
The Vaagso Raid, Joseph H. Devins
The Commandos, Charles Messenger
Operation Archery, Ken Ford
Storm from the Sea, Lt Col Peter Young
Commando, Brigadier John Durnford-Slater
The Green Beret: The Story of the Commandos 1940–45, Hilary
  St George Saunders

Operation BITING

The National Archives, Kew

By Air to Battle: The Official Account of the British Airborne Divisions

Most Secret War, R. V. Jones

The Red Beret: The Story of the Parachute Regiment at War 1940–45, Hilary St George Saunders

A Drop Too Many, Major General John Frost

The Bruneval Raid: Stealing Hitler's Radar, George Millar

Operation JUDGEMENT

Fleet Air Arm Museum & Archives, RNAS Yeovilton

War in a Stringbag, Charles Lamb

With Naval Wings, John Wellham

Swordfish: The Story of the Taranto Raid, David Wragg

Taranto 1940, A. J. Smithers

A Sailor's Odyssey: The Autobiography of Admiral of the Fleet Viscount Cunningham of Hyndhope, Andrew Browne Cunningham

Operation CHARIOT

The National Archives, Kew

Storming St Nazaire, James Dorrian

The Attack on St Nazaire, Robert Ryder

The Greatest Raid of All, C. E. Lucas-Phillips

List the Bugle: Reminiscences of an Irish Soldier, Major General Corran Purdon

Saint-Nazaire: Operation Chariot – 1942 (Battleground series), James Dorrian

The Green Beret: The Story of the Commandos 1940–45, Hilary St George Saunders

Turned towards the Sun, Michael Burn

www.stnazairesociety.org

Supplement to the *London Gazette*, 30 Sept 1947

Operation GUNNERSIDE

The National Archives, Kew

The Real Heroes of Telemark, Ray Mears

Skis Against the Atom, Knut Haukelid

Assault in Norway: Sabotaging the Nazi Nuclear Program, Thomas Gallagher

Operation Freshman, Richard Wiggan

Operation DEADSTICK

The National Archives, Kew

The Pegasus Diaries, John Howard & Penny Bates

Pegasus Bridge, Stephen Ambrose

The Devil's Own Luck, Dennis Edwards

The Pegasus and Orne Bridges: Their Capture, Defence and Relief on D-Day, Neil Barber

Pegasus Bridge, Will Fowler

Panzer Commander, Hans von Luck

With the 6th Airborne Division in Normandy, Richard Gale

Pure Poett: The Memoirs of General Sir Nigel Poett

Raiders

March Past: A Memoir, Lord Lovat

The Red Beret: The Story of the Parachute Regiment at War 1940–45, Hilary St George Saunders

By Air to Battle: The Official Account of the British Airborne Divisions, ed. Bob Carruthers

Index

THIS B